Constitutional Law, Democracy and Development

Uganda, like many African countries in the 1990s, adopted decentralisation as a state reform measure after many years of civil strife and political conflicts, by transferring powers and functions to district councils. The decision to transfer powers and functions to district councils was, in the main, linked to the quest for democracy and development within the broader context of the nation state. This book's broader aim is to examine whether the legal and policy framework of decentralisation produces a system of governance that better serves the greater objectives of local democracy, local development and accommodation of ethnicity. Specifically, the book pursues one main aim: to examine whether indeed the existing legal framework ensures the smooth devolution process that is needed for decentralised governance to succeed. In so doing, the book seeks, overall, to offer lessons that are critically important not only for Uganda but any other developing nation that has adopted decentralisation as a state-restructuring strategy. The book uses a desk-top research method by reviewing Uganda's decentralisation legal and policy frameworks.

Douglas Karekona Singiza is a serving Magistrate in Uganda. He is a former doctoral and post-doctoral fellow and currently an associate of the Dullah Omar Institute for Constitutional Law, Governance and Human Rights (University of the Western Cape, South Africa).

Constitutional Law, Democracy and Development

Decentralisation and Governance in Uganda

Douglas Karekona Singiza

Routledge
Taylor & Francis Group
LONDON AND NEW YORK

First published 2019
by Routledge
2 Park Square, Milton Park, Abingdon, Oxon OX14 4RN

and by Routledge
52 Vanderbilt Avenue, New York, NY 10017

First issued in paperback 2020

Routledge is an imprint of the Taylor & Francis Group, an informa business

British Library Cataloguing-in-Publication Data
A catalogue record for this book is available from the British Library

Library of Congress Cataloging-in-Publication Data
A catalog record has been requested for this book

ISBN 13: 978-0-367-66072-7 (pbk)
ISBN 13: 978-1-138-35347-3 (hbk)

Typeset in Galliard
by Deanta Global Publishing Services, Chennai, India

Contents

1 Introduction

1.1 Background to the study

This book describes the policy, constitutional and legislative framework of decentralisation in Uganda. The analysis of the institutional architecture is situated within the context of a normative and international discourse on decentralisation, the examination of which will form part of the study.

The book examines the history of district councils in Uganda and the latent features of both district councils and central government, beginning with the Buganda Agreement in 1900 with the British colonial government and the introduction of indirect rule across the country.

It explores current trends towards decentralisation and local government in Africa by describing and analysing international instruments of decentralisation. On the basis of these norms in the international legal framework, the book proceeds to restate the theoretical framework on decentralisation.

Thus, the book's description of the legal reforms introduced by the 1995 Ugandan Constitution is against the backdrop of the normative framework flowing from the emerging international 'soft' law on decentralisation.

1.2 Statement of the problem

For many African countries, decentralisation has been predicated on three important factors: the quest by local citizens for democracy; respect for human rights; and the pressure exerted by requirements that countries restructure themselves as a precondition for receiving financial assistance from developed countries and the World Bank.[1] Decentralisation is also associated with sustainable development,

1 World Bank 1992: 2. The World Bank *Study on Uganda's District Management* focused on the Structural Adjustment Programme as a means for macroeconomic management of the national economy; the Programme operated on the assumption that the country's public sector was too large and required an enabling environment for a market economy. The *Study* recommended that the decentralisation programme in Uganda had to focus on supporting macroeconomic reform in order to ensure management efficiency, popular participation at the local level and improved financial performance through increased revenue generation and rational expenditure decisions. See also Makara 2009: 27.

democratic governance, the promotion of diversity and political stability; essentially, it is meant to lead to improved accountability and transparency.

As stated, the book studies the policy, constitutional and legislative framework of Uganda's system of decentralisation, several features of which make it an attractive case study. First, as one of the first of Africa's large-scale decentralisation projects, it was adopted after a long spell of political instability and civil war. Second, whereas many less developed countries were forced to decentralise because structural adjustment programmes were a precondition for further financial assistance from the World Bank and/or the International Monetary Fund (IMF), Uganda's decentralisation process was a relatively 'home-grown' initiative. Consequently, the relatively 'voluntary' nature of Uganda's decentralisation implies that its constitutional and legal institutions were nurtured by local conditions that gave it better prospects for success than those in other countries. This book will identify six features, viz.: the integrity of local government institutions; functional local government authority; adequate fiscal autonomy; administrative autonomy; equitable intergovernmental transfers; and sound intergovernmental relations and links those features to what makes decentralisation more or less effective. When the six essential features are applied to Uganda's decentralisation progress, evidence of limited, intrusive, 'hard-edged' top-down centralism that is incapable of facilitating local democracy, local development and accommodation of diversity is revealed. Thus, Uganda's decentralisation fails to meet the test of the above proposition.

1.3 Research objectives

While much has been written about decentralisation in Uganda from a development-studies and public-management perspective, no study has been conducted yet from a legal background on the legal design of Africa's first large-scale decentralisation project. This book aims to examine whether the legal and policy framework of decentralisation produces a system of governance that better serves the greater objectives of local democracy, local development and accommodation of ethnicity.

The inquiry into the structure of Uganda's district councils and the powers and functions that devolve thereto pursues one main aim: to examine whether indeed the existing legal framework ensures the smooth devolution process that is needed for decentralised governance to succeed. In so doing, the study seeks, overall, to offer lessons that are critically important not only for Uganda but any other developing nation that has adopted decentralisation as a state-restructuring strategy.

1.4 Methodology

The study uses a desk-top research method in that its primary sources of information are the 1995 Constitution, different Acts of Parliament, Ministerial Declarations, case law, books, conference papers and articles in law journals. Relevant historical materials such as the Buganda Agreement of 1900, the 1962 Constitution, the

1967 Constitution, the Odoki Commission Report and Constituent Assembly (CA) debates are examined. Where foreign constitutional or legislative provisions are cited, this is done with minimal comparative intention but for the purpose of explaining the best practices in other jurisdictions. Likewise, where foreign case law is cited, this has been done not for comparative purposes but in order to aid interpretation of certain constitutional and statutory provisions in Uganda that are similar to ones found in other jurisdictions, an approach taken especially in situations where no relevant jurisprudence exists locally.

1.5 Structure

Chapter Two examines policy debates surrounding the system of decentralisation, and, in turn, reviews the different declarations that have been made both globally as well as in Africa on the subject of decentralisation. The review points to a growing international trend towards state decentralisation and provides the basis for assessing the main features of a decentralised system.

Chapter Three identifies six primary features for a good decentralised system of government, namely, the integrity of local government institutions; functional local government authority; adequate fiscal autonomy; administrative autonomy; equitable intergovernmental transfers; and sound intergovernmental relations. These features provide a basis upon which to examine the history of Ugandan decentralisation (discussed in Chapters Four and Five) as well as to critique the post-1995 constitutional and legal institutional architecture (undertaken in Chapters Six, Seven, Eight and Nine).

Chapter Four traces Uganda's local government from the historical perspective of the Buganda Kingdom and its role in British indirect rule, providing the background for the post-1995 local government reform. Chapter Five reviews the constitution-making process, the establishment of Uganda as a constitutional state and the role courts play as the ultimate arbiters of legal and constitutional conflicts; it also highlights the constitutional guarantees of the local government institutions, the recentralisation of Kampala City and the proposed establishment of the Regional Governments.

Chapter Six describes the intrusive institutional design and governance structures of the district councils, in the process raising the question of whether they are suitable for democracy, sustainable development and the accommodation of ethnic diversity. The chapter reveals how Uganda's decentralisation has not allowed for an adequate test for these three propositions.

Chapter Seven deals with the powers and functions that are devolved to the district councils. The chapter examines the legislative powers of the district councils, and in turn questions the intrusive role of the central government in the exercise of the district councils' legislative autonomy. The chapter also examines the administrative autonomy of district councils as well as the appointment and disciplining of senior district council managers. The recentralisation of district council senior managers not only undermines the political autonomy of district councils but places their development preferences under the central government's control.

Building on the assessment in Chapter Seven, Chapter Eight examines the nature of district council finances. In doing so, the chapter illustrates not only the narrow revenue raising discretion that vests in the district councils, but also discredits the intrusive role of the central government in the fiscal transfer system.

Chapter Nine highlights the nature of intergovernmental relations (IGR) in Uganda and draws a distinction between less and more intrusive IGR. District councils are generally over-regulated and the spaces afforded to them in their interaction with central government inadequate. The conclusion of this chapter is that Uganda emphasises the more intrusive or 'hard-edged' forms of IGR, whereas an appropriate decentralised system should favour 'soft-edged' IGR.

Chapter Ten concludes the book by pointing out that the existing constitutional and legal environment does not foster a democratic and responsive decentralised system.

1.6 Definition of key terms

Six key terms are deployed in this study: decentralisation; subsidiarity; deconcentration; delegation; devolution; and fiscal decentralisation. Their conventional meanings are defined in the discussion below, after which a working definition is set out in order to indicate the way in which their interrelationship is understood for the purposes of this book.

1.6.1 Decentralisation

Writers define the term 'decentralisation' differently. Some define it with reference to the transfer of powers and responsibilities. These powers generally include the power to plan, the power to manage and the power to mobilise and distribute resources. According to Work, decentralisation focuses on the transfer of authority to deliver services from central government to other orders of government, representatives or field offices.[2] This, therefore, means that the power formerly vested in the central government and its agencies goes to the lower orders of government. The United Nations Development Programme (UNDP) defines decentralisation as:

> the restructuring of authority so that there is a system of co-responsibility between institutions of governance at the central, regional and local levels according to the principle of subsidiarity, thus increasing the overall quality and effectiveness of the system of governance, while increasing the authority and capabilities of sub-national levels.[3]

Decentralisation is primarily about the transfer of political power. Accordingly, in this book the working definition is that decentralisation is the transfer of

2 Work 2000: 5.
3 The UNPD 2002: 7.

political power and authority from the central government to sub-national levels of government.

1.6.2 Subsidiarity

Decentralisation is grounded in the principle of subsidiarity, which is the notion that central governments should be limited to a subsidiary role and act only where a more immediate local level is unable, or fails, to do so.[4] Emphasising the advantages of institutional efficiency,[5] postmodern proponents of subsidiarity regard the devolution of powers to local communities as forming part of the principle. Unlike decentralisation, which acknowledges that power is devolved from the central government to local governments, the principle of subsidiarity rests on the legal and philosophical reasoning that local governments' powers naturally vest in them on the basis of preference for smaller orders of government.[6]

1.6.3 Deconcentration

Unlike decentralisation, 'deconcentration' means that, while the existing hierarchy is retained, authority and responsibility are distributed to more than one level of government, with a certain level of discretion being vested in civil servants as field agencies.[7] Deconcentration aims to improve service delivery by minimising directly central roles in the performance of certain tasks and thereby reducing inefficiency and underperformance.[8] It is hence a means by which the central government retains direct control over policy and finance while leaving the actual tasks in the hands of national civil servants who act as its agents at the lower order of government.[9]

1.6.4 Delegation

Delegation is the mechanism or system of transferring responsibility for a particular defined task to institutions that exist outside the parameters of the central government.[10] In other words, tasks are transferred to institutions that ordinarily do not form part of the delegating principal authority, namely, the central government.[11] The delegation of tasks is at its discretion; by implication, it has the power to prescribe the specific delegated power.

4 Bermann 1994: 336.
5 De Visser 2010: 18.
6 Føllesdal 1998: 196–202.
7 Work 2000: 6. De Visser 2005: 14.
8 Work 2000: 6.
9 Azfar, Kahkonen & Meagher 2001: 13.
10 De Visser 2005: 14.
11 Rondinelli 1983: 14. Work 2000: 7.

In theory, once a power has been delegated, the central government is barred from exercising that power.[12] In practice, however, the delegation of power and responsibility does not of itself take away the principal authority's legal obligation to perform. The principal authority may, for example, perform a delegated task once a delegated agency has failed to perform or has acted illegally in the exercise of its delegated power or responsibility.[13]

1.6.5 Devolution

Devolution is a process in which there is full transfer of responsibility to a public authority at local level; the latter must be autonomous of the authority that has devolved the power.[14] Key to devolution is the legal recognition of the autonomy of devolved orders of government from the original 'power', typically the central government.[15] To emphasise the autonomy of a lower order of government, the members thereof are usually elected, although this is not a criterion for their autonomous existence.[16]

1.6.6 Fiscal decentralisation

Fiscal decentralisation refers to the system of allocating revenue resources to lower levels of government. Revenue allocation is usually negotiated between central and local authorities, and based on a number of factors that include interregional equity, availability of revenue at all levels of government and local fiscal management capacity.[17] Fiscal decentralisation has its origins in a classic argument of fiscal federalism according to which sub-national government is seen as the most appropriate vehicle for matching public goods and services to preferences.[18]

1.6.7 Working definition

Within the discourse on decentralisation, it is held that whether power is merely deconcentrated or delegated, the ultimate decision remains with the centre. Given that some decentralised regimes evince both deconcentration and delegation, it is better to consider the latter pair as being distinct from decentralisation. Devolution, as distinguished from both deconcentration and delegation, describes the extent to which a lower order of government autonomously exercises power. The preferred definition of 'decentralisation' in this book is one that includes deconcentration and delegation of powers and responsibilities. This definition

12 De Visser 2005: 14.
13 Reynolds 1996: 159.
14 Rondinelli 1983: 24. Work 2000: 7.
15 De Visser 2005: 15.
16 Work 2000: 7.
17 Singiza & De Visser 2010: 12–16.
18 Azfar, Kahkonen & Meagher 2001: 24.

includes, furthermore, the devolution of authority thorough fiscal autonomy, on the basis of the principle of subsidiarity. In other words, 'decentralisation' is the umbrella concept that integrates all the above terms.

1.7 Conclusion

This chapter gives the background of the study, states the problem to be addressed and emphasises the overall research objective to be pursued. The chapter also demarcates the methodology and scope to be adopted in addressing the problem. In doing so, the chapter aims to establish clear research parameters. A clearly conceptualised research topic together with a narrowed scope helps in succinctly addressing the overall stated research goal. It is also noted that the six terms defined in this chapter are in turn employed to examine and to investigate the issues under discussion.

2 Decentralisation

International, political and policy context

2.1 Introduction

This chapter is divided into two broad areas. The first part of the chapter explores the ideological debates that surround the topic of decentralisation, while the second part reviews international 'soft' law on decentralisation. Evaluating decentralisation in terms of an international normative framework is important since doing so serves to establish benchmarks that may be used in reforming weak decentralised governments. The chapter restates the theories on decentralisation, locates good governance as the driving motive for decentralisation and identifies sustainable development, grassroots democracy and accommodation of ethnicity as key pillars on which the theory of decentralisation is predicated. This lays the ground for examining features that are crucial to the success of systems of decentralisation, particularly those in multi-ethnic developing countries.

2.2 Ideological background to the debate on decentralisation

2.2.1 Introduction

During the Cold War, many socialist scholars considered market economies as antithetical to social transformation because of their focus on profit maximisation. However, the alternative to a market economy was a strong, centralised, planned economy which, in many developing countries, left little room for grassroots democratic input in decision-making.[1]

2.2.2 The debate about the nature of the post-colonial state: 'African Socialism'

Most post-colonial leaders in Africa argued that the absence of a strong industrial base meant that the state had to play a dominant role as the engine for development, a conception of social organisation broadly known as 'African Socialism'.[2]

1 Pieterse 2003: 5.
2 Kanyeihamba 2002: 120.

Development was viewed as a common good not to be left in the hands of individuals.[3] In this regard, local government's role as a partner in development was a remote consideration. Most African countries looked to the Soviet Union and China as good models for development, preferring these command economies to the capitalist mode of production dominant in the West. The desire for a more centralised government was precipitated by the fact that many African central governments did not want to be restrained by independent institutions such as local governments.[4] By the same token, any articulation of democracy was rejected with the forceful claim that no country could have democracy where poverty, illiteracy, poor health and starvation prevailed. Thus, until African countries were 'liberated' from these ills, democracy remained shelved, with no institution of government capable of limiting the powers of central government.[5]

2.2.3 *The change in the ideological debates*

In the 1990s many African countries adopted structural adjustment programmes and privatisation as key strategies for undoing former state intervention in the economy.[6] While the free market doctrine was not disputed in the discourse on development, the requirement that markets ought not to lead to economic disparity was then a more favoured approach in the discourse on decentralisation for development.[7]

2.2.4 *The World Bank*

The World Bank's approach to development has undergone significant changes over time. Initially, its stance towards underdevelopment was to extend loans for reconstruction and development.[8] In the 1960s and 1970s, the Bank's philosophy widened to include 'growth with equity' through anti-poverty human development projects,[9] which included support for sectors such as education, agriculture, health and nutrition and rural development. The debt crisis that faced most developing and less developed countries in the 1980s and 1990s led the Bank to re-focus its strategies of relying on the field of macroeconomic structural-adjustment lending.[10] Thus, small government and fiscal discipline were conditions for further financial assistance.[11]

This economic model did not escape the criticism of academics and policy analysts, who argued that the Bank had ignored risks associated with macroeconomic

3 Nyerere 1968: 12.
4 Nkrumah 1963: 166.
5 Nyerere 1968: 12.
6 Pieterse 2003.
7 Trubek 2007: 235.
8 Carreau 1994.
9 Blanco 1999: 111–2.
10 Blanco & Carrasco 1999: 81.
11 Carrasco & Kose 1996: 29–31

discipline, such as hunger and unemployment.[12] Hence the design of the present World Bank development model: known as the Comprehensive Development Framework which aims at addressing previous development challenges. This framework 'advocates that the Bank and its country-clients pay more attention to the structural, social, and human side of development, and that development actors increase their co-operation in their efforts to eliminate poverty'.[13] Access to resources in order to address poverty is one of the core assumptions of micro-development theory.[14]

The World Bank takes the view that the obstacles to accessing resources are a result of power relations. Thus, according to the World Bank, in order to confront these power imbalances, development should be a continuous process.[15] Moreover, people on the fringes of development have a duty to organise themselves so as to 'overcome the obstacles to their social, cultural, and economic well-being'.[16] In this regard, poor communities must 'participate fully not only in identifying common problems, setting priorities, and designing strategies and programs, but also in carrying out project activities and distributing the benefits' so that other players can only respond to their efforts as partners.[17]

The changes in the World Bank's strategies for Africa from 1969 until now are testimony that economic models alone cannot address poverty and underdevelopment. In fact, there has not been evidence that reliance on strict fiscal economic austerity measures significantly reduces poverty.[18] There ought to be a multiplicity of approaches that are sustainable and result-oriented to ensure development. In the discussion below, local development is examined through the prism of good governance.

2.3 Decentralisation for development

This part of the book discusses the main arguments surrounding decentralisation. The discussion has three components: the link between decentralisation/local government and development; the link between decentralisation/local government and democracy; and the link between decentralisation/local government and the accommodation of diversity.[19]

12 Carrasco 1999: 124–6. See generally Adepoju (ed) 1993.
13 Cameron Blake 2000: 159.
14 James & Dias 1986: 65.
15 James & Dias 1986: 65–6.
16 Kleymeyer 1991: 38.
17 Kleymeyer 1991. Stiles 1987: 3.
18 Ebel & Yilmaz 2001.
19 Blank 2006: 11 argues that local communities have become transmitters, and enforcers, of international standards and thus ought to be considered as vehicles of transformation and economic empowerment. He argues further that local communities play a critical role in enhancing democracy and economic stability.

2.3.1 Economic arguments

2.3.1.1 Efficiency

In the discourse on devolution of power, the benefits and dangers of decentralisation are usually examined from an economic point of view.[20] First, decentralisation is important in helping the distribution of income, the maintenance of a stable economy and the efficient allocation of resources. Devolution of power is permissible as long as it reduces costs, promotes efficient production and does not disrupt macroeconomic policy and stability.[21] From a political-economy point of view, support for decentralisation considers both economic and political power as crucial in the devolution of powers and functions. Thus, devolution of power to lower orders of government must relate to the institutional capacity of lower orders of government to utilise that power.[22]

2.3.1.2 Accountability for development

Accountability is crucial to public management in that it ensures that elected political leaders constantly have to justify their actions to citizens: it implies a duty to offer explanations and justifications of actions taken by those charged with delivering services.[23] Accountability should not be viewed in terms of control, sanctions and punishment. As Callahan argues, such a view is simply the traditional negative approach to accountability, which centres on the enforcement of rules and regulations so as to limit bureaucratic power.[24] Rather, modern accountability is understood in broader terms that incorporate the legal constraints that minimise public administrators' discretion, fiscal constraints that reflect fiduciary responsibility and political constraints through voting.[25]

2.3.1.3 Distributive local government

Local governments play a vital role in distributing incomes to local communities. A common narrative is that central government is better positioned than the local government to affect the income redistribution that is key for development.[26] This is because strong fiscal decentralisation can compound regional inequity.[27] The counter-argument is that regional inequity can be countered with equalisation grants.[28]

20 Loughlin 1986: 1–4.
21 Loughlin 1986: 1–4.
22 Botchway 2001: 31.
23 Callahan 2007: 110.
24 Callahan 2007: 113
25 Callahan 2007: 113.
26 De Visser 2005: 27.
27 Peirce 1993: 17.
28 Bird 1994: 311–2. Sewell 1996: 144.

Local governments' dependence on intergovernmental fiscal transfers may undermine their ability to tailor service delivery to local needs and remain accountable to local communities. It is, however, also true that intergovernmental transfers, if well designed, can promote equitable local development.[29] In fragmented or ethnically diverse societies, central government transfers are a form of political bargaining and a means to share state resources and sovereignty.[30] In many countries, central government transfers to local governments are instead a form of political appeasement to ease local political pressures. Central government transfers are, that is to say, a kind of 'political glue' that keeps the country together.[31] In this regard, the peace-building potential of central government transfers in fragmented societies is significant.[32]

The conclusion is that while redistribution is generally better performed at national government level, this does not imply that decentralisation cannot foster redistribution of incomes altogether.

2.3.1.4 Corruption

Pessimists argue that decentralisation leads to 'decentralisation' of corruption without improving service delivery.[33] Indeed, some studies show that decentralisation may breed corruption as a result of the connivance between local bureaucrats and local interest groups,[34] making local government vulnerable to political capture by the wealthy elites.[35] De Visser argues that rather than blame corruption on decentralisation, the evidence suggests that corruption in local governments manifests a failure in the proper execution of decentralisation programmes.[36] Decentralisation fosters transparency in decision-making. And as Byanyima explains, '[t]ransparency is a great disinfectant' against corruption and a precursor to sustainable development.[37] Indeed, unless there are mechanisms to sufficiently limit corruption and abuse of power, decentralisation has little or no economic benefit at all. Establishing institutions of control and accountability at municipal/local government level creates a buffer against the 'fear' of corruption that may result from decentralisation.[38] In a nutshell, decentralisation does not

29 Bird 1994: 311–2. Sewell 1996: 144.
30 Bird 1994: 311–2.
31 Breton 1978: 11.
32 Prud'homme 1994: 202.
33 Azfar 2006: 234.
34 Prud'homme 1994: 10–1.
35 Bahl 2004: 4 cited in De Visser 2005: 29.
36 De Visser 2005: 29.
37 See W. Byanyima, 'To Sustain High Growth Rates, Africa Must Have Inclusive Policies in Place', *The Daily Monitor*, 9 May 2013, available at http://www.monitor.co.ug/OpEd/Commentary/To-sustain-high-growth-rates--Africa-must-have/-/689364/1844162//11d3idb/-/index.html.
38 Loughlin 1986: 1. See also Work 2002.

breed corruption but the high prevalence of corruption does nevertheless point to the need for adequate corrective measures.

2.3.2 Decentralisation for democracy

2.3.2.1 Introduction

It does not matter whether decentralisation is based on public management theory or economic efficiency theory. What is important is to point out that good governance through decentralisation leads to development in practice. Democratic local government ensures that development priorities are made after consultation with the local populations. In this respect, voting is an essential feature of local government democracy.[39]

Dahl defines the term 'democracy' by listing its determinants,[40] arguing that eight institutional guarantees are important determinants of democracy. These are: freedom to form and join organisations; freedom of expression; the universal right to vote; eligibility for public office; the right to compete for support and votes; alternative sources of information; free and fair elections; and governmental institutions' policies based on votes and other expressions of preference.

Democracy may be direct,[41] as in the case, for example, of referenda, where voters are asked to vote directly on certain contentious issues of national importance; it may also be indirect,[42] as in the case of a motion of censure, where Parliament passes a motion of disapproval against a sitting president, prime minister or MP on behalf of the electorate. It is noted that most, if not all, democratic systems are a combination of both representative and participatory democracy.

2.3.2.2 Democracy through traditional leadership in Africa

The debate in many African countries when decentralisation was rolled out as a policy initiative concerned the transformation of states from ones characterised by political instability, dictatorship, nepotism and corruption to ones that were more democratic, developmental and inclusive.[43] The traditional local institutions of governance were placed on the periphery of the debate on state reconstruction, notwithstanding the critical role of traditional institutions of leadership to this debate. There is a strong correlation between democracy and traditional leadership, especially on the African continent.[44]

39 Golooba-Mutebi 2000: 22–3.
40 Dahl 1971: 3, cited in Reynolds 1999: 20.
41 Callahan 2007: 154.
42 Callahan 2007: 154.
43 Oomen 2005: 110.
44 See Marry Morgan 'Can Democracy Deliver for Africa?', available at http://www.bbc.co.uk/news/world-africa-24228425 (accessed 25 September 2013).

In many African local communities, legitimacy emanates from age-old traditional institutions that were headed by chiefs and whose relation to the community is often described as being of a 'symbiotic, patron-client type'.[45] British indirect rule in many African countries, and indeed in other British spheres of influence, relied on chiefs as to exert their rule on the native communities. Pre-colonial traditional leaders were regarded as the keepers of community values and practiced a 'a high level of participatory democracy through assemblies of men'.[46] Arguably, the advent of colonial rule changed the traditional institutional arrangements and reduced traditional leadership to agents of colonial rule[47] and instruments of coercion and subjugation. Colonial rule created what Mamdani describes as 'decentralised despotism'.[48] In other words, post-traditional leadership institutions, having acquired a new blend of colonial authority, became tools of oppression. If traditional leadership is viewed as a shared value of a certain ethnic group, then liberal democracy, which emphasises competitive election, takes away that legitimacy. True traditional leadership is controversial, given that that leadership is hereditary and thus exclusionary. However, the exclusionary nature of leadership in traditional institutions may also play out in Western democracies that are dominated by the political elite class. It is true that the exclusionary nature of traditional institutions is simple while the exclusionary nature of democracies is a result of subtle factors such as power and class relations. However, some democracies have leadership positions that are dominated by one family or one racial group or gender.[49]

Democracies have term limits which traditional institutions do not. One could argue that even if a leader in a liberal democracy attempts to undermine the existing institutions that are supposed to limit his powers, the possibility of losing an election (if he or she does not rig that election) is a strong mitigating factor. However, traditional leaders also face a real possibility of abdication from the throne in a case of blatant abuse of power. In that regard, the leader can in theory lose power in the same way that Western democracy changes its leadership. There are, in fact, examples in Africa where traditional leaders have abdicated.[50]

45 Golooba-Mutebi 2007: 108.

46 Rugege 2003:172–3.

47 Mamdani 1996: 114.

48 Mamdani 1996: 23, 53, 58.

49 For example, since the declaration of American independence, the US had been led only by male whites until the election of Barack Obama in 2008. Similarly, the UK has had only one female prime minister, with no non-Caucasian prime minister.

50 For example, Markakis 2006: 30 writes that the secret conversion of Emperor Za Dengel of Ethiopia in the Horn of Africa in 1603–4 (he became a Jesuit) led to a violent rebellion. His successor, Susneyos 1607–32, who openly confessed Catholicism and forcibly converted his subjects to profess the Catholic faith, was forced to abdicate in favour of his son, Fasiladas.

Moreover, in a Westminster system, where there are no term limits, a bad leader can remain at the helm as long as his or her party is popular.[51]

Traditional institutions of leadership that focus on communitarian values counter the inadequacies of democratic systems.[52]

2.3.2.3 The contribution of decentralisation to democracy

Decentralisation creates spaces for democracy to flourish. Briffault argues that local governments must be looked at as potential hatcheries for democracy.[53] The evidence is that local communities learn about the essence of democracy (trade-offs and compromises) at local level better than at national level,[54] notwithstanding the possibility that in some cases local government structures may be prone to capture by elite groups. In this regard, local elections are an important feature for local democracy to flourish.

In the section below, the link between local elections and democracy is examined within the context of a broader multi-ethnic nation state.

2.3.2.4 The value of elections at local level

By its nature, local democracy may produce different outcomes in different jurisdictions. Yet, after elections, local political leaders, irrespective of their political or ethnic affiliations, will be 'forced' to work together under the broad umbrella of the nation state. The consensus-building nature of local elections therefore promotes co-operation and respect across the political spectrum. In that sense, multiparty democracy is learned. For example, South Africa and Ghana (two countries that previously experienced political instability) used local elections as a means of forging national political consensus over and above racial and ethnic differences.[55] The recognition of differences in local elections fosters democracy, development and tolerance across the social and political spectrum. Thus, contrary to some views that support monolithic politics,[56] multiparty politics has a more fertile ground for growth in a decentralised system of government than in a centralised one.[57]

51 For example, Margaret Thatcher, referred to as the 'Iron Lady', served as the British prime minister for more than 15 years. She only left office when her popularity within the Conservative Party plummeted; had her party not replaced her with a fellow Tory, she might have remained in office a few more years.

52 See Morgan 2013.

53 Briffault 1996: 1124.

54 Briffault 1993: 339.

55 Nohlen, Krennerch & Berhard 1999: 4–15.

56 Museveni 2000: 15.

57 Asbjørn 2002: 64.

2.4 Accommodation of diversity

2.4.1 Introduction

This section addresses the debate on the politics of identity and the role of ethnicity in decentralisation. Accommodation of ethnic identity has peace-building potential in a multi-ethnic national state and is vital to the success of a decentralised system.[58]

Ethnic groups in many African states were suppressed immediately after gaining independence from their colonial masters.[59] This had negative consequences: poverty, political despondency, alienation and civil strife. It also resulted in various ethnic groups directly challenging the legitimacy of those states.[60] Often a large number of people (in most cases minority and vulnerable groups) are politically and economically discriminated against and therefore outside the realm of the nation state. Thus, where an ethnic group has been alienated politically at a national level, an ethnically-based system of decentralisation guarantees their political participation.[61]

The word 'diversity' connotes a multiplicity of groups or categories of things or people. As a sociological term, the word presupposes the existence of different identifiable groups of people. The term 'diversity' acknowledges the existence of different groups which, taken individually, share unique and identifiable characteristics distinct from those of other groups or categories. Thus, the term relates to the uniqueness of a group's identity.[62]

Identities have evolved around different interests. For example, there are religious identities, in terms of which Muslims, Hindus, Buddhists, African traditionalists, Christians, atheists and pagans emerge as different identities. Even within these religious identities there are further subgroups such as Catholics, Protestants or Orthodox Christians. In Islam, too, there are subgroups such as the Sunnis or Shiites. Identities have also emerged along racial, gender and sexual lines. In most cases an identity is a construction in terms of which a dominant group is established as the 'norm' and a non-dominant group as its 'abnormal' other.[63] With this in mind, the next section focuses on ethnicity, given that the debate on decentralisation in multi-ethnic states revolves more strongly around questions of ethnic identity than it does around those to do with gender, religion and/or race.

A number of questions arise from this. What order of government is appropriate to accommodate ethnic interests? Should ethnic interests be accommodated at the regional level or in lower orders of government? Depending on the territorial manifestation of ethnicity, smaller orders of government may be appropriate to accommodate ethnic interests. The reasons are that, first, there is a lesser risk

58 Banks 2005: 1.
59 Kanyeihamba 2002: 1. Museveni 2000: 34–5.
60 See generally Mamdani 1983.
61 Kymlicka 2004: 27.
62 Kaplan 2008: 32–3.
63 Bernstein 2005: 49–50.

of secession from the rest of the nation state at smaller levels of government; and, second, smaller orders of government help to accommodate minorities within minorities.[64]

2.4.2 Why accommodation is important

Most states in Africa can hardly consider themselves as 'nations'. Instead, they are an amalgamation of different ethnic nationalities which were fused together at the time of colonisation and given 'legitimacy' on independence.[65] Accommodating ethnicity in lower orders of government may lead to additional political dividends in a given national state. That is to say, rights such as non-discrimination on the grounds of ethnic origin become part of the new political debate by virtue of tolerance of differences. The assumption here is that previous social and political prejudices within an autonomous cultural group may disappear with the passage of time, given that acceptance of differences is the common value for all groups that were previously marginalised.

The question that arises is how to share state power among different ethnic groups, some of which may be numerically as well as economically stronger than others.

2.4.3 Benefits and dangers of territorial accommodation through decentralisation

Ethnic diversity can be accommodated through territorial or non-territorial means. Territorial accommodation of ethnicity refers to the granting of self-government or autonomy to a specific ethnic minority group. Good examples are Quebec's asymmetric federalism in Canada or Zanzibar's greater political autonomy in Tanzania. Arguably, the territorial accommodation of ethnicity is different from decentralisation in that it is asymmetrical and of a unique kind.[66] By contrast, non-territorial accommodation of ethnicity entails devolving political power to ethnic groups irrespective of where they live. Here, the sole aim is to ensure that the ethnic minorities that may be in an area populated by major ethnic groups are not politically discriminated against.[67] According to Kymlicka,

> [s]elf-government claims ... typically take the form of devolving political power to a political unit substantially controlled by members of the national minority, and substantially corresponding to their historical homeland or territory.[68]

Self-government rights ensure that powers and functions are devolved to lower orders of government in the interests of particular social groups. For instance,

64 Siegle & O'Mahony 2006: 49.
65 Kanyeihamba 2002: 1.
66 Miller 1998: 66.
67 Asbjørn 2002.
68 Kymlicka 1995: 30.

devolving power to an indigenous peoples' self-governing political unit helps the group to tailor its services to local preferences. A political unit which is substantially controlled by indigenous people may help such communities determine their educational curriculum and language of instruction in schools. The protection of ethnically-based rights such as language may enhance the level of political participation of a given community in the affairs of the government.[69] In addition, as Mitra and Bhattacharyya argue, once ethnically based rights are politically accommodated, the real questions of how to share the national 'pie' replace narrow identity issues. Ultimately, the risk of freezing ethnicity in a nation state is averted.[70]

The following questions thus present themselves:

- Should ethnic interests be accommodated territorially or culturally?
- What institutional guarantees are needed to accommodate ethnic diversity as a key consideration in a decentralised system?

Preference is usually given to non-territorial cultural autonomy, given its ability both to protect minorities who might be living in a given territory and to protect inherited borders within which many other ethnic groups have lived historically.[71] However, where devolution of power is aimed at protecting a particular ethnic group with a unique history, territorial autonomy or asymmetrical decentralisation is preferred. The accommodation of ethnicity is attained if it becomes a major consideration in the overall decentralisation scheme.[72]

Accommodation of ethnicity in the process of devolution of powers is usually rejected for the wrong reasons. For example, opinions abound to the effect that ethnic or regional autonomous governance and identity would override national development interests.[73] In this respect, ethnicity is viewed as a retrogressive notion undesirable in the context of attempts to achieve a country's developmental goal.[74] Thus, the argument goes, strong autonomous lower orders of government may exacerbate ethnic tensions and national disintegration.[75] Ethnic identity is only a small part of what makes one a citizen and a member of a nation. As the American president Barack Obama succinctly put it, 'None of us wants to be defined by one part of what makes us whole'.[76]

Recognising the different ethnic identities is not without any risks in that certain ethnic groups may question the legitimacy and existence of the nation state.[77]

69 Howard 1983: 479–80.
70 Mitra & Bhattacharyya 2000:130.
71 Asbjørn 2002.
72 Singiza 2010: 8–9.
73 Howard 1991: 418–9.
74 Howard 1983: 482.
75 Bayart 1993: 41–59.
76 See President Barack Obama's address to the Gay Rights Group, Washington 10th October 2009, available at http://www.whitehouse.gov/the-press-office/remarks-president-human-rights-campaign-dinner.
77 Erk 2010: 37.

In fact writers such as Smith express the fear that the use of decentralisation to accommodate ethnicity may backfire. The risk is that in multi-ethnic societies, decentralisation may lead to discrimination against 'minorities' within minorities. The argument is that decentralisation creates an artificial majority in local communities. In turn, the new 'majority' may discriminate against those who become minorities within local governments.[78]

Even when the real risk associated with secession in ethnically based decentralisation is not far-fetched, the devolution of state power to strong and autonomous local governments helps to accommodate ethnic identities without compromising national identity. The argument is that the devolution of state power through a decentralisation process that takes into account ethnic diversity is an incentive for peace and apolitical stability,[79] and can never threaten the wider nation state's identity.[80]

In order to accommodate ethnic diversity, in a decentralised system, institutions of local governments should be designed through a boundary demarcation process that takes into account indigenous peoples' rights. It also means that preferential treatment may be given in the design of the electoral system to ensure that indigenous peoples access political offices through free and fair elections. Finally, it means that the central government fiscal transfer system may take into account the special needs of indigenous peoples as a form of affirmative action.

Having discussed the arguments on which decentralisation is based, the book now turns to the international law context of decentralisation, a review of which is discussed below.

2.5 Manifestations of decentralisation in international law

2.5.1 Introduction

International law can generally be divided into two parts: 'hard' law and 'soft' law.[81] The focus in this chapter is on international 'soft' law.

International 'soft' law refers to standards that emanate from declarations, diplomatic conferences and the resolutions of international organisations. The intention of these instruments is to serve as guidelines for the conduct of states; on their own, however, they do not enjoy the position and status of law.[82] According to Romero, '"[s]oft law" ... refers to sets of standards, principles or guidelines, and codes of conduct which may be useful for governments to incorporate into their national law, coupled with a plan or agenda of action'.[83] For Craik, '[w]hile there is no generally accepted definition of soft law, its

78 Smith 2007: 113.
79 Siegle & O'Mahony 2006: 49.
80 Stauffer & Topperwien 2000: 48.
81 Brownlie 1998.
82 Dugard 2007: 38–9.
83 Romero 2005: 532.

essential characteristic is that ... soft law does not create formally binding obligations'.[84] Dugard argues that with the passage of time such declarations, or 'soft' international law, may be turned into customary international law.[85]

A number of questions are raised in this chapter. The first is whether there is, within international law, a right to local government. As shall be discussed, the answer is clearly in the negative; however, a relationship exists between decentralisation and the right to participate in government. Moreover, the consensus in the emerging international 'soft' law is that local governments are appropriate institutions for the provision of social services to local communities. Various declarations about decentralisation also emphasise the need to bring every social group into the realm of the state. As a result, the chapter highlights the role of decentralisation in protecting the rights of special interest groups such as women, ethnic minorities and those with disabilities.

The second question is: is there an international obligation on states to devolve power through decentralisation? The answer, again, is no. Nevertheless, there is a trend, discernible through a flurry of statements, made particularly in Africa, that links decentralisation to sustainable development. While it is acknowledged that ministerial declarations do not amount to international law and are little more than expressions of the political wishes of government functionaries, the seemingly unrelenting succession of declarations indicates all the same that a vital role is being accorded to decentralisation and that this may create the momentum for driving forward an evolving debate on decentralised governance. Ministerial declarations are a statement of intent upon which future international 'hard' law regarding the practice of local government may develop.

This section demonstrates that there is an emerging trend at the regional level towards decentralisation, one which is manifested in international 'soft' law.

For example, the World-Wide Declaration of Local Self-Government (WWDLSG)[86] deals with the emerging worldwide effort to promote decentralisation through a charter on which 'the theory of decentralisation' as a system of government could be based, an effort that was frustrated by the international geopolitical interests. In spite of resistance from other world powers,[87] the UN Governing Council Habitat Section (UNGCHS) requested that the Advisory Group of Experts on Decentralisation (AGRED) formulate policy guidelines on local government,[88] the result of which is the UN Draft Guidelines on Decentralisation (UNDGD) – the first attempt by the United Nations to adopt a

84 Craik 1998: 573.

85 Dugard 2007: 38–9.

86 Available at http://www.bunken.nga.gr.jp/siryousitu/eturansitu/charter/iuladecltxt.html.

87 Opposition to the UN efforts towards creating a UN charter on local government mainly came from China and the US, two of the five permanent members of the Security Council.

88 See the UNGCHS Resolution 19/12 of 9 May 2003. The draft guidelines were made by the members of the AGRED. The full citation of the draft guidelines is 'Draft Guidelines on Decentralisation and the Strengthening of Local Authorities' 3 HSP/GC/21/2/Add.2, hereinafter referred to as the UNDGD.

charter on decentralisation.[89] However, as the term 'draft' implies, no such charter has been adopted yet by a formal resolution.[90] The British Commonwealth member states have also adopted a specific set of principles dealing with local government which all member countries must be adhere to. The Aberdeen Principles assert that 'effective, elected local government is an important foundation for democracy'.[91] The Aberdeen Principles call on member states to adhere to democracy, the rule of law, good governance, freedom of expression and the protection of human rights as core common values.[92] The Aberdeen Principles proceed from the premise that local democracy and good governance, community empowerment and effective decentralisation are important vehicles for poverty reduction and necessary tools in the implementation of the UN Millennium Development Goals.[93] In addition, the Aberdeen Principles regard local democracy as indispensable in mitigating reconstruction challenges in less developed countries that are prone to natural disasters.[94]

Within the European Union, a specific European Charter of Local Self-Government (ECLSG)[95] has also been adopted that addresses the status of local governments by postulating democracy and development as the main rationale for decentralisation.[96] It is arguable that the adoption of the ECLSG by the Council of Europe influenced the formulation of the Aberdeen Principles (which are applicable only to members of the British Commonwealth).

The trend towards decentralisation in Africa, as manifested in the flurry of statements is also noted. A number of commitments, declarations and ministerial statements in Africa address decentralisation. The majority focuses on those adopted in Anglophone and/or Commonwealth African countries, specifically the Victoria Falls Declaration and the Kigali Declaration,[97] both of which are

89 Hoffschulte 2008: 114

90 Hoffschulte 2008: 114–6. Writers on the development of the international discourse on local governments place emphasis on the correlation between the ECLSG and the UN efforts to adopt a charter on local government. The correlation between the ECLSG and the UN's efforts for a charter on local government is that the UNDGD were published after the ratification of the ECLSG by a substantial number of European countries. In fact, it is now acknowledged that ratification of the ECLSG was one of the benchmarks for countries that sought to join the European Union. It is argued that the success of the ECLSG served as an inspiration for UN efforts to adopt a world charter on local government.

91 CLGF 2005: 3 para. 2.

92 CLGF 2005: 3 para. 4.

93 CLGF 2005: 3 para. 6 and 9.

94 CLGF 2005: 3 para. 11.

95 The European Charter on Local-Self Government, available at http://www.google.com/search?ie=UTF-8&oe=UTF-8&sourceid=navclient&gfns=1&q=European+charter+on+local+government.

96 Hoffschulte 2008: 114.

97 Besides the Victoria Falls and the Kigali Declarations, numerous African summits on local government have taken place. These include the 2nd Africities Summit held in Windhoek, Namibia, 2000; the 3rd Africities Summit held in Yaoundé, Cameroon, 2003; the Eastern African Ministers of Local Government Conference on Decentralization and Local

broadly representative of the debate on local government in sub-Saharan Africa. These instruments are nevertheless similar to those instruments that have been applied in other, non-Anglophone African countries.

Last is the African Charter on Democracy, Elections and Governance (ACDEG). The ACDEG has its origin in Articles 3 and 4 of the Constitutive Act of the African Union which emphasise the relationship among good governance, popular participation, the rule of law, the protection of human rights and sustainable development. The ACDEG therefore aims to promote the universal values and principles of democracy, respect for human rights and peace-building.[98] These values are held to be necessary for building consensus among different political players and advancing sustainable development in Africa.[99]

The ACDEG lists the following as crucial in institutionalising political and economic social governance: effective public sector management; transparent public financial management; combating corruption; efficient management of public debt; equitable allocation of national resources; poverty alleviation; and investor-friendly tax policies and systems.[100] Immediately after listing these factors, the ACDEG obliges member states to 'decentralize power to democratically elected local authorities as provided for in national laws'.[101] This is the ACDEG's most vital provision in that is the only hard law on the continent that specifically instructs member states to decentralise. It also emphasises the vital role of traditional authorities, enjoining member states to 'strive to find appropriate ways and means to increase traditional authorities' integration and effectiveness within the larger democratic system'.[102] The ACDEG recognises that decentralisation has an essential role to play in political and economic social governance in Africa.

2.6 Overview and assessment

A matrix extracted from the instruments under discussion is presented in Table 2.1. The matrix reveals critical aspects of decentralisation that are excluded

Development held in Mombasa, Kenya, 2004; the Conference on Decentralization: the new Dimension of Peace, Democracy and Development, held in Florence, Italy, 2004; the Eastern African Ministers for Local Government Consultative Meeting held in Nairobi, Kenya, 2004; the Arusha Conference on the Foundation of the Eastern Africa Local Government Association held in Arusha, Tanzania, 2005; the 4th Africities Summit held in Nairobi, Kenya, 2006; the Ministerial Conference on Participatory Planning and Budgeting for Effective Local Level Delivery of Services held in Maseru, Lesotho, 2006; and the African Governance Conference, on the theme 'the Capable State for Poverty Reduction in Africa', held in Ouagadougou, Burkina Faso, 2007. See para. 1 of the Preamble to the Yaoundé Communiqué on Leadership Capacity Building for Decentralized Governance and Poverty Reduction in Africa, 30th May 2008. See also para. 1 of the Kigali Declaration.

98 Para. 2, 3 and 4 of the Preamble to the ACDEG.

99 See Kane 2008: 43–5.

100 Article 33 of the ACDEG.

101 Article 34 of the ACDEG.

102 Article 35 of the ACDEG.

Table 2.1 Summary of the six instruments under review

International instrument	*Legal status: International Law/Soft Law/or Draft*	*Geographical application*	*Increased role of LG in development*	*Constitutional recognition*	*Statutory protection*	*Transfer of powers*	*Elected local governments*	*Supervision (monitoring and intervention) of LG*	*Co-operation with LG*	*Sharing of national revenue*	*Own revenue sources*	*Due process in boundary demarcation*	*Inclusive institutions and processes*
WW D	Soft law	Worldwide	✓	✓	✓	✓	✓	✓	X	✓	✓	✓	X
UNDGD	Soft law	UN member states	✓	X	X	✓	✓	✓	✓	X	X	X	✓
Aberdeen Principles	Hard law	British Commonwealth	✓	✓	✓	✓	✓	X	✓	✓	✓	X	✓
ECLSG	Hard law	Member states to the Council of the European Charter	X	?	X	✓	X	✓	✓	✓	✓	✓	X
VFD	Soft law	Anglophone sub-Saharan Africa	✓	✓	X	✓	✓	✓	✓	✓	✓	X	✓
KD	Soft law	Africa	✓	?	✓	✓	?	X	✓	✓	✓	X	X
ACDEG	Hard law	Member states of the African Union	✓	X	X	✓	✓	X	X	X	X	X	✓

Source: Adapted from the six international instruments under review

and the key features of decentralisation. There is, for instance, little regard for the accommodation of diversity as a function to be carried out by local government. Even where accommodation of diversity is called for, it is lumped together with democracy. The instruments also do not indicate the role of traditional leaders in local government, even though extant literature on the traditional leaders stresses their peace-making and conflict-management roles, ones undergirded by long-earned legitimacy in local communities.[103] Furthermore, the instruments do not give prominence to the role of co-operative government. Whereas the instruments call for central government to support local government, this should be provided on the understanding that the two orders of government are partners and that 'support' ought not to amount to a veiled form of control.

Notwithstanding the above inadequacies, the instruments establish important benchmarks for the analysis of decentralisation in any context, but particularly so in the case of countries in Africa.

Table 2.1 is a summary of the six instruments discussed so far. In each case, it indicates the instrument's background, legal status and geographical focus as well the rationale it provides, and the role it envisages, for local government. The table also shows the importance that is attached to the recognition of local governments, to the supervision of local governments and to the importance attached to a boundary-demarcation process.

The overview of international instruments reveals, to varying degrees, a number of common features. These features are: increased role of local government (LG) in development; constitutional recognition; statutory protection; transfer of powers; elected local governments; supervision (monitoring and intervention) of LG; co-operation with LG; sharing of national revenue; own revenue sources; due process in boundary demarcation; and inclusive institutions and processes. For instance:

1 The WWD, categorised as soft law in international law, with a worldwide geographical focus, calls for most of these features except the transfer of powers, co-operation with LG and inclusive institutions and processes.
2 The UNDGD, which is also categorised as soft law and applicable to member states of the UN, calls for only six features: increased role of LG in development, transfer of powers, elected LG, supervision of LG, co-operation with LG and inclusive institutions and processes.
3 The Aberdeen Principles, categorised as hard law and only applicable in the British Commonwealth, provides for all features except supervision of LG and due process in boundary demarcation.
4 The ECLSG, categorised as hard law and only applicable to member states to the Council of the European Charter, only provides for transfer of powers, supervision of LG, co-operation with LG, sharing of national revenue, own revenue and due process in boundary demarcation.

103 Oomen 2005: 110.

5 The VFD, categorised as soft law and applicable mainly in Anglophone sub-Saharan Africa, calls for all the features except statutory recognition of LG, due process in boundary demarcation and inclusive institutions and processes.
6 The KD, categorised as soft law and applicable on the entire African continent, calls for all other features except constitutional recognition of LG, elected local governments, supervision (monitoring and intervention) of LG, due process in boundary demarcation and inclusive institutions and processes.
7 The ACDEG, categorised as hard law and applicable to member states of the African Union, calls only for the increased role of LG in development, transfer of powers, elected LG and inclusive institutions and processes.

On average, each of the seven instruments calls or provides for at least six features, leading to the conclusion that:

- Free and fair local elections are crucial in the promotion of grassroots democracy. The latter should be inclusive, responsive and reflect the interests of the local electorate.
- Sharing revenue between central government and local governments is important not only for sustainable economic development but protecting the institutional autonomy of local government. Once a system of revenue-sharing is legally provided, central government transfers cease to be viewed as 'favours' from central government but as legal entitlements instead.[104]
- Local governments should be constitutionally recognised. When decentralisation is recognised constitutionally, it is able to serve its objectives better than when it is merely recognised by a statute.[105] Genuine and effective decentralisation[106] must have a constitutional character for the purposes of predictability and stability.[107]
- Local government powers should be clearly defined and based on the principle of subsidiarity. The underlying reasoning is that local governments are better placed than the central government to regulate and manage the provision of services to local communities.
- Central government should supervise local governments, with two tools being emphasised: monitoring and intervention. Supervision of, and intervention in, local governments by central government should be legally justifiable and respectful of their autonomy.
- Creating or altering local government boundaries should take place within boundary demarcation processes built upon public engagement and consultation.

104 Breton & Scott 1978: 11.
105 See generally Steytler & Fessha 2007.
106 Part II of the KD para. 6.
107 Seidman, Seidman & Walde 1999: 1.

2.7 Further support for decentralisation in international human rights instruments

The role of decentralisation is also discernible from the international human rights instruments. Article 21 of the Universal Declaration of Human Rights (UDHR) provides for a right to every person 'to take part in the government of his country, directly or through freely chosen representatives', and states that the source of every government's authority must be derived from people's consent. According to Article 21 of the UDHR, every government's authority must 'periodically' and 'genuinely be elected by secret ballot of every person of voting age'. In essence the UDHR merely calls for free and fair elections without necessarily stating how such a right can be realised. Article 25 of the International Covenant on Civil and Political Rights (ICCPR) provides that it is an 'opportunity' as well as a 'right' for every citizen 'to take part in the conduct of public affairs, directly or through freely chosen representatives'. The ICCPR repeats the UDHR's provision on free and fair elections and adds that the right of every citizen to take part in 'genuine periodic elections' should be guaranteed. Again, the ICCPR does not specifically state how such an opportunity and right should be achieved.

The international legal framework for the right to public participation through elections does not state how in practice such a right may be realised. In fact, the drafting debates on the ICCPR zeroed in on political participation as an important ideal, with little emphasis placed on the institutions that could realise that ideal.[108]

Markku examines the provisions of Article 21 of the UDHR and Article 25 of the ICCPR on the right to public participation from the point of view of accessibility, inclusiveness and competition.[109] According to the author, the word 'genuine', as used in Article 21 of the UDHR, is in reference to the choice between the different political participants made by the voter when he or she votes: 'The term "genuine" would thus introduce an element of competitiveness in the electoral process'.[110] For Markku, the idea of universal suffrage makes the right to public participation somewhat more inclusive.[111]

Article 13(1) of the African Charter on Human and Peoples' Rights (ACHPR) provides for the right to public participation. By virtue of Article 2 of the ACHPR, the right to public participation is enjoyed by all without discrimination on any grounds such as 'race, ethnic group, colour, sex, language, religion or political opinions'.[112]

The realisation of the right to public participation under Article 13(1) of the ACHPR and the prohibition of discrimination on any of the prohibited grounds under Article 2 of the ACHPR is nothing more than a restatement of similar

108 Steiner 1988: 85.
109 Markku 2002: 206–22.
110 Markku 2002: 220.
111 Markku 2002.
112 Article 2 of the ACHPR.

rights in other international human rights instruments. A decentralised system is more inclusive in supporting the right to public participation than a centralised one. Some writers pour scorn on this argument on the grounds that sometimes localities are parochial and have with little interest in national integration; in addition, they reject the argument that, because local residents can demand explanations more quickly than an entire national constituency, smaller units promote responsive democracy.[113]

It is reiterated that the right to public participation through elections may be better realised through elections at the lower orders of government than at national level. Elections at the lower orders of government are more inclusive and more easily accessible; in a well-designed electoral system, they are also more competitive and better suited to promoting grassroots democracy than elections at national level.[114]

2.8 Indigenous peoples/tribal identity

International human rights law's call to protect ethnic minorities can be linked to the ability of decentralisation to accommodate ethnic diversity. For some time now, efforts to formalise a treaty for protecting indigenous peoples have been unsuccessful. Part of the opposition to recognising indigenous peoples' rights in a specific or dedicated treaty arises from the internal social dynamics of states worldwide.[115] However, a number of general international human rights instruments offer protection to indigenous peoples as minorities.[116] Crucial to the protection of indigenous peoples' rights is Article 27 of the ICCPR. It provides thus:

> In those states in which ethnic, religious or linguistic minorities exist, persons belonging to such minorities shall not be denied the right, in community with the other members of their group, to enjoy their own culture, to profess and practise their own religion, or to use their own language.

The Human Rights Committee, when commenting on Article 27 of the ICCPR, details categories of people protected, and argues that they ought to be 'a group and who share in common a culture, a religion and/or a language' or 'persons belonging to minorities which "exist" in a State party'. It notes that the 'existence of an ethnic, religious or linguistic minority in a given State party does not depend upon a decision by that State party but [is] require[d] to be established

113 Reynolds 2003: 106.

114 Smith 2007: 107.

115 The United Nations Declaration on the Rights of Indigenous Peoples was adopted by a record vote of 30 to 2 votes with 12 abstentions.

116 For instance, the Convention on the Prevention and Punishment of the Crime of Genocide 1948, UNESCO Convention against Discrimination in Education (1960) and International Convention on the Elimination of All Forms of Racial Discrimination (CERD) (1965) show advances in the quest for protection of minority rights.

by objective criteria'.[117] In other words, minorities such as indigenous peoples do not exist at the whim of the state but as a matter of right.

The Working Group for Minority Rights has produced the draft Declaration on the Rights of Persons Belonging to National or Ethnic, Religious and Linguistic Minorities (DRPBNELM).[118] The fundamental criterion in the definition of an 'indigenous person' is self-determination.[119] However, no generally acceptable definition has so far emerged. The International Labour Organisation's (ILO) definition of 'indigenous peoples' is preferred. According to the ILO definition, 'indigenous persons' refer to tribes that are socially, culturally and economically distinctly regulated by customs or traditions or by some other special laws. The ILO definition also makes reference to the fact that indigenous peoples are historically connected to a country or region before conquest or colonisation, but still retain all or part of their social, cultural and political institutions.[120]

The United Nations Declarations on the Rights of Indigenous Peoples (UNDRIP)[121] provides a platform for establishing a relationship between decentralisation as a system of government and the protection of indigenous peoples' rights. The connection between the UNDRIP, on the one hand, and decentralisation, on the other, is twofold.

First, the recognition and protection of indigenous peoples' rights can be achieved if the legal framework acknowledges diversity in the form of autonomous entities like local governments. Second, local government offers meaningful spaces for consultation to local communities.[122] Thus, given the responsive nature of local government, devolving powers to lower orders of government creates a legitimate institutional structure and appropriate forum for indigenous peoples as a vulnerable and disadvantaged group.[123]

The UNDRIP acknowledges that diversity is the epitome of civilisation for the benefit of the common good of humanity.[124] Furthermore, the view that one ethnic group is naturally superior to another is racist, scientifically baseless, legally invalid and morally unjust.[125]

Principally, the UNDRIP proposes to address the historical injustice of discrimination against indigenous peoples. The recognition of indigenous peoples' rights creates a linkage between a land right and political, economic and social development, as well as spiritual history and philosophy.[126] The Declaration

117 General Comment No. 23 para. 5.1–5.3.
118 Adopted by UNGA in December 1992 (Resolution 47/137).
119 See Article 1(2) of the United Nations Declaration on the Rights of Indigenous Peoples.
120 See Articles 1(1) (a) & (b) of the United Nations Declaration on the Rights of Indigenous Peoples.
121 Available at https://www.ohchr.org/en/issues/ipeoples/pages/declaration.aspx.
122 Scheinin 2002: 42.
123 See 'Local Government and Human Rights: Doing Good Service', Report of the International Council on Human Policy 2005, ATAR Roto Press SA, Vernier, Switzerland, p. 20.
124 See para. 2 of the Preamble to the UNDRIP.
125 See para. 3 of the Preamble to the UNDRIP.
126 See para. 5 and 6 of the Preamble to the UNDRIP.

asserts that while development must be linked to the identity and aspirations of the people, development must be pursued in a co-operative manner with the central government.[127] Indigenous peoples' rights are linked to self-determination and self-identity.[128] Institutions established under a decentralised system of government help ethnic minorities to 'govern' themselves.

The World Bank presently links poverty reduction and sustainable development to the protection of indigenous peoples' rights. This view is reflected in the Bank's borrowing policy, which makes access to funding conditional on consultation and engagement with indigenous peoples.[129] The Bank also views indigenous peoples as a socially and culturally vulnerable group which, though marginalised,[130] has a distinct identity.[131] Decentralisation creates institutional democratic spaces for ethnic minority groups to have a say on international capital inflow that is necessary for a developmental state.

2.9 Concluding remarks

This chapter has made a case for decentralisation as a means to tackle the governance challenges that face many developing countries. Whereas the umbrella argument is good governance, the role of decentralisation in promoting sustainable development, nurturing democracy and accommodating ethnic diversity has been emphasised. The chapter also disputed the argument that decentralisation is only an ideal with limited practical application, especially in developing countries. Harnessing the benefits of decentralisation, on the one hand, and seeking to limit the risks associated with it, on the other, can lead to the development of an effective system of decentralised government. The institutionalised design features of such a system are discussed in the next chapter.

127 See para. 7 of the Preamble to the UNDRIP.
128 See also Article 3 & 8 of the UNDRIP.
129 See the 'OP 4.10- Indigenous People's, available at http://web.worldbank.org/WBSITE/EXTERNAL/PROJECTS/EXTPOLICIES/EXTOPMANUAL/0,contentMDK:205653~mnuPK:4564185~pagePK:64709096~piPK:6.4709108~theSitePK:502184,00.html.
130 See para. 2 of the Policy Principles.
131 See para. 3 of the Policy Principles.

3 Critical features of decentralisation

3.1 Introduction

The institutions of local government that are created under a decentralised system must serve the purpose of local development, grassroots democracy and accommodation of diversity.[1] This chapter discusses critical features for the design of a system of local government. Six key features are identified as important for a successful decentralised system of government. These are: (a) integrity of local government institutions; (b) functional local government authority; (c) adequate fiscal autonomy; (d) administrative autonomy; (e) equitable intergovernmental transfers; and (f) sound intergovernmental relations.

What follows is a brief analysis of what each of the six features entails. The argument is that these features are not only critical for establishing and maintaining a functional decentralised system, but also necessary for minimising or eradicating the possible negative effects of devolving power to lower orders of government.

3.2 Integrity of local government institutions

The following discussion of the integrity of local government institutions focuses on constitutional recognition, the boundary demarcation process, the electoral system and traditional leaders.

3.2.1 Constitutional recognition

'Constitutional recognition' of local government means that local government institutions acquire a status under the constitution just like any other order of government.[2] Constitutional status in a decentralised system of government is a precondition for the existence of local governments as distinct orders of government and not mere extensions of the central government administrative hegemony in a centralised system.[3] In the landmark case of *Fedsure Life Assurance Ltd*

1 Chapter Two § 2.1.
2 Article 2 of the ECLSG. See also the Vancouver Draft Guidelines, para. C1.1.
3 See para. 4(iv) of the Preamble to the VFD. See also Part II of the KD, para. 6.

v Greater Johannesburg Transitional Metropolitan Council,[4] the Constitutional Court describes the evolution of the status of local government in South Africa and held that '...a local government is no longer a public body exercising delegated powers. Its council is a deliberative legislative assembly with legislative and executive powers recognised in the Constitution itself'.[5]

3.2.2 Boundary determination

The determination of local government boundaries may have either a political or a social dimension. In fact, there is a link between the territorial spaces of local governments and their political organisation.[6] Thus, a boundary demarcation process is a critical factor in the success of any decentralisation programme as boundaries help local government determine identity groups, voting rights and its tax base.

There are four criteria on which local government boundary demarcation can be based. These are: promotion of democratic citizenship; improvement of efficiency in public service delivery systems; determination of territories of communities; and the role of boundaries in relation to powers and duties of local governments.[7]

In the process of creating or altering local government boundaries, local communities and all the stakeholders should be consulted. It can compromise the objectives of decentralisation if the central government changes a local government's boundaries out of political expediency. The manipulation of local government political boundaries can affect the democratic and developmental role of a decentralised system of government.[8] Given the importance of public participation, investigating the input of local citizens by an independent body is crucial.[9]

3.2.3 Adequate electoral model for local government

There are two main electoral systems: 'winner-takes-all' and proportional representation. In the 'winner-takes-all' or 'first-past-the-post' system, the candidate who gets the highest number of votes wins the election. In a system of proportional representation, on the other hand, seats are allocated to candidates according to the percentage of votes they have obtained.[10] In a 'winner-takes-all' system, a party or an individual that supported a losing candidate(s) loses the

4 *Fedsure Life Assurance Ltd v Greater Johannesburg Transitional Metropolitan Council* 1998 (12) BCLR 1458.

5 *Fedsure Life Assurance Ltd* para. 26. This case confirmed the cases of Robertson and Another v City of Cape Town and Another, Truman-Baker v City of Cape Town 2004 (9) BCLR 950 (C) and *City* of *Johannesburg Metropolitan Municipality v Gauteng Development Tribunal* and *Others* (CCT89/09) [*2010*] *ZACC 11.*

6 Paddison 2004: 24.

7 Briffault 1996: 1123–33. Cameron 2004: 217.

8 Cameron 2004.

9 Cameron 2004: 208.

10 Reynolds 1990: 90.

chance of political representation and participation. In contrast, in a proportional representation system, the party members or individuals who supported a candidate with the least number of votes in an election may still be represented. The ultimate aim of a good electoral system should be to guarantee the free expression of the will of the voters.[11]

3.2.3.1 Criteria

Reynolds identifies five crucial considerations in the design of the electoral system in fragmented societies.[12] These considerations are relevant to local governments in many African countries. They are: (a) representativeness; (b) accessibility; (c) accountability; (d) inclusive political mobilisation; and (e) stability of governments.

3.2.4 Traditional institutions

Given the influence of traditional institutions on the African continent, these institutions should be vested with powers to resolve disputes involving customary land-holding.[13] They should also be allowed to participate in the formulation of local governments' plans and budgeting processes in instances where they have strong institutional links with the local communities. For the above reasons, the institutional design of local government should adequately recognise the role of traditional institutions in local governments.

For instance, a quota for representatives of traditional leaders may be legally provided for in local government councils. These quotas should ensure that women are adequately represented. Further, a house of traditional leaders should be legally established as an advisory body to both the central and local governments.

3.3 Local government's functional mandate

3.3.1 Introduction

Decentralisation has the potential to promote efficiency and accountability in that local authorities' delivery of goods and services match local preferences better than central government.[14] Further, decentralisation may potentially enable local citizens to have a say in how resources are used on the assumption that local governments generate the revenue themselves from local citizens and spend it with a higher degree of discipline, minimising waste.[15] In the discussion below,

11 Markku 2002: 223.
12 Reynolds 1990: 91–2.
13 Makumbe 2010: 95
14 See Chapter Two § 2.3.1.1.
15 See Chapter Two § 2.3.1.1.

the proper tools necessary for local governments to deliver services are examined. The nature and extent of the functions that should be devolved to local governments are also assessed.

3.3.2 Equipping local governments with the right governance tools

Local governments, as lower orders of government, must be vested with adequate tools to exercise their discretion on their jurisdictional mandates. This view is supported by De Visser, who argues: 'It is only when local government is afforded substantial powers that the notion of development, driven at local level, can really take root. Local government must be allowed to govern, to make mistakes, learn from its mistakes and, importantly, establish a sound and interactive relationship with its citizenry'.[16] The role of local governments in the economic transformation of local communities was discussed in detail in Chapter Two. It was emphasised that local governments' capacity to perform their tasks is critical for the success of decentralisation.[17] Local governments' capacity to perform their task relates to their ability to effectively govern.

3.3.3 Decentralising the right functional matters

The type of functions that vest in local governments must be relevant to the overall objective of decentralisation.[18] There are various mechanisms to transfer power to local governments. Powers and functions can be transferred to lower orders of government by devolution, delegation and deconcentration. The detailed discussion of these three mechanisms was given in Chapter One.[19] The allocation of powers may also take the nature of 'concurrence', where powers are attributed to both orders of government, but with one order of government, often the local government permitted to exercise a power until the central government steps in to legislate.[20] Powers may also be shared where different orders of government have powers that are related to each other with a requirement for consent before such a competency may be exercised.[21] Plenary powers (an offshoot of subsidiarity) may be transferred to local governments to execute matters that are not excluded from their explicit competencies.[22] The key issue is whether the mechanism used to transfer powers vests sufficient discretion in local governments.

16 De Visser 2005: 35.
17 See Chapter Two § 2.3.
18 Chapter Two § 2.3.1. See also De Visser 2005.
19 See Chapter One § 1.5.
20 LaCroix 2007: 366. See also Garner *et al.* 2004: 1288 who define the term 'concurrency power' as 'a political power independently exercised by both federal and state governments in the same field of legislation'.
21 Watts 2008: 88–9.
22 Article 4(2) of the ECLSG.

In Chapter Two, while discussing the international context of decentralisation, it was noted that local governments should be allocated 'full and exclusive' powers.[23] After powers have been transferred, using any of the mechanisms, local government should be afforded sufficient discretion to pursue local policies.

3.3.4 *Incremental transfer of power*

In Chapter Two, the justification for vesting full and exclusive powers to lower orders of government was given. The argument was that local governments better match local preferences and service delivery than the central government.[24]

However, some studies, especially of developing countries, show reservations about devolving powers to lower orders of government that lack the necessary capacity to fully execute their tasks.[25] Moreover, fragmentation of service delivery could lead to inefficiency and create barriers to the provision of more efficient services.[26] These findings are, however, contested as highly generalised, and ignore instances where local governments have adequately performed their role.[27] Arguably, local preferences, as well as the local capacity to fully execute local government tasks, can never be homogenous. These differences in 'tastes' and abilities call for the asymmetrical allocation of powers and functions. As Steytler argues, in countries where there is an uneven distribution of resources and skills, the wisdom of a uniform system of allocation of powers and functions becomes questionable.[28] Consequently, a good design of local government institutions should ensure that the competencies vested in local governments match the capacities of those institutions.[29]

3.3.5 *Clarity*

A clear and simple scheme of allocation of powers promotes efficiency and accountability, as discussed in Chapter Two,[30] and this is critical for the success of decentralisation.[31] There are three main arguments for clear local government competencies. First, unclear local government functions may result in the duplication of services, whereby both the central government and local government perform the same functions.[32] Second, an unclear definition of local governments' competencies may create uncertainty and confusion, leading to poor

23 See Chapter Two § 2.8. See for instance Article 3(4) of the WWDLSG.
24 Chapter Two § 2.3.1.1.
25 Azfar *et al.* 2001: 48–60.
26 Reynolds 2003: 105.
27 Lambright 2011: 221.
28 Steytler 2005: 208.
29 Steytler 2005.
30 See Chapter Two § 2.31.1 to 2.3.1.2.
31 De Visser 2005: 40–1.
32 Young 2006: 19.

service delivery.[33] Third, poorly defined functions and powers of local governments are likely to confuse local citizens in that they may not be certain which order of government is responsible for the poor service delivery.[34]

3.4 Fiscal authority

Local government fiscal discretion entails, on the one hand, the discretion to raise the local government's 'own revenue', and on the other hand, the discretion to determine tax rates and exemptions.[35] The term 'own revenue' has a wide meaning; it denotes much more than taxes. It includes not only local taxes but also charges, fees and other related sources of income.[36] Fiscal autonomy of local governments also presupposes the authority to engage in public and private partnerships, have a share in sales and local income taxes and regulate private sector investment and lending/borrowing programmes for infrastructure development.[37]

In order for local governments to perform their mandate, they should determine what to spend, and when and how to spend it. Ultimately, local governments should determine not only their tax revenue sources but also tax rates and exemptions.

3.5 Administrative autonomy

Local government administrative autonomy refers to the power or discretion to appoint local government staff, and the capacity to harness human resources for the purposes of improved service delivery in local communities. Local government administrative autonomy should, therefore, be both a discretionary power that vests in local government and a capacity and resource issue which the local government has to manage independently of the central government.[38] As Stanton argues, administrative autonomy in a decentralised system of government is only possible when local governments have the leverage and discretion to appoint and dismiss their employees.[39]

Three types of personnel systems are usually adopted by local governments: the separate, the unified and the integrated personnel systems.[40]

33 Hooja & Mathew 2006: 26.
34 Steytler & Fessha 2007: 322.
35 Bird & Slack 2003: 1.
36 Devas 2008: 19.
37 See for example the 'Federation of Canadian Municipalities, Strengthening Municipalities: On the Path to Economic Sustainability' 2002: 3, cited in Meehan *et al.* 2007: 55.
38 Kakumba 2008: 99.
39 Stanton 2009: 47.
40 Kumar 2011: 54. See also Report on the Commission of Inquiry into the Local Government System 1987: 75.

Administrative autonomy is important, but given the risk of elite capture and localised corruption, it is extra important to separate politics from administration, and this separation enhances local government accountability since the administration of a local government does not depend on the whims of politics and local manipulation.[41]

3.6 Intergovernmental fiscal transfers

Designing a proper system of intergovernmental fiscal transfers is crucial to the success of decentralisation.[42] As argued in Chapter Two, fiscal transfers are vital for equitable development, and in fragmented societies, fiscal transfers are a form of political appeasement with a peace-building potential.[43]

In most developing countries, and indeed developed countries, most revenue sources accrue to the central government.[44] The central government usually allocates funds to local governments through a system of intergovernmental fiscal transfers. The main purpose of intergovernmental fiscal transfers is to ensure that the functions that have been devolved to local governments are effectively performed, given the low revenue-raising capacities of local governments.[45] These transfers ensure resource distribution, compensation for spill-over effects and harmonisation of national objectives with controlled local discretion and accountability mechanisms.[46] Further, they have the effect of a re-distribution of resources between local governments, hence ensuring a minimum standard of service delivery.[47]

Intergovernmental transfers should be based on three main considerations, namely: predictability, inclusiveness and redistribution. Crucial to the existence of formula-based transfers is the need for intergovernmental consultation. In fact, as Shah argues: 'Fiscal rules accompanied by "gate keeper" intergovernmental councils/committees provide a useful framework for fiscal discipline and fiscal policy coordination'.[48]

3.7 Intergovernmental relations

The discussion below deals with the different types of intergovernmental relations (IGR) and the impact of the adoption of either of the types to the devolution of powers. There are two major types of IGR: the more intrusive or 'hard edge' IGR and less intrusive, 'soft edge' IGR. In this chapter, 'hard edge' refers to the supervision of local government. 'Soft edge' refers to co-operation between

41 Kumar 2011: 54.
42 Devas 2008: 83.
43 Chapter Two § 2.3.1.3.
44 Bird 1994: 311–2.
45 Watts 2001: 25.
46 Watts 2001: 26.
47 Watts 2001: 27.
48 Shah 1998: 34.

central government and local government. The adoption of a particular type of IGR depends on the extent of devolution of powers from the central government to lower orders of government.[49]

3.7.1 Supervision

Supervision is an intrusive measure intended to correct local government failures.[50] The rationale for supervision is that the central government must retain some level of leverage so that the autonomy granted to lower orders of government does not exacerbate the negative consequences associated with decentralisation.[51] In a way, supervision neutralises the dangers of decentralisation. The absence of supervision may lead to a dysfunctional system of local governance.[52]

Supervision is characterised by three main instruments: regulation, monitoring and intervention. Supervision of local governments must be predictable, must respect the autonomy of local governments[53] and must be proportional.[54]

3.7.1.1 Predictability

A framework for the supervision of local government affairs should be stable and certain. This means that the circumstances under which the central government may supervise must be known to local governments. The key test is whether central government supervision has been 'confined to *a posteriori* verification of the legality of local authority acts'.[55] The idea is that once local governments know precisely when the central government may supervise, then they will have to confine their authority to their constitutional democratic and developmental role.[56] Unpredictability in the nature and manner of supervision is a disincentive for democratic nurturing, economic development and peaceful co-existence of diverse groups in a given country. In order to have a predictable system of supervision, any administrative supervision of local authorities should be conducted according to clearly defined procedures.[57]

3.7.1.2 Autonomy of local governments

Whenever central government exercises its supervisory powers, it should be in the context of promoting institutional autonomy of local governments. The objective

49 Azfar *et al.* 2001: 48–60.
50 De Visser 2005: 170.
51 See Chapter Two § 2.4.5.
52 Shah 1998: 30.
53 De Visser 2005: 174–98.
54 De Visser 2005: 199.
55 See AGRED para. C 11.
56 Article 8(1) ECLSG. AGRED para. C 10.
57 Article 8(1) ECLSG.

of supervision by the central government should be to be to ensure that the devolution process succeeds. Particularly during an intervention, the legislative powers of the local government should be left intact, as it manifests the constitutional autonomy of any local government.[58]

3.7.1.3 'Proportionality test' in supervision

The key principle in supervision of local government is the proportionality test.[59] In other words: is the supervision commensurate with the object and purpose of decentralisation? Supervision of a local government should not diminish the local government's power to take initiative and make decisions.[60] Thus, supervision is a form of intrusion[61] which requires independent bodies, such as courts of law, to oversee the nature and extent of the supervision by central government.[62]

3.7.2 Co-operation

Co-operation is the 'soft edge' of IGR because of its less intrusive nature in the local governments by the central government. Chapter Two presented an overview of principles derived from international soft law. A number of declarations relating to, or dealing with, decentralisation make a case for co-operation.[63] Co-operation, in principle, 'neutralises' the negatives effects of autonomy, on the one hand, and limits the central government's tendencies to re-centralise local governments, on the other. As Levy and Tapscott state, 'co-operative government is an imperative for stability and peace'.[64]

Haysom juxtaposes the competitive federalism as espoused in the Canadian federal system with the co-operative federalism as espoused under the Germany federal system to make a case for co-operative government in IGR as a collective exercise of power.[65]

De Visser, building on Murray's synthesis of a framework for South Africa's local governments,[66] explains that each individual local government exercises its autonomy for the common good of the county as a whole, through co-operation.[67] Co-operation is a condition for a local government to achieve democracy,

58 See AGRED para. C 11.
59 Article 8(3) ECLSG.
60 Article 8(4) WWDLSG (the Toronto Declaration).
61 De Visser 2005: 179.
62 See AGRED para. C 14.
63 See Chapter Two § 2.8.9.
64 Levy & Tapscott 2001: 9.
65 Haysom 2001: 52.
66 Murray 2001: 67. According to Murray, the Constitution of South Africa provides an innovative standard of formal description of the allocation of powers to local government with clear-cut parameters on how the system should operate. For instance, section 40 provides that the spheres of government are 'distinctive', 'interdependent' and 'interrelated'.
67 De Visser 2005: 214.

development and peace. Thus, 'co-operative government means that national policy must be sensitive to local ... needs and concerns and must not ignore or ride roughshod over them'.[68]

3.7.3 Instruments of supervision

3.7.3.1 Regulation

The phrase 'regulation of local government' in its literal sense refers to the act of establishing the framework within which local government autonomy may be exercised.[69] De Visser distinguishes regulatory powers dealing with local governments' institutions and the regulatory powers affecting local governments' functions.[70]

Through regulation, the central government may design the local government institutions and their powers and functions to fit with the objectives of decentralisation.[71]

3.7.3.2 Monitoring and evaluation

The discussion below illustrates the importance of monitoring as a feature of supervision in IGR. The discussion also highlights the relationship between monitoring and supervision and concludes that monitoring is a form of supervision. Although the term 'monitoring' in the discourse of decentralisation is sometimes described as an antecedent to the power to 'support', 'promote' and 'supervise' local government, it is distinguishable from the power to control.[72] Generally, the power to monitor is not a power to intrude into the affairs of local government. The Constitutional Court of South Africa, while examining the central government's power to monitor local governments, held that '[w]e do not interpret the monitoring power as bestowing additional or residual powers of provincial intrusion on the domain of LG, beyond perhaps the power to measure or test at intervals LG compliance with national and provincial legislative directives ...'[73]

Reporting is part and parcel of monitoring in IGR. There ought to be a mechanism by means of which the framework set by the central government can be enforced. Consequently, if '*monitoring* of local governments by "senior" governments is necessary in order to pick up early signals of problems that require intervention of some sort',[74] the means by which monitoring can be achieved

68 Murry & Nijzing 2002: 42.
69 Kavanagh 2002: 985.
70 De Visser 2005: 170.
71 Steytler 2008: 518.
72 See the South African case of *Re Certification of the Constitution of the Republic of South African* 1996 (10) BCLR 1253 (CC) para. 371–3, cited in De Visser 2005: 179.
73 See Re Certification of the Constitution of the Republic of South Africa para. 373 cited in De Visser 2005: 179.
74 De Visser 2005: 260 (emphasis in the text).

have to be clarified. Indeed, some writers on local governments in Africa now place emphasis on self-reporting as a means through which local governments endeavour to ensure compliance with their obligations.[75] Reporting is a key compliance measure of local governments' constitutional and legislative obligations. International human rights law offers a good example of reporting as a means of ensuring compliance with standards of state party obligations.[76]

Reporting on the performance of local governments provides a way of correcting errors. Reporting may also help poorly performing local governments adopt better practices.[77] It is emphasised that the aim of reporting should ordinarily be concerned with information gathering and should never be used as a means to penalise any local government for poor performance.

3.7.3.3 Intervention

Where monitoring of local governments by the central government reveals evidence of failure on the part of local governments, intervention may be triggered. Strictly speaking, a power to intervene may appear oppressive,[78] and may in fact run counter to the notion of local government autonomy. However, as De Visser points out, intervention is part of an institutional design that seeks to promote the objects of local governments.[79] The author further explains that interventions 'can work as "insurance policies" for the central governments in that these governments will let go of some of their traditional areas of governance in return for security that, if there are serious failures, there are instruments available to address them'.[80] The question then becomes: what does an intervention as an instrument of supervision entail and what are its parameters?

As a rule, intervention must be exercised within the parameters of promoting the integrity and the objectives of local government. Intervention in local governments must be predictable, must respect the autonomy of local governments and must be proportional.[81]

3.7.4 Instruments of co-operation

The discussion below focuses on co-operation as a type of IGR. As noted above, the powers and functions devolved to local governments require regulation and

75 De Visser 2005: 160.

76 See CESCR General comment 1, Reporting by States parties UN doc. document E/1989/22, 24/02/1989 para. 1, available at http://www.unhchr.ch/tbs/doc.nsf/%28Symbol%29/38e23a6ddd6c0f4dc12563ed0051cde7?Open document (accessed 20 September 2010).

77 Kugonza 2012: 5.

78 Murray 1999: 335.

79 De Visser 2005: 185.

80 De Visser 2005: 197.

81 De Visser 2005: 199.

supervision by the central government. Yet over-regulation of local government institutions and supervision of local government may impede decentralisation. Co-operation is about relations of equality of different orders of government in the exercise of their distinct powers. Therefore, the two distinct orders of government ought to work together in executing their different mandates.

Co-operation as a type of IGR focuses on the role of local government associations, joint plans and dispute resolutions. IGR may either be horizontal or take the nature of intergovernmental agreements.

3.7.4.1 Associations of local governments

Emerging international 'soft' law on decentralisation provides for the right of local governments to form associations[82] and calls on central government to 'consult associations of local authorities when passing legislation affecting local government'.[83] Associations of local governments provide a more reliable way of engaging in negotiations with central government than a single local government on its own.[84]

3.7.4.2 Integrated planning

The devolution of powers to local governments calls for co-operation in the planning process between the central government and local governments,[85] hence the notion of integrated planning (joint planning) characterised as the epicentre of development.[86] Integrated planning as an instrument of co-operative local government is foundational to local democracy.[87] In South Africa, for instance, integrated planning is defined as 'a participatory process of planning, through which the municipality assesses its needs, prioritises them and formulates objectives and strategies to address these needs'.[88] Local governments cannot address their needs and priorities outside the overall national policy framework and priority areas.[89] As a strategy, IGR joint planning ensures that the local governments' needs form part of the umbrella state policies and development goals. As an instrument of co-operative governance, integrated planning requires 'bottom-up development': the 'institutionalisation of integration refers to a legal framework that enables local government to participate, as an equal partner, in the integration of various levels of government'.[90]

82 See Chapter Two § 2.9.8.
83 Article 9(2) of the Toronto Declaration.
84 Murray (2001). See also Article 10 of ECLSG.
85 Katono 2007: 76.
86 De Visser 2005: 85.
87 Okidi & Guloba 2006: 6.
88 De Visser 2005: 85.
89 Katono 2007: 75.
90 De Visser 2005: 211.

3.7.4.3 Intergovernmental agreements

Intergovernmental service agreements are mutual undertakings between units of state or local governments with each other to provide common services in a local government or in different local governments.[91] Essentially, intergovernmental agreements focus on the 'overlapping of powers'.[92] For example, two or more organs of state may each have distinct powers that relate to one common project. In such cases, they may conclude an agreement about their powers to make that one common project work.[93] Intergovernmental agreements amongst different local governments can result in delivery of certain large-scale services, such as water and education. When an IGR agreement is between local governments, it is a manifestation of horizontal IGR.[94]

Intergovernmental agreements can promote efficiency in resource allocation and create a forum for mutual discussion amongst different local government units.[95] Intergovernmental agreements are therefore crucial instruments for fostering co-operation and peace in a nation state.[96]

3.7.4.4 Intergovernmental dispute resolution

The essence of a dispute resolution mechanism in IGR is an honest admission that there are bound to be conflicts between organisations.[97] Within the context of devolution of powers to lower orders of government, it is preferable that a mechanism for a fair resolution of conflict is in place. For instance, a dispute may arise by passing a law in an area where both the central government and local governments exercise a concurrent or residual power. Without a mechanism for resolving disputes amongst the different orders of government, the real benefits of decentralisation are endangered. The legal framework should provide for a forum to deal with IGR disputes outside the traditional adjudication structures.

3.8 Conclusion

The above discussion highlights the critical features necessary for a successful system of decentralisation. The argument has been that in order to protect the integrity of local governments, constitutional recognition of local government, demarcation of boundaries, electoral systems and traditional institutions that underpin the system of decentralisation must be constitutionally recognised and

91 Flood *et al.* 1997: 112.
92 Gillette 2001: 194, cited in Reynolds 2003: 123.
93 De Visser 2005: 212.
94 Mohnach 1999: 164.
95 Mohnach 1999.
96 Mohnach 1999.
97 Steytler 2001: 175–80.

entrenched. In multi-ethnic countries, local governments should adopt an electoral system that is not only inclusive but fosters political stability.

An adequate decentralised system should ensure that local governments are vested with the discretion to fully exercise executive and legislative powers. Thus, preference is placed on sharing of power between the central government and local governments. Creating lower orders of government with no independent revenue-generating capacity and little or no discretion to spend such revenue according to local priorities is antithetical to the theory of decentralisation. Invariably, the integrity of local government is unrealistic unless local government institutions are vested with the discretion to generate their own revenue and spend it. The argument for independent local government fiscal powers is also mindful of the role of central government transfers: hence the emphasis placed on the role of central government transfers in local economic development.

A successful decentralised system of government should recognise the role of traditional leaders by vesting them with special seats in the local government councils as well as the right to veto local government laws and policies. This may lead to a mutual influence of traditional leadership with modern democratic values. Further, a 'one-size-fits-all' design of local government may exacerbate some of the inadequacies of decentralisation. In countries where there are strong ethnic or economic disparities among communities, an asymmetrical form of local government is desirable. The discussion also highlighted the importance of local governments' discretion to hire and fire their own staff in order to have a meaningful decentralised system. Reiterating the relationship between development and political stability, the chapter identified IGR as an all-encompassing feature of a successful decentralised system of government.

4 Decentralisation in Uganda

History and overview

4.1 Introduction

This chapter provides a historical background to local government in Uganda and in turn documents the historical political-social-scientific variables that account for an intrusive centralism in Uganda's decentralisation. In this chapter, demographic, ethnicity identity, the power of the elite and the phenomenon of the rural urban divide are highlighted as critical variables in Uganda's top-down decentralisation system. These variables are further examined through the prism of the historical political institutions of governance and how these institutions have over time shaped the incentives of the decision-making processes of district councils.

The introduction of Western European institutions of governance alienated most communities from participating in decision-making. The pre-colonial organisation in Buganda that was rolled out to the rest of the Uganda Protectorate soon after the Buganda Agreement will be the chapter's point of departure. The political and constitutional developments, regarding local governments, from the pre-colonial period and the independence period up to 1995, are also examined.

The Buganda Kingdom is the focus of the chapter for two main reasons. First, the system of Buganda Kingdom's administration that predated colonial rule was replicated in all other parts of the country by the British colonial rulers through the method of indirect rule. Secondly, the system of the Buganda Kingdom's political organisation was similar to that of other kingdoms in Uganda, like the Ankole, Toro and Bunyoro Kingdoms. Thus, the Buganda Kingdom's traditional pre-colonial system of administration is fairly representative of the general administrative structures in the entire country before the advent of foreign rule.

The questions that this chapter proposes to answer are as follows. Is the decentralisation phenomenon new in Uganda? Do the pre-colonial political and institutional features of the Buganda Kingdom have any role to play in the discourse on decentralisation in Uganda today? Did the sharing of powers, under the 1962 Constitution, between the central government and the traditional Kingdoms in Uganda, then provide a model for reforming the present decentralisation legal and policy frameworks? The above questions will help us to understand the connection between law, history and politics with regard to local government in Uganda.[1]

1 Kunal 2003: 6.

4.2 Political and administrative structures of Buganda before British rule

Even before the coming of the European missionaries, Arab merchants, and later colonial rulers, the Buganda Kingdom had had a long history as a sophisticated model of political organisation which rivalled the political organisation of many pre-industrial Western European countries.[2] Ssekandi and Gitta trace the Buganda Kingdom's history well back to the 14th century, explaining the hereditary nature of a leader as a hierarchical system of chiefs. At the helm of political and cultural leadership was the King (the *Kabaka*), who was also referred to as the chief land owner (*Sabataka*). His ascendance to power took place through clan lineage. The *Kabaka* is considered to be the giver of grace and favour and an embodiment of Bugandan cultural identity.[3]

Below the *Kabaka* was the Prime Minister, known as the *Katikiro*, who presided over the Parliament (the *Lukiiko*). Below the *Katikiro* was the Chief Justice (the *Omulamuzi*), who presided over all matters of dispute resolution, with a right of appeal by an aggrieved party to the King. Below the Chief Justice was the Treasurer (the *Omuwanika*), who was responsible for the collection of revenue from all subjects and the semi-independent states within Buganda. Finally, there was the Queen mother (the *Namasole*) who played an advisory role to the King. In other words, a King could not take a decision without notifying all the other officials mentioned above as well as the Queen mother.[4]

The Buganda Kingdom's system of administration was highly decentralised through a system of chiefs who were appointed by the *Kabaka*.[5] The county chief (the *Saza* chief) was the highest in the hierarchy of chiefs (historically there were 20 *Sazas* in the Buganda Kingdom), followed by the sub-county chief (the *Gombolola* chief). Below the *Gombolola* chief was the Parish chief (the *Muluka* chief). The lowest level of administration was the sub-parish chief (the *Mutongole*). Generally speaking, the term *mutongole* also means a local leader.[6] Mamdani argues that while chiefs in the pre-colonial period were limited by the King's powers, they were limited too by the will of the populace.[7] According to Mamdani, this was a form of peer mechanism in leadership to ensure discipline.

The Buganda Kingdom had different clans, whose leaders served as chiefs in different administrative roles. These clans were organised according to their different totemic connections. The leaders of these clans, also known as the *Abataka*, controlled the land tenure system and supervised the observance of the customs concerning marriage, succession and other social relationships.[8] The different clans indicate that even within homogenous kingdoms like Buganda, there

2 Apter 1967: 63–4.
3 Ssekandi & Gitta 1994: 194.
4 Apter 1967: 44.
5 Nabudere 1980: 19.
6 Apter 1967: 95.
7 Mamdani 1996: 46.
8 Ssekandi & Gitta 1994: 194.

existed social groups which were not only respected but culturally accommodated for the purposes of political cohesion.[9]

4.2.1 The role of the traditional Lukiiko

As mentioned, the *Lukiiko* was the traditional parliament of the Buganda Kingdom. The *Lukiiko* consisted of three native ministers as *ex officio* senior members thereof. These were: the Prime Minister (the *Katikiro*); the Chief Justice (the *Omulamuzi*); and the Treasurer or Controller of the *Kabaka*'s revenues (the *Omuwanika*). The term *Lukiiko* loosely translates into the word 'meeting' or a traditional assembly or meeting place. Traditionally, admission to the *Lukiiko* was limited to chiefs and the *Kabaka*'s appointed ministers, who were usually old men. The debates in the *Lukiiko* were open to the public and relatively democratic. The *Lukiiko* passed resolutions regarding war and mercy, and ensured an orderly coronation process for a new king. It also passed laws for the Kingdom.[10] It is for this reason that even after interaction with modern European systems of parliamentary democracy, the Buganda Kingdom was keen to preserve the *Lukiiko*, rather than abandon it, albeit with limited success.[11]

4.2.2 Boundary demarcation in pre-colonial Buganda

Before colonial rule, traditional leadership boundaries were determined by geographical features, such as rivers, mountains, swamps and lakes. In addition, language and cultural differences played a role in determining the physical boundaries of an identified ethnic group. Rarely were any stone markers or maps used to clearly delineate where a boundary of one *Saza* began or ended. However, somehow its boundaries were known and accepted by the different *Sazas* within Buganda. Similarly, the boundaries of the Buganda Kingdom itself were drawn along geographical, linguistic and cultural lines.[12]

4.2.3 Analysis of the traditional leadership

The first conclusion that one may draw from the above description of the pre-colonial Buganda Kingdom's traditional institutions of governance, is that devolution of power as a form of governance, as discussed in Chapters Two and Three, is not an entirely new phenomenon in Uganda.[13] The different traditional governments that existed before colonial rule were either centralised or decentralised. In both cases, there existed a hierarchy of power. Rugege, writing on traditional leadership in Africa, argues that these leaders were the keepers of values

9 Ssekandi & Gitta 1994: 194.
10 Twaddle 1993: 12–30.
11 Nabudere 1980: 30.
12 Apter 1967: 96.
13 Chapter Two § 2.3 and Chapter Three § 3.2.5.

and responsible for the defence of the kingdom as well as for food production.[14] The author further argues that there was a high level of participatory democracy, where decision-making took place in assemblies of men.[15] The Buganda Kingdom's pre-colonial traditional government conforms to the above view.

Commenting on the effect of colonial rule in Africa, Oomen[16] describes it as both a nightmare and a cultural dialogue. According to the author, colonial rule was a nightmare because of the dehumanising nature of foreign rule, and a dialogue because of the interaction between two different political and legal orders.[17] Starting with the 'nightmare' Oomen describes, this part of the chapter examines how colonial rule disrupted existing local government structures.

Much has been written about European colonial administration in Africa, which requires no further inquiry in this book.[18] However, it is necessary to examine the nature of the colonial state that was adopted in Uganda during the period 1900–62. In British colonial Africa, the method of rule was indirect. Indirect rule, a method espoused by Captain Lugard,[19] ensured that the natives had a say in the day-to-day administration of the territories under British rule.[20] In order to better exploit the African resources at the time, it was imperative that Africans were granted a stake in their native lands.[21] The Buganda Agreement of 1900 was one of the instruments through which the natives' resources could be exploited. The British colonial government thus adopted the system of indirect rule by signing an agreement with the native rulers of the Buganda Kingdom, known as the Buganda Agreement of 1900, by apparently vesting the Buganda Kingdown with a unique status within the protectorate government. As has been documented by many historians, the Buganda Kingdom's special status under the Buganda agreement of 1900 was very much limited.

4.2.4 The impact of colonial rule on the Buganda Kingdom's institutional structures

Constitutional lawyers and writers have often ridiculed the Buganda Agreement as a relic of colonialism, and as a symbol of loss of traditional autonomy.[22] However, as the first legal document introducing modern local administrative structures in Uganda, the Agreement plays a central role in the understanding of Uganda's constitutional history.[23]

14 Rugege 2003: 172–3.
15 Rugege 2003.
16 Oomen 2005: 13–29.
17 Oomen 2005: 13–29.
18 See Milner 1948: 12; Speak 1863; Margery 1960; Nsibambi 1968; Morris & Read 1966; Nabudere 1980; Museveni 1997; Ibingira 1973; Karugire 1988.
19 Lugard 1965: 18.
20 Lugard 1965: 18.
21 Lugard 1965: 18.
22 Mugambwa 1987: 244; Morris & Reed 1972; Apter 1961: 109–33.
23 Ibingira 1973: 19.

As explained, there was no political vacuum in the Buganda Kingdom before the advent of British rule. There existed traditional political mechanisms that placed emphasis on consensus and dialogue. Thus, when the colonial administrators took over, they not only undermined these mechanisms but also 'liberated' the chiefs from 'all institutionalised constraint'.[24] The laws with which the British administered the entire Uganda Protectorate were inimical to the existing traditional structures of the Buganda Kingdom at the time, such as the notion of clan meetings.[25] Rugege argues that whereas clan meetings in pre-colonial times were characterised by open debates, colonial rule was characterised by decrees and ordinances.[26] Moreover, none of the laws made during the colonial period were made by Africans. In this regard, traditional institutions of local democracy were replaced by centralised repression.[27]

The idea of colonial rule was based on the interests of the elites who formed and monopolised the centres of power.[28] Thus, as Mamdani explains, whenever colonial administrators sought to change local power dynamics, they created new political institutions, such as the 'warrant chiefs', that were unknown to the local citizens.[29] Further, Mamdani argues, colonial rule stratified local administration into two worlds: the urban, which was 'civilised'; and the rural, which lacked proper amenities such as good sanitation, electricity, good schools and hospitals.[30] The institutional segregation that was a consequence of this stratification not only supported racial discrimination, but 'nurtured' local institutions of leadership *to become* inferior, meek and undesirable.[31]

4.3 Contested political questions before 1962 Independence

The constitutional negotiations for independence were preceded by two reports compiled by the British Colonial Office: the Wild Constitutional Committee Report (1959) and the Munster Constitutional Committee Report (1960). Although the Final Report of the Munster Committee made a case for a single democratic state with a strong central government, it also recommended granting the Buganda Kingdom federal status within Uganda.[32] During the

24 Mamdani 1996: 122.

25 Kanyeihamba 2002: 55. See also *Daudi Ndibarema and Others v The Enganiz of Ankole and Others*, 1960: 47. In this case the High Court disputes the view that traditional leaders were the sole custodians of Kingdoms. See also Rugege 2003: 173 and *Nyali, Ltd v A.G. of Kenya* (1956) Q.B 15.

26 Rugege 2003: 172–3.

27 Kanyeihamba 2002: 16. Ndulo 1998: 76.

28 Seidman 1984: 285.

29 Ndulo 1998–9: 77.

30 Mamdani 1996: 122.

31 Mamdani 1996.

32 Ssekandi & Gitta 1994. Morris & Read 1966: 70.

Constitution Conference on Uganda's Independence in London in 1961,[33] Buganda's delegates' demand for separate autonomous federal status within Uganda was granted.[34]

Thus, the 1962 Constitution of Uganda was to a large extent a compromise document after numerous negotiations between different ethnic and political groups. It was after the negotiations had been completed that the British government enacted an Act of Parliament granting Uganda self-government.[35] Notwithstanding the negotiations before the grant of independence to Uganda from British colonial rule, the historical traditional 'value' that was attached to the culture of dialogue and consensus-building in the traditional authorities was missing in the democratic process. In the discussion that follows, the political institutions under the 1962 Constitution are explained.

4.4 The 1962 Uganda Constitution: a general overview

The most contentious political questions before the promulgation of the 1962 Constitution related to the competition for leadership positions and power rather than to issues, such as a genuine devolution of power to local governments. Ironically, there was no mention of, or attempt at reforming, the colonial state, as evidenced by the political institutional design that emerged. Kanyeihamba asserts that the 1962 Ugandan Constitution created a 'hotchpotch' form of government that was both federal and unitary, with vague delineation of the boundaries of the different regions within the country.[36] Nonetheless, the 1962 Constitution placed emphasis on power-sharing and co-operative government between the central government and federal states, especially in the areas of service delivery.[37]

33 Seidman 1984: 56, cited in Ndulo 1998: 81, describes most independent constitutions in former British colonies in Africa as 'an elaborate buffet, with elaborate constitutional provisions from other existing constitutions spread across the glittering sideboard, from which the constitutional maker filled her plate to her taste … sentences, paragraphs, whole sections and chapters float from one constitution to the next'. Constitutional Conferences, also known as Lancaster Conferences, were common in former British colonies before independence. Constitutional Conferences were aimed at negotiating with former British colonies in preparation for their independence. Kanyeihamba 2002: 61 explains that for 'all British colonies which gained independence, in the 1960 and 1970s, a constitutional conference held in London was always a prelude to "self-determination"'.

34 See Schedule I to the 1962 Constitution of Uganda – the Constitution of the Kingdom of Buganda which granted a special federal arrangement for Buganda within Uganda.

35 See Uganda Independence Act 1962.

36 Kanyeihamba 2002: 78.

37 Section 79(1) of 1962 Constitution.

4.4.1 Buganda's federal status and other federal states under the 1962 Constitution

The Constitution provided for 'federal states', 'districts' and 'territories'.[38] The federal states were the Kingdoms of Buganda, Ankole, Bunyoro and Toro, the 'Territory of Mbale' and the 'Territory of Busoga',[39] each of which was dealt with in a separate schedule.[40] The federal states and territories were designed along the lines of the Buganda Kingdom's political structures.[41]

4.4.2 Buganda's political and institutional structures

The Buganda Constitution provided for the *Kabaka* as the '*ruler*' of the Buganda as long as he was elected by the majority of votes in the *Lukiiko*.[42] However, candidacy for the *Kabakaship* was limited to those of royal lineage.[43] The Buganda Kingdom's Constitution established the *Kabaka*'s Council consisting of the *Katikiro*; the *Omulamuzi*; the *Omuwanika*; the Minister of Health and Works; the Minister of Education; the Minister of Natural Resources; and the Minister of Local Government.[44] The *Kabaka*'s Council was vested with the executive authority of the Buganda Kingdom's government.[45] All members of the *Kabaka*'s Council, with the exception of the *Katikiro*, were appointed by the *Kabaka*.[46] The *Katikiro* was elected by the *Lukiiko* from a list of five persons nominated by the *Kabaka*.[47]

4.4.3 Local government administration under the 1962 Constitution

The Constitution provided for the districts of Acholi, Bukedi, Karamoja, Kigezi, Lango, Madi, Sebei, Teso and West Nile, outside the kingdom areas.[48] The 1962 constitutional design acknowledged the political and developmental uniqueness of the non-kingdom areas, especially those found in the northern parts of the country. Because most of them had less cohesive traditional political structures than in the kingdom areas, it was appropriate for the central government to retain a significant role in the political control of those areas. In addition, the areas of the northern part of the country were less developed compared to those of the

38 Section 2(1) of 1962 Constitution.
39 Section 2(2) 1962 Constitution.
40 Section 5(1) of 1962 Constitution.
41 See Milner 1963: 1–63.
42 Article 2(1) of the Constitution of Buganda.
43 Article 2(2) of the Constitution of Buganda.
44 Article 4 of the Constitution of Buganda.
45 Article 8(1) of the Constitution of Buganda.
46 Article 10 & 12 of the Constitution of Buganda.
47 Article 12(2) of the Constitution of Buganda.
48 Section 5(1) of 1962 Constitution.

southern parts of the country. It would not have been appropriate to grant semi-federal status to areas that had no means of revenue generation.

Uganda's local administrations in the 1960s were described as a colonial inheritance, given that the legal framework at independence was prescriptive and rule-oriented, based on command and control. In fact the local administration legal framework was developed along the lines of English urban and rural district councils.[49] The legal framework categorised local governments as either (rural) local administration or urban authorities. However, these categories of local government had similar powers and functions. The main legislative enactments made pursuant to the Constitution were the Local Administration Act (LAA)[50] and the Urban Authorities Act (UAA).[51] The features of these two pieces of legislation will be examined below.

4.4.4 *The Local Administration Act: district administration in non-kingdom areas*

Compared to the manner in which the federal states' powers were provided for under the Constitution, the articulation of local government was rather limited. Besides, the power to regulate local governments in kingdom areas was vested in the respective federal states.

The Constitution left the task to Parliament to make laws dealing with local administration.[52] Though the Constitution mentioned that there would be district councils in every district, their functions were mainly administrative.[53] It is also noted that the national assembly empowered local administrations to make laws for the establishment of the 'Districts Constitutional Heads', their appointment to office, tenure and ceremonial functions.[54]

4.4.5 *The Urban Authorities Act*

Under the 1967 Constitution local governments were further categorised as urban authorities. The designation of an area as a municipality depended on an area's level of development and urbanisation.[55] Under the UAA, the Minister of Local Government could simply declare, by a statutory order, an area to be

49 Hubert & Andersen 1932. Mamdani 1996: 18.

50 Its long title stated that it was '[a]n Act to make provision for the establishment and regulation of administrations in and for Districts and to provide for matters incidental thereto and connected therewith'. This Act was amended by Act 13/66 to become the Administrations (Districts) Act.

51 Its long title stated that it was '[a]n Act to establish and regulate Urban Authorities and to provide for matters incidental thereto and connected therewith'.

52 Section 88(1) of the 1962 Constitution.

53 Section 88(1) of the 1962 Constitution.

54 Section 89(1) of the 1962 Constitution. Section 2(1) of the LAA.

55 See The Local Governments (Classification of Towns) Order pursuant to sections 3(5) and 7(1) of the Urban Authorities Act.

a municipality. He or she could assign it a name and define its boundaries, or declare that an area had ceased to be a municipality.[56]

However, no alteration to the boundaries could be made of a town in the Buganda Kingdom unless the alteration was in accordance with the agreements between the central government and the *Kabaka*'s government.[57]

4.4.6 Assessment of the 1962 Constitution

Unlike many African constitutions at independence, which were highly centralised,[58] the 1962 Ugandan Constitution catered for the sharing of political power between central government, the federal states and district administrations. When its basic institutional design is reviewed against the principles of local development, democracy and accommodation of diversity, it appears that the legal framework of local government at the time was considerably well articulated.

First, the Buganda Kingdom had a measure of political and financial autonomy entrenched in the Constitution. The other traditional kingdoms also enjoyed political autonomy though not to the same degree as the Buganda Kingdom. Another element to be considered here is that the local government design relating to urban areas was different to that for rural areas. The legislative framework of local administration, which provided for rural administrative structures separate from urban ones, in effect polarised the urban local administration from the rural local administration.[59]

Lastly, the constitutional design entrenched institutions of colonial rule, such as the office of the chief, who retained untrammelled powers at the local level. While the institutional design for devolution of powers to local administrations and urban authorities was reasonably elaborate, the institutions that were established thereunder were not fully democratic. By placing much of the political power in the hands of unelected kings, the constitutional design promoted monarchical rule to the detriment of democratic principles. Thus, the 1962 Uganda Constitution, just like in many other first post-independence African Constitutions, may then be described as 'a false start' in that, other than for the Buganda Kingdom, there was no proper transfer of powers to local communities.[60]

4.5 Abrogation of the 1962 Constitution

*4.5.1 The '*Kabaka *crisis' and the recentralisation of state power*

The abrogation of the 1962 Constitution followed what is referred to as the '*Kabaka* crisis' in Uganda's legal and constitutional history. The *Kabaka* crisis

56 Section 3 of the UAA.
57 Section 63 of UAA.
58 Prempeh 2007: 479.
59 Mamdani 1996: 23.
60 Prempeh 2007: 469.

heightened tensions between the central government and the Buganda Kingdom and heralded the total loss of power for the Buganda Kingdom and other federal states, and the centralisation of power. It is referred to as a 'crisis' because of the legal and institutional instability that resulted.[61]

On 22 February 1966, amidst allegations of an alleged coup plot against the government, the Prime Minister suspended the 1962 Constitution, abolished the posts of president and vice-president and assumed all executive powers. On 24 February 1966, the cabinet made proposals for a new Constitution. An interim constitution was debated and promulgated the same day. On 15 April, the National Assembly (NA) turned itself into a Constituent Assembly, leading to the adoption of the 1967 Constitution. In response to these events, the federal legislature of the Buganda Kingdom passed a resolution barring Buganda's representatives in the National Assembly from being sworn in, in terms of the new Constitution. Furthermore, the Buganda Kingdom resolution demanded that the central government officials leave the territory of Buganda.[62]

The suspension of the old constitutional order was challenged in the case of *Uganda v Commissioner of Prisons Ex Parte Matovu*.[63] The Court dismissed the application and held that the new Constitution had established a new order, whose legitimacy could not be questioned in court. The Court, based its decision on Kelsen's theory of revolution,[64] and took the view that a military coup could legitimately change a government. The Court held that the events that took place in 1966 amounted to a coup d'état that lawfully changed the old legal order. The Court stated:

> The series of events which took place in Uganda from February 22 to April, 1966, were law creating facts appropriately described in law as a revolution; that is to say there was an abrupt political change not contemplated by the existing Constitution, that destroyed the entire legal order and was superseded by a new Constitution, namely, the 1966 Constitution, and by effective government.[65]

The *Ex parte Matovu* case had two important implications for the history of decentralisation and power-sharing in Uganda. First, the decision ended all the pretences of power-sharing between the central government and the federal states, and increased the role of central authority.[66] Secondly, the decision militarised the relationship between the central government and local government

61 The Odoki Commission 1993: 51.
62 Kanyeihamba 2002: 103–13.
63 Reported as *Uganda v Commissioner of Prisons Ex Parte Matovu* (1966) EA p 514. Mr Matovu, a chief in the Buganda Kingdom government, had mobilised his subjects not to pay taxes to the central government.
64 Kelsen 1945: 117–18.
65 See *Ex Parte Matovu* holding no 5.
66 Prempeh 2008: 323.

and projected the central government of the day as invincible.[67] Oloka-Onyango, commenting on *Ex parte Matovu*, considers the Court's decision as a constitutional 'ghost', in that it was a precursor to militarism in Uganda's politics.[68]

4.5.2 *Demise of local government institutions under the military government*

The political uncertainty and the economic meltdown that started in 1966 partly explain the military takeover of the government in 1971.[69] When the then Prime Minister 'lawfully' abrogated the Constitution and used the military to establish his rule as the Head of State, he as a consequence introduced the army into active politics in the country.[70]

In 1971, the Army Commander, Major General Idi Amin, staged a military coup d'état. One reason given by the coup d'état leaders was to save a 'bad situation from getting worse'.[71] The examples of 'a bad situation' referred to above were: the economic stagnation at the time, collapse of state democratic institutions and loss of political legitimacy because of the alienation of the majority of the population from decision-making at local levels. By the time Idi Amin took power, the state structures were already highly centralised. Idi Amin merely formalised the militarisation of those institutions. He also ended all pretence of parliamentary oversight of government by vesting the law-making power in himself.[72]

After initially allowing political parties to operate, a decree was promulgated to suspend and ban all political activities. The earliest clampdown on former leaders particularly targeted former local government leaders.[73] In the place of local government leaders, military personnel were appointed. The country was divided into ten provinces, each placed under the leadership of military officials. Each district was headed by a district military commissioner, who was assisted by militias at different levels of local government as chiefs.[74] They arrested, killed and extorted people at will.[75]

4.5.3 *The role of the local communities in the liberation struggle*

Local communities played a key role in the liberation struggle from the days of President Amin's regime to the second Obote regime. The role of local

67 Kanyeihamba 2002: 128.
68 Oloka-Onyango 1996: 14.
69 Kanyeihamba 2002: 126.
70 Kanyeihamba 2002: 131.
71 See The Soldiers Statement, 1971, Government Notice No. 82/1971, cited in Kanyeihamba 2002: 160.
72 See Legal Notice No. 1 of 1971 that suspended the Constitution and vested all powers in the President. See also Decree No 5 of 1971.
73 Kanyeihamba 2002: 146–7.
74 The Odoki Commission 1993: 485.
75 Museveni 2000: 13. Kanyeihamba 2002: 150.

communities can be explained by two main factors: extreme oppression and material deprivation.

First, local people in the villages bore the brunt of the local militias without having recourse to any disciplinary mechanism against the perpetrators.[76] People suspected of engaging in subversive activities were arrested and tortured (and in some cases killed) by local officials.[77] Secondly, local communities experienced the effect of the absence of basic amenities, such as clean water, drugs and good schools for their children.[78] The material deprivation and repression of communities were important reasons for communities to resist the military government.[79] The local community became a breeding ground for resistance, and thus, armed opposition groups found it easy to recruit local people.[80]

The first government after the fall of President Idi Amin was led by Prof Yusufu Lule, under the umbrella organisation of the Uganda National Liberation Front/Army (UNLF/A).[81] Prof Yusufu Lule was removed by the Uganda National Liberation Army (UNLA) and immediately replaced by President Godfrey Binaisa.[82] President Binaisa was also deposed by the Military Commission, headed by the late Paulo Muwanga.[83] The national elections, held in 1980 under the heavy influence of the Military Commission, resulted in the second Obote regime from 1980 to 1985.[84] The rigged elections led to a rebellion headed by the current President, Yoweri Museveni, that lasted for five years.[85]

During President Obote's second regime, local government structures were dominated by hand-picked party faithful of the UPC and members of the party youth wing. These officials wielded tremendous power and were responsible for many deaths and disappearances of people suspected of having been rebel collaborators.[86] The second Obote regime was also overthrown by a military junta led by General Tito Okello Lutwa.[87]

When the National Resistance Movement/Army (NRM/A) finally gained state power in 1986, after removing General Lutwa's military junta, the solemn promise to Ugandans was that the change of government was not 'a mere change

76 Kanyeihamba 2002: 158–63.
77 Kanyeihamba 2002: 162.
78 Museveni 2000: 32–3. Kiyaga-Nsubuga 2000: 2.
79 Golooba-Mutebi 2000: 16.
80 Kanyeihamba 2002: 163. Lambright 2011: 24.
81 This government was formed after numerous negotiations between two main factions. The one faction, known as *Kikosi Maalum*, was led by President Obote, and the other, known as the Front for National Salvation (FRONASA), was led by the current President, Yowerri K Museveni. See Kanyeihamba 2002: 183.
82 President Binaisa was the Attorney-General of Uganda in the 1960s and was the lead government counsel in the *Commissioner of Prisons Ex Parte Matovu* case.
83 Kanyeihamba 2002: 197.
84 Museveni 2000: 117.
85 Kanyeihamba 2002: 200–1.
86 Kanyeihamba 2002: 232.
87 Kanyeihamba 2002.

of guards, but a fundamental change'.[88] Onyango-Obbo explains the historical and political context of the events preceding the NRM government thus:

> Uganda was broken, bloodied by war, poor, and its citizens exhausted by marauding military goons when Museveni took power. They [Ugandans] were willing to support NRM as long as it didn't take the country back to the nightmarish past. And they were willing to be forgiving of any crime that was not as worse [sic] as Amin's or Obote II's.[89]

4.5.4 Assessment

The period between 1967 and 1986 can be summarised as a period of over-centralisation of all political powers in Uganda, with local government structures serving as mere extensions of central government. This period also marked a general decline in the rule of law, economic collapse and material deprivation of the majority of the people. The period was characterised by military government, disrespect for human rights, civil wars and dictatorship.

However, this period was also one in which the foundation for democratic revival was laid. Most people became disillusioned with the prevailing circumstances; hence the desire for a fresh start. The desire for a new beginning started with opposition to the military government of Idi Amin and developed into a civil war against the misrule of President Obote. A consensus seemed to emerge that in order to have a sustainable democratic future, an inclusive government was needed. It was for this reason that the period after 1986 witnessed attempts to decentralise powers and functions from the centre to local communities.

4.6 Local government reforms between 1986 and 1995

In 1986, immediately after the overthrow of the military government that had overthrown the civilian government, the NRM government legalised itself by proclamation. The proclamation also adopted the 1967 Constitution.[90]

A statement by the Minister of Local Government at the time summarises the history of the reforms introduced after 1986. According to him, the principal object of decentralisation reform was to enhance local democracy through citizens' participation in sustainable development. In order to strengthen local democracy, it was imperative to change the nature of the state at the local level through institutional reform and capacity-building.[91]

88 See President Museveni's speech on February 1986 cited in Kanyeihaba 2002: 200–38.

89 Onyango-Obbo, C 'Kony has survived for 25 years by stealing Museveni's secrets' *Daily Monitor*, available at: http://www.monitor.co.ug/OpEd/OpEdColumnists/CharlesOnyangoObbo/Kony+has+survived+for+25+years+by+stealing+Museveni+s+secrets/-/878504/1411184/-/7nm435z/-/index.html.

90 See Legal Notice No. 1 of 1986.

91 See Hansard of the Parliament of Uganda 1993.

The decision to decentralise power to local government was made in 1986. However, decentralisation reform gained currency only in 1993 through the Presidential Policy Statement.[92] In 1993 the President issued a statement on decentralisation. According to the statement, the objectives of decentralisation were as follows:

- to transfer power to the local communities as an initial stage in decentralisation;
- to reduce the workload on remote and unfunded central government technocrats;
- to evenly distribute resources to local communities;
- to gradually increase the political autonomy of local communities;
- to enhance local administrative autonomy by linking local service delivery to local tax payment;
- to promote public participation in the formulation of local government policies; and
- to improve the quality of public sector performance by ensuring that the decision-making process was participatory.[93]

4.6.1 Resistance councils

The transition from a highly centralised state to a more decentralised system of government started with the enactment of two pieces of legislation: the Local Governments (Resistance Councils) Statute (LGRCS) and the Resistance Committees (Judicial Powers) Statute (RCJPS).[94] These two pieces of legislation provided for the establishment of the five-level local government structures known as Resistance Councils (RCs). The RCs ranged from level one, known as RC I, to the district level, known as RC V.[95] The structure of the RC system is represented in Figure 4.1.

Only RC III and RC V were bodies corporate.[96] Every district, city, municipality, sub-county, city and municipal division and town was vested with executive and legislative powers.[97] The county, ward, parish and village were vested with mainly administrative roles.[98] The RCJPS vested RC I–III with limited judicial powers and functions.[99] The political heads of all the different levels of local government were elected by local people through a procedure that involved a voter

92 The Uganda Government (MOLG) *Decentralization: The Policy and Its Philosophy*. Kampala: Ministry of Local Government/Decentralisation Secretariat 1993a.
93 The Uganda Government (MOLG) *Decentralization: The Policy and Its Philosophy*. Kampala: Ministry of Local Government/Decentralisation Secretariat 1993a.
94 The RCJPS 1/87: Golooba-Mutebi 2000: 20.
95 Section 4 of the LGRCS. Golooba-Mutebi 2000: 18.
96 Section 6 of the LGRCS.
97 Section 11(1) of the LGRCS.
98 Sections 11(2) and 18 of the LGRCS.
99 Section 2 of the LGRCS.

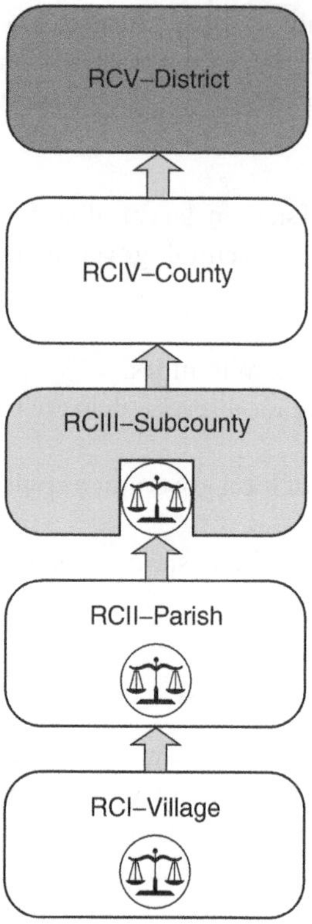

Figure 4.1 Structure of transitional resistance council committees.

Source: Adopted from the LGRCS and the RCJPS; see also Golooba-Mutebi 2000: 18.

standing behind his or her preferred candidate. The candidate with the biggest number of people behind him or her was declared the winner.[100]

4.6.2 Central government oversight institutions

The LGRCS replaced the District Commissioner (DC) with the District Administrator (DA) in every district. The DA was a presidential appointee and the overall (transitional) political head in every district.[101] He or she was responsible for government policy implementation, security and development.[102] The district administrative head, however, remained separate from the political head. The exercise of what had remained of the powers of the DC was vested in a new

100 Odoki Commission 1993: 487.

101 Section 23 of the LGRCS. Golooba-Mutebi 2000: 19–21.

102 Section 23(4) of the LGRCS. the Odoki Commission 1993: 488.

official, known as the District Executive Secretary (DES). The powers of DES were very limited,[103] given the pervasive ministerial control of district administrations at the time.[104] For instance, the Minister, upon a recommendation from the DA, had powers to suspend a district council based on a DA's 'belief' of wrongdoing by the council.[105] The LGRCS also provided for the establishment of a district development committee (DDC) in each district chaired by the DA. A DDC had the power to formulate and implement the district local government development plans.[106]

4.7 Conclusion

The description above has earmarked important periods in the development of local government law in Uganda since the pre-colonial period. In answering the three questions posed at the beginning of the chapter, three points have been made. First, decentralisation is not a new idea in Uganda. Second, the Buganda Kingdom illustrates the multi-ethnic uniqueness of many communities, the recognition of which in a decentralisation system has real political and developmental dividends. The Buganda Kingdom affirms the multi-ethnic nature of Uganda as a nation state given the historical process through which the different ethnic groups were brought together under the 'protectorate' during the period of British colonial rule. Third, the sharing of powers between the central government and the Buganda Kingdom in 1962 is useful in understanding the proper sharing schemes that needed to be adopted for a successful decentralised system.

It is further noted that the contribution of RCs in 1986, as a new form of local government at that time, in rallying local democracy and political legitimacy, was limited.[107] The fusion of both political and judicial powers into one institution was clearly undesirable at a time when local government reform was seen as part of the strategy to democratise the country.[108] The absence of secret voting undermined the claim to democracy. The reforms introduced by decentralisation at this stage were intended to consolidate the quasi-military government and were never intended to democratise the country at all.[109] Further consultations on the form of new local governments that would be suitable for a more democratic order were preferred. The next chapter discusses the political and legal debates that preceded the 1995 Constitution which provided for an entrenched decentralised system of government.

103 Sections 30 and 31 of the LGRCS. Odoki Commission 1993: 488. Golooba-Mutebi 2000: 19–22.
104 A minister could declare an area part of local government or could delegate the central government's functions to local governments. See sections 7(3) and 12 of the LGRCS.
105 Odoki Commission 1993: 488.
106 Sections 19 and 20 of the LGRCS. Odoki Commission 1993: 488.
107 Kanyeihamba 2002: 239.
108 Kanyeihamba 2002: 262.
109 Makara 2009: 132–3.

5 Local governments' institutional integrity, sub-national ethnic questions and politics in the post-1995 Constitution

5.1 Designing the 1995 Constitution: the Odoki Commission

In this chapter, the genesis of intrusive centralism in Uganda's decentralisation is systematically documented. The six-part framework on key features of decentralisation which were highlighted in Chapter Three is discussed in the context of the 1995 Constitution-making process.

In 1995 a new Constitution was promulgated, replacing the unitary Constitution of 1967. The promulgation of the 1995 Constitution followed the Odoki Commission Report whose mandate was to gather the views of the people and make recommendations to the Constituency Assembly (CA).[1] The discussion in this chapter deals with three main themes: the Odoki Commission recommendations on decentralisation; the promulgation of the 1995 Constitution; and the establishment of the local government institutions. The chapter also assesses the relationship between the abuse of central governmental political power, the proliferation of districts, the recentralisation of Kampala City and the tepid establishment of Regional Governments (RGs) as a means of undermining the institutional integrity of local governments.

There were two main reasons why it was important to gather people's views on reforming democratic institutions such as local government. First, in order to have a sustainable democratic reform process, public involvement was needed at the outset. Secondly, the act of collecting views from the public was a healing process that was needed for a country that had emerged from years of conflict and political neglect.[2] The Commission was mandated to collect views from the public on the new Constitution that would guarantee national independence, territorial integrity, democratic governance, viable political institutions, demarcation of responsibilities between the different state organs, creation of public participation

1 See sections 4 & 5 of the Uganda Constitutional Commission Statute No 5 of 1988.

2 Kanyeihamba 2002: 254–5. For instance, Ndulo 1998: 93 argues that '[t]he process of adopting a constitution is both important and substantive. The process must be legitimate and legitimacy requires inclusiveness. It should represent the interests of all the people in the country, and the people must be made to feel that they own the process as well as the product'.

spaces, free and fair electoral systems and the establishment and upholding of a culture of accountability.[3]

The Commission published a report which influenced the Constituent Assembly's debate on local governments and the eventual adoption of the new Constitution that provided for a decentralised system of government. The Commission addressed several issues concerning local government, including its constitutional status, governance structures, finances, staff, electoral systems, competencies and Buganda's quest for federal status.

The Commission recommended protecting the integrity of local government institutions by calling for a gradual and smooth transfer of powers and responsibilities from the central government to local government.[4] It held that decentralisation requires a sound financial base for local governments so as to enable the exercise of devolved planning powers through the initiation of appropriate policies at all levels.[5] Further, the Commission made a case for the control and supervision of the civil service by local government authorities,[6] and emphasised the need to base local governments on democratically elected councils.[7] All of these recommendations accord with the arguments made in Chapters Two and Three,[8] as will be discussed in more detail below.

5.1.1 Constitutional guarantee of local government

The Commission recommended that a decentralised system of government upon which local governments were to be based should be constitutionally protected. This, as already noted, protected against arbitrary changes in the future by the central government.[9] The Commission recommended vesting powers in Parliament to regulate local government.[10] In Chapter Three of this book, the significance of a constitutionally protected local government as a key feature of a good decentralised system is emphasised.[11]

5.1.2 Demarcation of district as the basic unit of decentralisation

The Commission recommended that the district should be the basic unit of local government. Although existing districts could be retained, there was a need for a mechanism for boundary changes, especially for people who sought to have separate districts. However, the existing boundaries would be appropriate starting

3 See Principal Objectives of the Odoki Commission.
4 Odoki Commission 1993: 513.
5 Odoki Commission 1993: 504.
6 Odoki Commission 1993: 495.
7 Odoki Commission 1993: 494.
8 Chapter Two § 2.8.9 and Chapter Three § 3.1.
9 Odoki Commission 1993: 495.
10 Odoki Commission 1993: 524.
11 Chapter Three § 3.2.

5.1.10 Intervention in local governments

The Commission acknowledged that, although the sanctity of local government status was important, situations could arise requiring some level of central government intervention. The Commission listed circumstances under which the central government, through either the executive or the legislature, could intervene in local government. Such circumstances included a state of emergency, widespread corruption, abuse of office, financial mismanagement, breakdown of law and order or any actions that may threaten 'national unity or the sovereignty of the country'. However, it was recommended that as soon as the conditions for taking over the administration of a district no longer existed, local administration should be restored.[45] Nonetheless, no specific types of intervention were suggested. It is important to note that the Commission specifically recommended against vesting any power in the Minister of Local Government to suspend a local government council or any of its committees.[46]

Insofar as it laid out clear criteria for the central government to intervene in the affairs of district councils, the Commission sought to protect the integrity of district council institutions. Equally, the long list of reasons for intervention gave central government a wide ambit for correcting any errors in district councils. This recommendation therefore does not fully accord with the arguments against arbitrariness in the intervention process advanced in Chapter Three.[47]

5.1.11 The 'Buganda Question'

The Commission reviewed the history of the Buganda Kingdom within the context of the development of Uganda as a modern nation state.[48]

The Commission emphasised five aspects of the Buganda Kingdom's uniqueness: (a) its geographical position in Uganda; (b) its population size; (c) its early interaction with Islam and Christianity; (d) its pre-colonial political organisation; and (e) its fear of loss of identity.[49] According to the Commission, the majority of the views from the Buganda region favoured the return of power-sharing between the central government and the Buganda Kingdom, as it existed under the 1962 Constitution.[50]

The Commission Report, without first clarifying the issue of the Buganda Kingdom's special demand for federal status, decided to discuss 'the Buganda Kingdom question' together with the question of traditional leaders. After reviewing the merits and demerits of institutions of traditional leaders, the Commission recommended that traditional institutions should be governed by

45 Odoki Commission 1993: 513.
46 Odoki Commission 1993: 513.
47 Chapter Three § 3.9.3.
48 Odoki Commission 1993: 525–33.
49 Odoki Commission 1993: 534.
50 Odoki Commission 1993: 536. See Chapter Four § 4.7.1.

a separate constitutional arrangement. The Commission held the view that given the feudal nature of traditional institutions, they were inimical to the promotion of democratic values, human rights and development. Nonetheless, the role of traditional institutions as in fostering peace, prosperity and national unity was acknowledged.[51] Yet in a manner that appeared to target the Buganda Kingdom, the Commission recommended not involving traditional leaders and their institutions in national politics; instead, traditional leaders were limited to 'purely cultural and developmental roles'.[52] Two issues were conflated by the Commission: traditional leaders and the Buganda Kingdom's request for a special federal status. The question of traditional leaders related to their constitutional restoration, whereas the Buganda Kingdom's question related to its demands to share power with the central government. In the end, the Commission never truly addressed the political alienation of the Buganda Kingdom within the nation state.

5.2 Uganda as a constitutional state under the 1995 Constitution

Most of the Commission's recommendations were adopted by the CA delegates, leading to the promulgation of the 1995 Constitution. However, some important recommendations were either rejected or radically altered.[53] The discussion that follows reviews the general reforms introduced by the 1995 Constitution on the nature of the state in Uganda, and the protection of the institutional integrity of district councils as constitutionally recognised lower orders of government.

5.2.1 Supremacy and separation of powers

The Preamble to the 1995 Constitution of Uganda provides for a durable constitutional order, outlining in essence the essential features of a constitutional state. According to the Preamble, attributes such as 'unity, peace equality, democracy, freedom, social justice and progress'[54] are central features of a constitutional state.

The 1995 Constitution is 'supreme'[55] insofar as it was derived from a mandate of the electorate through its democratically elected leaders.[56] Besides the provision for the sanctity of the Constitution, there are special protection measures under Article 3 of the Constitution. The 1995 Constitution is one of the few in common law countries that bestows on every citizen a right as well as the obligation to resist any form of unconstitutional usurpation of political power. Thus, every citizen is obliged to resist any attempt to 'overthrow the established

51 Odoki Commission 1993: 547.
52 Odoki Commission 1993: 549.
53 Kanyeihamba 2002: 250.
54 Para. 4 of the Preamble to the Constitution.
55 Article 2 of the Constitution.
56 Article 1(4) of the Constitution.

constitutional order'.[57] The above provision was a response to the abolition of the 1962 and 1967 Constitutions through the force of arms, as explained in Chapter Four.[58]

Article 126 of the Constitution provides for the separation of powers[59] by providing for the Parliament,[60] the Executive,[61] and the Judiciary.[62]

5.2.1.1 The Parliament

Members of Parliament (MPs) are elected in three broad ways: directly by universal adult suffrage where the county serves as the constituency; allocation of seats for women in every district; and by a collegial system for special interest groups representing persons with disabilities, the workers, the youth and the army. Except for the army representatives (who, in theory, are politically neutral), all other MPs can either be nominated by a political party or compete as independent candidates. The Constitution adopts the winner-takes-all electoral system in that the person who gets the majority of the votes in any of the categories becomes the elected MP. The Vice President and Ministers are *ex officio* MPs. MPs are elected every five years.[63] The Parliament is headed by a Speaker assisted by the deputy Speaker, both of whom are elected from among the MPs in the first session of Parliament.[64] Parliament is mandated to enact laws and protect the 'Constitution and promote the democratic governance of Uganda'.[65] Further, Parliament plays a critical oversight function on all public accounts, including those dealing with local governments. For instance, Parliament is empowered to withhold central government transfers to a district council, if evidence of financial abuse in a district council is presented.[66]

5.2.1.2 The executive

The executive arm of government is headed by the President who is directly elected by universal adult suffrage. He or she must obtain more than 50% of the valid votes cast. The President is the Head of State, the Commander-in-Chief of the armed forces, the 'Fountain of Honour' and takes precedence over all other persons in the country. The President also enjoys absolute judicial immunity

57 Article 3(6) of the Constitution.
58 Chapter Four § 4.8.
59 Aristotle 1932: 1297b–1298a; Conway 2011: 305.
60 Article 77 of the Constitution.
61 Article 99 of the Constitution.
62 Article 126 of the Constitution.
63 Article 78 of the Constitution.
64 Article 82 of the Constitution.
65 Article 78 of the Constitution.
66 See Rule 155 of the Rules of Procedure of the Parliament of Uganda, 2006 made Pursuant to Article 90.

while still in office.[67] The executive is composed of the Vice President, Prime Minister and Ministers who are appointed by the President from among the MPs and approved by a simple parliamentary vote.[68] The President as the head of the executive arm of government has a duty 'to abide by, uphold and safeguard this Constitution and the laws of Uganda and to promote the welfare of the citizens and protect the territorial integrity of Uganda'.[69] The President, Vice President, Prime Minister and Ministers form the Cabinet, whose main function is to initiate, formulate, and execute government policies, in accordance with the Constitution.[70]

5.2.1.3 The judiciary

The judiciary, as the third arm of government, has a duty to adjudicate disputes. It is also vested with the duty to enforce and interpret the Constitution independently of the other arms of government.[71] Should either of the other two arms of government exceed their constitutional mandate, the judiciary has to intervene as a fair and independent arbiter. Uganda's court structure consists of the Supreme Court as the highest court, the Court of Appeal, the High Courts and the subordinate courts.[72] The Supreme Court is composed of the Chief Justice and no fewer than six other justices.[73] The Supreme Court is the final court of appeal.[74] The Court of Appeal is composed of the Deputy Chief Justice and not less than six other justices.[75] The High Courts are composed of the Principal Judge and judges of the High Court whose number is determined by Parliament.[76] The High Courts have original jurisdiction in all matters except those relating to the interpretation of the Constitution.[77]

The jurisdiction to interpret the Constitution vests in the Court of Appeal sitting as the Constitutional Court.[78] Article 50 of the Constitution allows any person whose rights have been violated to seek redress from any court of competent jurisdiction. On the other hand, Article 137 vests the exclusive jurisdiction to interpret the Constitution and to grant redress in the Constitutional Court.[79]

67 Article 79 of the Constitution.
68 Article 108, 108A and 111 of the Constitution.
69 Article 99 of the Constitution.
70 Article 111(2) of the Constitution.
71 Article 128 of the Constitution.
72 Article 129 of the Constitution.
73 Article 130 of the Constitution. At the time of writing the book, Uganda had no substantive Chief Justice since March 2013 and no Deputy Chief Justice since 2012.
74 Article 132(1) of the Constitution.
75 Article 134(1) of the Constitution.
76 Article 138 of the Constitution.
77 Article 139(1) of the Constitution.
78 Article 137(1) of the Constitution.
79 *Attorney-General v Tinyefuza* Supreme Court Constitutional Appeal No. 1 of 1997 arising from Constitutional Petition No. 1 of 1996.

In Chapter Three, the protection of local government by means of constitutional recognition (and not as a mere creature of statute) was argued as one of the attributes of a decentralised system of government.[80] It is noted that only the Constitutional Court is vested with the power to strike down laws that violate the Constitution. Implicitly, if any laws dealing with local government undermine the Constitution, such laws can be invalidated by the Constitutional Court.[81]

5.3 The new constitutional status of local government

The Constitution entrenches local governments in three broad ways. First, the Constitution's stance seems to adopt the principles of subsidiarity in the allocation of powers and functions to local governments by providing for residual powers which devolve to district councils. For instance, the Constitution provides for 29 areas of exclusive central government competence, on the assumption that what remains is a residual function of district councils.[82] Thus, in part, the Constitution adopted the recommendation of the Odoki Commission on the transfer of functions.[83] Secondly, the Constitution itself grants every district council political and administrative powers. For example, the Constitution makes provision for the district council as the legislative authority in a district. The Constitution also provides that the district council chairperson is the political head of the district. Further, the Constitution provides for the district Chief Administrative Officer (CAO) as the senior district manager.[84] Thirdly, the Constitution provides for the protection of the district council by establishing a special procedure by which the institutions and powers of local government may be altered. For instance, the Constitution provides local governments with a right to veto any changes to the powers and institution of local government.[85]

5.3.1 The institutional structure of local government

Uganda's local government is a two-tiered structure.[86] District councils on the one hand, and sub-county councils on the other, are legal persons with capacity to sue and to be sued, and are vested with executive and legislative powers.[87]

80 See Chapter Three § 3.2.1.
81 Oloka-Onyango 1996: 144.
82 See Article 189 and the Sixth Schedule of the Constitution.
83 It is noted that the Odoki Commission had only recommended 13 areas of exclusive central government competencies.
84 Article 188(1) of the Constitution.
85 See Article 261 of the Constitution. The constitutionally entrenched provisions are in Articles 5(2), 152, 176(1), 178, 189 and 197 of the Constitution.
86 Some writers hold different views. See Tusasirwe 2007: 14 and Oloka-Onyango 2007: 12. See also Lady Justice Arach-Amoko's judgment in *Victor Juliet Mukasa and Another v Attorney-General*, Miscellaneous Cause no. 247/06.
87 Section 3(2) read together with section 6 of the LGA.

Under Article 181(3) of the Constitution, a sub-county is also a constituency for electing district council councillors.

5.3.1.1 Constitutional framework

The Constitution of Uganda provides for district councils as the basis of the local government system.[88] This provision adopted essentially what the Odoki Commission recommended.[89] Under Article 207 of the Ugandan Constitution, a reference to a local government includes: a district council, an urban council, a sub-county council or any other unit prescribed by law to replace any of the councils mentioned above. District councils are entrenched under the Constitution, in that it requires a special procedure to amend any of the governance structures and functions of district councils.[90] The Constitution vests Parliament with the discretion to establish other institutional structures below the district.[91]

The demarcation of districts is governed by the 1995 Constitution.[92] Parliament is empowered to alter district boundaries or create new ones. Changes of boundaries must be supported by the majority of the members of Parliament.[93] Demarcation is based on three factors. First, the change to a district boundary must be based on the need for effective administration. Second, it must be based on the need to bring services closer to the people. Third, the means of communication, geographical features, population density, economic viability and the 'wishes of the people concerned' must be considered.[94] There is no specific injunction on Parliament to assess these wishes through a consultative procedure.

5.3.1.2 Legislative framework

The LGA is the main legislation dealing with district councils.[95] The LGA repeats the provisions of Article 207 of the Constitution on district councils or

88 Article 177 of the Constitution states: '(1) Subject to the provisions of this Constitution, for the purposes of local government, Uganda shall be divided into the districts referred to in article 5(2) of this Constitution. (2) The districts referred to in clause (1) of this article shall be taken to have been divided into the lower local government units which existed immediately before the coming into force of this Constitution'.

89 See Odoki Constitution Commission 1994: 496 para. 18.81.

90 See Article 261 of the Constitution. The constitutionally entrenched provisions are in Articles 5(2), 152, 176(1), 178, 189 and 197 of the Constitution.

91 Article 176(1) of the Constitution.

92 Article 179 of the Constitution.

93 Article 179(2) of the Constitution.

94 Article 179(1)(a) and (b) of the Constitution.

95 The long title to the LGA states that it is an Act to 'consolidate and streamline the existing law on local governments in line with the Constitution to give effect to the decentralisation and devolution of functions, powers and services; to provide for decentralisation at all levels of local governments to ensure good governance and democratic participation in, and control of, decision making by the people; to provide for election of local government councils and for any other matters connected to the above'.

Local Council Five (LC5), a term that takes over from RC5, as the basic unit of decentralisation.[96]

5.3.2 *Rural councils*

Under the district council, the LGA provides for the county councils (the LCIVs), sub-county councils (the LCIIIs),[97] the parish councils (the LCIIs) and village councils (the LCIs) for rural local governments.[98] The legal position of LIVs, LCIIs and LCIs as structures in local government in Uganda is contested. The Constitutional Court nullified the elections of the office-bearers of county, parish and village councils in 2007,[99] and at the time of writing this book, no fresh elections have been conducted. In fact, there have been suggestions to disband county, parish/ward and village/cell councils altogether.[100] The description thereof thus may only serve academic purposes. Thus, the depoliticisation of LCIV, LCII and LCI (discussed in Chapter Four),[101] formerly known as *Ssaaza*, *Muluka* and *Mutongole* under the 1962 Constitution,[102] may also be linked to the central government desire to further weaken the Buganda Kingdom's most powerful political structures and exclude it from the overall decentralisation process.

5.3.2.1 *Enhancement of local council courts' powers*

As explained in Chapter Four, from 1986 to 1996, Resistances Councils (RCI-IIIs) exercised limited judicial powers.[103] In 2006, the Local Council Courts Act (LCCA) was enacted,[104] enhancing the judicial powers of LCIIIs on the one hand, and LCIIs and LCIs on the other in disputes that are of a customary nature.[105] The LCIIIs were designated as appellate courts, hearing appeals of the

96 Section 4(a) of the LGA.
97 Section 3(2)(a) & (b) of the LGA.
98 Section 45(1)(a) of the LGA.
99 See Rubaramira Ruranga v Electoral Commission and Another, Constitution Petition No. 21 of 2006.
100 'Gov't to review local councils' *The New Vision* on 2 May 2009, available at http://www.newvision.co.ug/detail.php?mainNewsCategoryId=8&newsCategoryId=13&newsId=753296.
101 See Chapter Four § 4.9.2.
102 See Chapter Four § 4.7.2.
103 See Chapter Four § 4.9.2.
104 See Part I and II of the Local Council Courts Act Cap 13 of 2006. The long title to the LCCA provides '[a]n Act to establish local council courts for the administration of justice at local level, to define the jurisdiction, powers and procedure of the established courts and to provide for other related matters'. The LCCA came into force on 8 June 2006, and repealed the Executive Committees (Judicial Powers) Act Cap 8.
105 Under the Second Schedule of the LCCA, local council courts can hear cases dealing with simple contracts, assault and battery. These courts have the power to hear cases of custody of children, conversion, damage to property and the infringement of district

decision of LCIIs and LCIs courts.[106] As already noted, the Constitutional Court nullified the elections of the office-bearers of county, parish and village councils in 2007,[107] and at the time of writing the book, no fresh elections have been conducted. Even if the LCIIIs have duly elected political office-bearers, they cannot exercise any original judicial jurisdiction at all in the absence of legally constituted LCIIs and LCIs courts. The vagueness of these courts explains in part the underlying bias against traditional adjudication systems.[108]

5.3.2.2 Designation of urban councils

Urban councils are categorised as town councils, municipal councils or city councils (Table 5.1). Municipal councils (LCIV/IIIs), municipal division councils (LCIIIs), ward councils (LCIIs) and cell councils (LCIs) within a district council are designated as urban local councils.[109]

The number of inhabitants in a given area and its level of economic development determine the designation of that area as an urban council. Thus, for an area to be designated a town it must have more than 25,000 inhabitants.[110] For any urban area to be designated as a municipality it must have more than 100,000 inhabitants.[111] An urban area must have more than 500,000 inhabitants to be designated a city.[112] In addition, the LGA provides that before any area is declared and gazetted as an urban area, it must have the capacity to meet the costs of the delivery of services, have offices, a water source and a master plan for land use.[113] The practical implication of this provision is that it is next to impossible to declare any area an urban local government because of the resource and human capacity limitations of many local councils. Besides, most local governments depend on central government transfers.

Urban councils are further categorised from A to D.[114] The level of economic activity of a given urban council determines its category.[115] The categorisation of urban councils overlaps with the categorisation of town, municipal and city

council bylaws. Under the Third Schedule of the LCCA, these courts can also hear cases dealing with civil debts governed by customary law such as customary bailment, customary joint land ownership and customary land tenure, customary marriages, customary divorce, customary separation and customary declaration of parentage.

106 See Part X of the LCCA.

107 See *Rubaramira Ruranga* (2006).

108 See the detailed discussion on the history and politics of traditional institutions in Uganda in Chapter Four §4.2.1.

109 Section 45(1)(a) of the LGA.

110 Section 32(1)(a)(i) of the LGA.

111 Section 32(1)(a)(ii) of the LGA.

112 Section 32(1)(a)(iii) of the LGA.

113 Section 32(1)(b) of the LGA.

114 See the Local Governments (Classification of Towns) Order pursuant to sections 3(5) and 7(1) of the Urban Authorities Act.

115 See O.2 of the Local Governments (Classification of Towns) Order.

Table 5.1 Criteria for a declaration of urban councils

Population (number of inhabitants)	*Categorisation*
<25,000	Town council
<100,000	Municipal council
<500,000	City council

Source: Adopted from section 32 of the LGA.

categorisation. There is no legal consequence for categorisation of urban councils as either A or B. The categorisation thereof merely shows that most urban councils are colonial remnants.[116]

5.3.3 Consequences of categorisation of an urban council

A municipal council falls under the political jurisdiction of the district council in which it is situated (Figure 5.1).[117] The uniqueness of a municipal council is that it enjoys a degree of administrative, fiscal and planning autonomy from the district council, as provided for by Article 197 of the Constitution.[118] Ordinarily, municipal councils are county councils but of a unique kind.[119]

As a further consequence of urban categorisation, the LCIIIs below the municipal councils become known as municipal division councils (the equivalent of rural subcounty councils),[120] while all LCIIs and LCIs below the municipal division councils become known as ward and cell councils respectively.[121] It is noted that only municipal and municipal division councils have legal personality.

116 A municipality is an area which, because of its level of development and urbanisation, is designated as such by a minister. See the Local Government (Declaration of Towns) (No.1) Order. This Statutory Instrument was made under the Urban Authorities Act, 1964 Revision Cap 27. The Act was later repealed by the Local Governments (Resistance Councils) Statute, No 15/1993. Section 48(2) of the Statute saved the subsidiary legislation made under the Urban Authorities Act. The Local Governments (Resistance Councils) Statute was repealed by the Local Governments Act, 1/1997. Section 177 of that Act saved subsidiary legislation made under the Local Governments (Resistance Councils) Statute. Source: Laws of the Republic of Uganda Revised Edition 2000 Vol. XXIV p 5145. It noted that under Section 32(2) of the LGA every district headquarters is declared as a town.

117 Section 5 of the LGA provides that a municipality is a lower council of the district council in which it is situated.

118 Oloka-Onyango 2007: 12 describes municipal and town councils as a hybrid of a county and sub-county councils. See also section 79 of the LGA. Makara Makar 2009: 156 clarifies that municipal and town councils are of a hybrid nature as they are not under the direct control of district councils. According to the author, municipal councils have independent executive powers in the performance of their functions. The author adds that these councils receive their central government transfers, collect local government revenue and spend it 'according to their own priorities'.

119 Oloka-Onyango 2007: 12.

120 It is noted that where a sub-county council as an LCIII is designated as an urban area, it becomes a town council.

121 Section 45(1)(b) of the LGA.

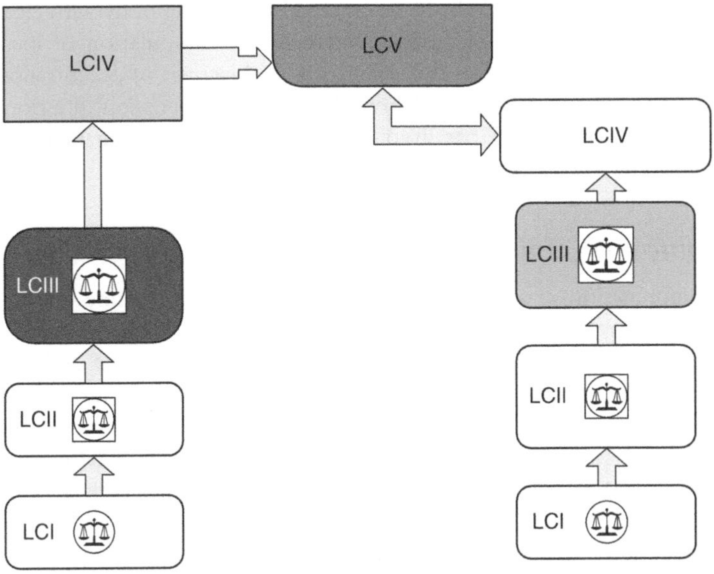

Figure 5.1 Structure of a district council in Uganda.

Source: Ministry of Local Government/Articles 5 and 178 and Fifth Schedule to the Constitution, and sections 3–5 and 45 of the LGA. The squares on the right with a grey border refer to the rural local governments from LCI-LCV while the grey border on the left refers to the urban local governments from LCI to LCV. The medium to dark grey fill refers to local governments LCIII, LCIV and LCV with corporate personality. The square in the top left-hand corner refers to the hybrid nature of municipal councils as an urban LCIV. The local governments with a court symbol refer to local council courts.

Notwithstanding the elaborate legal framework for Uganda's local governments, there has been a systematic manipulation of these institutions over a period of time, the discussion of which takes place below.

5.4 Manipulation of district councils: sub-national politics and the re-emergence of autocracy

In the first three parts of the chapter the institutions of local government (LG) have been described. In the discussion that follows three manifestations of manipulation of local government institutions are presented: the political undercurrents in the proliferation of many districts,[122] the recentralisation of Kampala City and the continuous rejection of Regional Governments (RGs). Districts, as manifestations of local governments' institutional integrity in Uganda, are important units through which local development, local democracy and accommodation of

122 Oloka-Onyango 2007: 12.

ethnic diversity may be supported. For local governments units to execute their ultimate objectives above, they ought to be created by a neutral body with clear criteria.[123] The description thereof assesses whether the manipulation of local government institutions undermines the integrity and objectives of decentralisation as discussed in Chapters Two and Three. In turn, the discussion questions whether the central government has lived up to its constitutional mandate of protecting the institutional integrity of district councils.

5.4.1 The proliferation of districts

Uganda has a population of about 29.7 million people.[124] At the time of writing the book, there were 122 districts in Uganda, up from 33 when the current regime came into power in 1986.[125] This translates into an average of 243,443 people per district. Between 1986 and 1997, 11 new districts were created. In 2000, a further 11 districts were created, while in 2005, the year preceding the 2006 elections, 22 new districts were created. In 2006, the year that followed the elections, nine districts were created. It had been expected that only 14 new districts would be approved in 2010.[126] However, by the end of 2010, the total number of districts had risen to 122, up from 79 in 2006.[127]

Table 5.2 shows that there was a 559% growth in the number of districts from independence in 1962 to 2010. The phenomenal rate of growth in the number of districts can be illustrated by looking at three periods. There was a 24% growth in the number of districts in 2000 from 1997. There was also a 25% growth in the number of districts in 2005 from 2000. Lastly, there was an unprecedented 160% growth in the number of districts in 2010 from 2005. In 2013, the President placed a moratorium on creating new districts.[128]

5.4.2 The recentralisation of Kampala City

Since the commencement of decentralisation, Kampala City has been part of the local government system, and has had the status of a district. Its five divisions were considered sub-counties. Before 2005, Kampala City formed part of the local government structures and was known as the KCC. The KCC was regulated in the main by the LGA, with similar structures and powers to any other district council. The elected political leader of KCC was the City Mayor, while

123 Chapter Three § 3.3.3.

124 Bahemuka 2006: 8.

125 *The Daily Monitor* July 21, 2009. The number districts above includes Kampala City, which was formally centralised in 2010.

126 *The Daily Monitor* July 21, 2009.

127 See a List of Districts, Municipalities and Town Councils in Uganda as of July 2010, available at http://molg.go.ug/2010/11/05/list-of-districts-municipalities-and-town-councils-in-uganda-as-of-july-2010/ (accessed 10 July 2010).

128 Lumu D & Waluusimbi D 'Museveni tired of new districts' *The Observer*, 11 March 2013.

Table 5.2 Growth of districts (1962–2010)

Year	*No. of districts*	*Percentage growth of districts*
1962	17	–
1968	18	6%
1971	19	6%
1974	37	95%
1979	33	−11%
1990	34	3%
1991	38	12%
1994	39	2.60%
1997	45	15%
2000	56	24%
2005	70	25%
2006	79	13%
2010*	112*	42%*

Source: ACODE Policy Research Series, No. 27, 2009 p 42, excluding the percentages and figures with asterisks, which are adopted from the author's previous work.

the administrative head was known as the City Town Clerk.[129] With the amendment to the Constitution in 2005 and the adoption of the Kampala Capital City Act (KCCA), the administration of Kampala, designated as the Capital City, was re-vested in the central government.[130] The Constitution now vests powers in Parliament to determine the boundaries of the Kampala City Council Authority (KCCA).[131] Parliament is also empowered to determine the administration and development of KCCA.[132]

129 The detailed discussion of the district council's governance structures and powers is given in Chapters Six and Seven. It is noted that before the centralisation of district senior managers in 2005, the Town Clerk was appointed by the Kampala City Service Commission.

130 Article 5(4) of the Constitution. See also Constitution (Amendment) Act 2005. See also the Kampala Capital City Act (KCCA), 2010, whose long title states:An Act to provide, in accordance with Article 5 of the Constitution, for Kampala as the capital city of Uganda; to provide for the administration of Kampala by the central Government; to provide for the territorial boundary of Kampala; to provide for the development of Kampala City; to establish the Kampala City Authority as the governing body of the City; to provide for the composition and election of the members of the Authority; to provide for the removal of members from the Authority; to provide for the functions and powers of the Authority; to provide for the election and removal of the Lord Mayor and the Deputy Lord Mayor; to provide for the appointment of, powers and functions of an executive direct and deputy executive director of the Authority; to provide for lower urban council under the Authority; to provide for the devolution by the Authority of the Functions and Services; to provide for the Metropolitan Physical Planning Authority for Kampala and the adjacent districts; to provide for the power of the Minister to veto decisions of the Authority in certain circumstances and for related matters.

131 Article 5(5) of the Constitution.

132 Article 5(46) of the Constitution.

The KCCA provides for three important offices that are pertinent in assessing the recentralisation of the former KCC as a local government institution: the Kampala City Authority (KCA) as the legislative body of the City;[133] the office of the Lord Mayor;[134] the Executive Director (ED);[135] and the Ministry in charge of Kampala City.[136] These structures are briefly described below.

5.4.2.1 The City Authority

The KCCA provides for the 'Authority'[137] as a corporate body with the capacity to sue and to be sued. The Authority has the mandate to govern the city on behalf of the central government. The City Authority is composed of the Lord Mayor, the Deputy Lord Mayor and a directly elected councillor representing each electoral area in the city.[138] The KCCA provides for two youth councillors representing the youth, and two councillors with disabilities representing persons with disabilities. In both cases, one of the councillors must be a woman. The KCCA provides for the elections of councillors representing each of the following professional bodies: the Uganda Institute of Professional Engineers, the Uganda Institute of Architects, the Uganda Medical Association and the Uganda Law Society. The electoral system adopted for electing the Authority's councillors is similar that that of electing district council councillors.[139] The procedure for removing the Authority councillors from office is also similar to that of removing district council councillors from office.[140]

The KCCA lists 29 areas of the City Authority's competencies. The most pertinent ones are initiating and formulating policies of the Authority, determining service delivery standards and determining tax levels. The City Authority monitors the general administration of the Authority and is mandated to deliver services in the divisions and to promote economic development in the city. The Authority's other functions are physical planning and the control of development of the city.[141] It is noted that the Authority exercises legislative powers similar to those of the district councils.[142]

133 Section 9(1) of the KCCA.
134 Section 9(1) of the KCCA.
135 Section 17 of the KCCA.
136 Section 79 of the KCCA.
137 Section 2 of the KCCA defines the term 'Authority' to mean 'the Kampala Capital City Authority established by section 5'.
138 The Electoral Commission is mandated to demarcate the city electoral areas for the purposes of conducting elections for directly elected councillors.
139 A detailed discussion of the district council elections is provided in Chapter Six.
140 Section 11 of the KCCA.
141 Section 7 of the KCCA.
142 Section 8 of the KCCA.

5.4.2.2 The Lord Mayor

The KCCA provides for the office of the Lord Mayor, elected directly by universal adult suffrage and by a secret ballot. The qualifications of a person to stand as a candidate for the office of the Lord Mayor are similar to those of a Member of Parliament.[143] The Lord Mayor is answerable to the Minister and the City Authority.[144] The Lord Mayor may be removed from office using the same procedure as that of removing the district council chairperson from office.[145] The office of the Lord Mayor is a full-time job.[146]

The Lord Mayor is the political head of the Capital City and not the political head of the Authority.[147] Nonetheless, the Lord Mayor presides over all meetings of the City Authority and performs both ceremonial and civic functions, including hosting foreign and local dignitaries. Besides the political and ceremonial roles of the Lord Mayor, he or she is mandated to monitor the administration of the Capital City and to provide guidance to the division administrators. The Lord Mayor also represents the Capital City on the Metropolitan Authority.[148]

5.4.2.3 The Executive Director

The KCCA provides that the ED is the chief executive of the City Authority. The ED is appointed by the President on the advice of the Public Service Commission. For a person to be appointed as the ED of the Authority, he or she must qualify to be a permanent secretary in a government ministry.[149] The ED is under the disciplinary control and direction of the Public Service Commission.[150]

The ED is the head of public service in the Authority. The ED is the Authority's accounting officer responsible for the management of public funds. The ED is accountable to Parliament and coordinates and implements national and Authority policies, laws, by-laws, regulations, programs and projects. The ED advises the Authority on the central government's policies and advises the Authority on technical, administrative and legal matters. The ED is mandated to implement lawful Authority decisions.[151] Thus the functions of the ED are similar to those of the district Chief Administrative Officer (CAO).[152]

143 Section 9 of the KCCA.
144 Section 11 of the KCCA.
145 Section 12 of the KCCA.
146 Section 9 of the KCCA.
147 Section 2 of the KCCA defines the term 'capital city' to mean the 'Kampala Capital City'.
148 Section 11 of the KCCA. Section 2 of the KCCA defines a 'Metropolitan Authority' as 'the Metropolitan Physical Planning Authority established by section 20' [sic]. Under section 21 of the KCCA, the Metropolitan Authority is mandated to deal with the planning matters of the capital city and the neighbouring districts of Mukono, Mpigi and Wakiso.
149 Section 17 of the KCCA.
150 Section 18 of the KCCA.
151 Section 19 of the KCCA.
152 See the detailed discussion on the role of the district CAO in Chapter Six.

5.4.2.4 The mandate of the Kampala Capital City Authority's Minister

Section 2 of the KCCA defines a 'Minister' as the Minister responsible for the Capital City.[153] The KCCA provides for extensive powers of the Minister for the Kampala City Authority. For instance, the Minister has the powers to change or overturn the decisions of the Authority should he or she form the opinion that the Authority's decisions contradict government policy. All that the Minister needs to do thereafter is seek the approval of the cabinet for his or her decision to be valid. The Minister has the power to appoint a Commission of Inquiry should he or she form the opinion that something serious has arisen in the Authority. The Minister oversees the performance of the Authority by presenting yearly reports to Parliament. A Minister's directive on any matter cannot be questioned by the Authority. Besides, the Minister can veto any decisions taken by the Authority if in his or her opinion such a decision is illegal.[154]

5.4.2.5 Historical context of the recentralisation of Kampala City

Whereas administrative efficiency might have been the reason for recentralisation of the Kampala City, given the evidence of past mismanagement of the city,[155] the evidence of political undercurrents leading to the change of status is too overwhelming to ignore.

Since 1996 the opposition has won the majority of elective seats of Kampala City. In fact, in the last local council election of 2006, the ruling party managed to win only one in five council seats, representing 20% of all the seats.[156] In the 2011 national and local council elections, the Lord Mayoral seat was won by the opposition party with 64% of the votes cast. However, the ruling party won the majority of city council seats.[157] The decision by the central government to legally take over the control of Kampala City is mainly explained by political reasons rather than the desire to improve the management of the city.[158] According to the President, Kampala voters had hanged themselves by voting Mr. Lukwago and other opposition-leaning politicians. The President explained that by recentralising the city administration he had 'cut them off from the ropes' [sic].[159]

153 Currently, the Minister of Kampala Capital City Authority is also the minister in charge of the presidency.

154 Section 79 of the KCCA.

155 Makara 2009: 9.

156 Oloka-Onyango 2007: 39.

157 See generally the 2011 Uganda Elections Results.

158 See Oloka-Onyango 2007: 12, who argues: 'The more telling reason was political; Kampala has for a long time been a hotbed of political opposition; by recentralizing control over its administration, it was hoped that the political problem could be handled. While no bill has yet been presented to Parliament, the draft which is circulating takes away the remaining vestiges of autonomy originally enjoyed by the Capital city and places it under the thumb of the president'.

159 Kafeero 'Museveni tells off Lukwago in city tour' *The Daily Monitor*, available at http://www.monitor.co.ug/News/National/Museveni-tells-off-Lukwago-in-city-tour/-/688334/2284166/-/mtmwia/-/index (accessed 18 April 2014).

The controversy surrounding the removal of the Lord Mayor of the Kampala City Authority from office is evidence of the highly charged political context/animosity between the central government and the elected political leaders of Kampala City.[160] In 2013, the Minister for Kampala Capital City Authority appointed a tribunal chaired by a High Court Judge to investigate the allegation against the Lord Mayor of abuse of office and incompetency. The tribunal found the Lord Mayor guilty on eight of the 12 impeachable offences.[161] The Lord Mayor was subsequently 'impeached' from office[162] and his seat declared vacant.[163] The tribunal's report, the decision to impeach him from office and the declaration by the Attorney General, the ED and the Minister that the Lord Mayor's seat was vacant have been challenged in the High Court.[164] Given the strict nature of *sub judice* rule in Uganda, I propose not to make any further comments on the subject matter.[165]

5.4.3 Assessment

That the integrity of local government institutions is vital for the success of decentralisation is all but clear at this point.[166] As noted earlier, the Odoki Commission recommended constitutionally protected local governments in order to guard against arbitrary institutional changes. The Commission also recommended clear criteria to be met before local government can be changed or altered.[167] But the above three narratives indicate that many districts have been arbitrarily created, hence undermining the constitutional objective of decentralisation. A district may be created on account of promoting local democracy. Local democracy as a process affords voters the power to select their local leaders and allows them

160 See *Lukwago Elias and 3 Others v the Attorney General and Another* Miscellaneous Cause NO. 362 OF 2013. See also *Lukwago Elias and 3 Others v Attorney-General and Another* Misc Application No. 445 of 2013, where the High Court Judge stayed the Authority's Councillors' meeting that purported to impeach the Lord Mayor. The alleged meeting was in fact chaired by the Minister of Kampala City Authority. The Court order was openly defied by the Minister, hence the numerous litigations on the subject matter.

161 GOU: The Report of the KCCA Tribunal (2013) Constituted to Investigate Allegations against the Lord Mayor of Kampala Capital City Authority Pursuant to a Petition of Councillors of the Kampala Capital City Authority 2013: 66–192.

162 Masereka 'Drama as Lukwago is impeached' *The Red Paper*, available at http://www.redpepper.co.ug/lukwago-impeached (accessed 20 February 2014).

163 'Lukwago returns to court to fight tribunal report' *The Observer*, available at http://www.observer.ug/index.php?option=com_content&view=article&id=29608:lukwago-returns-to-court-to-fight-tribunal-report&catid=34:news&Itemid=114 (accessed 9 April 2014).

164 Okanya A 'Court to hear Lukwago petition on tribunal today' *The New Vision*, available at http://www.newvision.co.ug/mobile/Detail.aspx?NewsID=644110&CatID=1 (accessed 30 February 2014).

165 The rule of *sub judice* is an old English common law rule that bars discussion of court cases before their determination. In Uganda this rule is still strictly enforced.

166 Chapter Three § 3.2.

167 Odoki Commission 1993: 495.

to participate in local decision-making process. Furthermore, communities can demand explanations from their elected local leaders more quickly from smaller local governments than bigger ones. Downsizing local governments units therefore enhances the state's ability to address local developmental challenges.[168]

Despite the existence of criteria for creating new districts under Article 179(1)(a) and (b) of the Constitution, there is evidence that some of the newly-created districts serve as inducements to communities to vote for a specific political party (usually the ruling party). As long as the ruling party has the numbers in Parliament that it does,[169] it can create as many districts as it wants without significant input from independent stakeholders. The process of the creation of districts was assessed in a recent report as follows:

> The creation of the districts did not follow any established parameters, neither was the process informed by administrative necessity or economic rationale. Instead, the President announced their creation via presidential decrees, often to reward politicians threatening to withdraw support for the NRM, or to punish those who had.[170]

The evidence of arbitrariness in the creation of many districts in Uganda shows that the 1995 Constitution did not fully adopt the recommendation of the Commission that called for considerations such as language, culture, geographical features, economic viability, population density and 'the desire of the people concerned' as the major criteria for creating new districts.[171] Oloka-Onyango remarks that 'the strategy of district proliferation has also been adopted by President Museveni as a means of dispensing patronage, and ultimately of splintering challenges to the central government hegemony and control'.[172]

Thus, rather than ensuring the realisation of socio-economic rights, the objective of the creation of districts appears to be to benefit a few local politicians in the new districts in order to strengthen the central government's political clout.[173] The same views are applicable to the recentralisation of Kampala City.

The rancour against ethnicity in Uganda notwithstanding, the consideration of culture and ethnicity in the drawing of local government boundaries is not uncommon and may enable communities to participate in local politics.[174] However, the evidence of the creation of ethnic-based districts by the central

168 Singiza & De Visser 2010: 23–4.

169 Currently the ruling National Resistance Movement (NRM) has a two-thirds majority in Parliament.

170 ARD *Democracy and Governance Assessment: Republic of Uganda*, 2005, Kampala: USAID 2005: 41.

171 Odoki Commission 1993: 497.

172 Oloka-Onyango 2007: 12. The central government's narrative is that it amounts 'tribal chauvinism' to consider ethnicity in the boundary demarcation of local government boundaries.

173 Oloka-Onyango 2007: 12.

174 Singiza & De Visser 2010: 10.

government in Uganda seems to be diametrically opposed to its official decentralisation policy framework which aimed to exorcise ethnicity altogether. The recent Parliamentary and Presidential moratorium on creating any more districts is a matter of 'too little too late', and of no remedial value.[175] The relationship between increases in the number of districts and changes in voting trends and distribution of patronage in Uganda is easy to find. When the voting trend in the country from 1996 to 2011 is juxtaposed with the proliferation of districts over the same period of time, it is discovered that when the regime's political support was high, there was little incentive to create many districts compared to when its support had somewhat reduced as illustrated by Figure 5.2.[176]

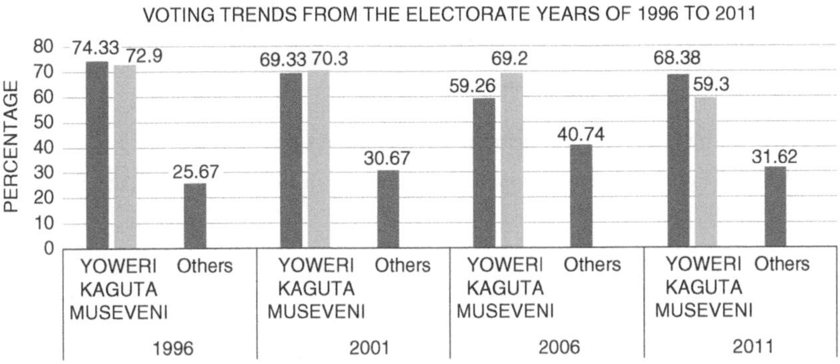

Figure 5.2 Voting trends in Uganda (1996–2011).

Source: Adopted from the Uganda Electoral Commission results from 1996 to 2011. Yellow represents the ruling NRM led by President Museveni, the grey represents the voter turnout, while the mixture of red, green and blue represents the combination of the UPC (whose traditional colour is red), the Forum for Democratic Change (FDC) (whose traditional colour is blue) and the DP (whose traditional colour is green). Indigo represents the independent candidates and smaller political parties. From the above table it can be seen that the voter turnout in the 2011 elections was slightly lower than 59.6% compared to an average of 70% voter turnout in 2001 and 2006. Between 1996 and 2006 the President's share of votes declined from 75% to 59%.[177]

175 Lumu D & Waluusimbi D 'Museveni tired of new districts' *The Observer*, 11 March 2013.

176 See Chapter Five § 5.4.1.

177 See Uganda Electoral Commission, available at http://www.ec.or.ug/eresults.php. In May 1996, Yoweri Kaguta Museveni obtained 74.33%, Paul Kawanga Ssemogerere 23.61% and Muhammad Kibirige Mayanja 2.06%. There was a 72.9% voter turnout. In 2001 March elections, Yoweri Kaguta Musevi obtained 69.33%, Kiiza Besigye 27.82%, Aggrey Owor 1.41%, Muhammad Kibirige Mayanja 1%, Francis Bwengye 0.31% and Karuhanga Chapaa 0.14%. The voter turnout was 70.3%. Both the 1996 and 2011 elections were held under the non-party political system. In 2006, a year after the introduction of political pluralism, Yoweri Kaguta Museveni of the National Resistance Movement (NRM) got 59.26%, Kiiza Besigye of the Forum for Democratic Change (FDC) 37.39%, John Ssebana Kizito of the Democratic Party (DP) 1.58%, Abed Bwanika (Independent) 0.95% and Miria Obote of Uganda the People's Congress (UPC) 0.82%. The voter turnout was 69.2%. In 2011, Yoweri Kaguta Museveni (NRM) got 68.38%, Kiiza Besigye (FDC) 26.01%, Norbert Mao

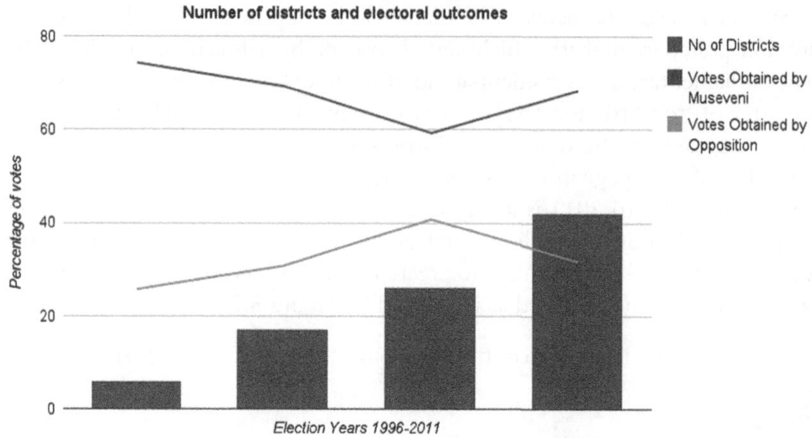

Figure 5.3 Number of electoral districts and electoral outcomes.

Source: Adopted from the Electoral Commission Results from 1996 to 2011 and the number of districts created over the same period.

For instance, in the election year 1996, only six districts were created at the time when the President's share of votes was at 74.33%. In the election year 2001, 17 new districts were created when the President's share of votes was at 69.33%. In the election year 2005, 26 new districts were created when the President's share of votes had declined to 59.26%, while in 2010, the year preceding the election year 2011, 42 new districts were created, resulting in the increase in the President's share of votes to 68.38%. Thus, the more districts were created, the greater the 'stability' (in statistical terms) of the President's share of the national vote. Districts have therefore been used as a form of 'vote buying' that stabilised the President's decline in political popularity, as illustrated by Figure 5.3.

The recentralisation of Kampala City not only threatens the notion of local governments as hatcheries of democracy, as discussed in Chapter Two,[178] but also fundamentally undermines the integrity of decentralisation. The recentralisation of Kampala City is therefore a clear example of the arbitrariness on the part of the central government, and affirms the very risks that the Odoki commission had sought to overcome. A point has already been made that constitutionally recognised local governments endure, can be predicted and are legally ascertainable.

(DP) 1.86%, Olala Otunu (UPC) 1.58%, Betty Kamya of Uganda Federal Alliance (UFA) 0.66%, Abed Bwanika of the *People's Development Party* (PDP) 0.65%, Jaberi Bidandi Ssali of *People's Progressive Party* (PPP) 0.44% and Samuel Lubega (independent) 0.41%. The voter turnout was 59.3%

178 See Chapter Three § 3.2.4. See also Onyango-Obbo 'Mayor Lukwago and the new truth his victory reveals about Uganda's politics' *The Daily Monitor*, available at http://www.monitor.co.ug/OpEd/OpEdColumnists/CharlesOnyangoObbo/-/878504/1131088/-/h5xbc6/-/index.

However, when this argument is applied to the recentralisation of the former KCC, it is clear that over and above the constitutional protection, the role of political players is equally vital in protecting local governments. The political manipulation of local government institutions is not limited to the arbitrariness with which many districts have been created and the recentralisation of Kampala City. The deliberate misunderstanding of the Buganda Kingdom's special federal demands points to the continuation of further political manipulation. It is in the context of the Buganda Kingdom's special federal status demands that Regional Governments (RG) are discussed below.

5.4.4 Regional Governments (RG)

The historical uniqueness of the Buganda Kingdom was discussed in Chapter Four.[179] The Buganda Kingdom's separate demand for independence, its special federal status under the 1962 Constitution and the nullification thereof under the 1967 Constitution were pointed out. The nullification of the Buganda Kingdom's special power-sharing arrangement with the central government partly explains the constitutional and political instability from 1967 to 1995.[180] It was also noted in Chapter Five that the Odoki Commission did not favour the reintroduction of the Buganda Kingdom's greater political autonomy, a position that was adopted by the CA delegates.[181] The point made in Chapter Two is that where there are clear dividends for greater political autonomy because of an ethnic group's unique history, asymmetric federalism should be adopted.[182] Rather than provide for asymmetrical federalism, the central government sought to appease the Buganda Kingdom with a nebulous version of asymmetrical federalism called Regional Government. This is discussed in the paragraphs below.

In 2005, ten years after the promulgation of the Constitution, the Constitution was amended to provide for Regional Governments (RGs).[183] Under Article 178(3), the districts of Buganda, Bunyoro, Busoga, Acholi and Lango are deemed by the Constitution to have agreed to form Regional Governments. However, no RGs have so far been established under the terms of this article. While the RGs are constitutionally specified, parliamentary approval thereof is still required.[184]

The Constitution also provides for the establishment of RGs by mutual consent through an agreement between two or more districts.[185] The agreement

179 See Chapter Four § 4.3.
180 See Chapter Four § 4.8.1.
181 See Article 178 of the Constitution and Chapter Five § 5.1.2.11.
182 See Chapter Three § 3.2.4.4.
183 See Constitution (Amendment) (N0.2) Act, 21/2005.
184 Article 178(4) of the Constitution provides: 'The headquarters of the Regional Governments deemed to have been established in clause (3) of this article shall be as follows: (a) in Buganda, Mengo Municipality which shall be created by Parliament; (b) in Bunyoro, Hoima Municipality which shall be created by Parliament; (c) in Busoga, Jinja Municipality; (d) in Acholi, Gulu Municipality; and (e) in Lango, Lira Municipality. (5) The districts forming the Regional Government shall form a regional Assembly'.
185 See Article 178 of the Constitution

to co-operate is with a view to performing the functions specified in the Fifth Schedule to the Constitution dealing with RGs. Before any district decides to enter into a co-operation arrangement to form an RG, a proposal to join must be approved by a two-thirds majority resolution of the district council, and ratified by a two-thirds majority of the sub-county councils.[186]

Article 178(7) of the Constitution provides that '[n]otwithstanding article 180',[187] an RG is 'the highest political authority within its region' with 'political, legislative, executive and cultural functions in the region'. Article 180 of the Constitution underscores the political authority of the RG in its area of jurisdiction. This provision underlines the significance of the RGs as political entities.

5.4.4.1 Regional Assembly (RA)

The RA is composed of representatives directly elected by universal adult suffrage in the region.[188] Unlike districts which are vested with political authority by the Constitution, RAs are merely clothed with cultural powers and therefore are a forum for regional cultural matters. In the Ugandan context, it is difficult to separate cultural matters from politics. Aside from providing for special representation of women, youth and persons with disabilities, the Constitution provides for representatives for the indigenous cultural interests in areas where there is a traditional or cultural leader.[189] In principle, indigenous cultural interests are represented by persons who are nominated by the traditional or cultural leader in a region. However, the number of these representatives should not exceed 15% of the members of the RA.[190] The representatives of indigenous and cultural affairs are not permitted to vote in a partisan manner.[191] It is undemocratic to limit the voting rights of elected representatives. Besides, it is unclear how this will be enforced. The chairpersons of the district councils in the region are *ex officio* members of the RA, but have no voting rights.[192]

186 See Article 178(2) of the Constitution.

187 Article 180 of the Constitution underscores the political authority of the district local government council in its area of jurisdiction.

188 Paragraph 2(1)(b) Fifth Schedule pursuant to Article 178 of the Constitution.

189 Paragraph 2(1)(d) Fifth Schedule pursuant to Article 178 of the Constitution.

190 Paragraph 2(1)(d) Fifth Schedule pursuant to Article 178 of the Constitution.

191 Paragraph 7(1) Fifth Schedule pursuant to Article 178 of the Constitution. Paragraph 7(2) Fifth Schedule pursuant to Article 178 of the Constitution provides: 'A matter shall be considered to be of a partisan nature if in the course of its being tabled or debated in a regional assembly it is declared by a majority vote of the directly elected representatives to be partisan'.

192 Paragraph 2(1) Fifth Schedule pursuant to Article 178 of the Constitution. Under paragraph 2(4) Fifth Schedule pursuant to Article 178 of the Constitution, the members of a RA can only serve for the same term of office as members of district councils in the region. Thus, on the expiry of the term of office of district councils, the term of office of members of RA automatically ends. It is noted that under paragraph 2(2) Fifth Schedule pursuant to Article 178 of the Constitution the RA elects its own Speaker.

5.4.4.2 Functions

The Constitution calls on RAs to establish 'standing and other committees or organs for the efficient discharge of its functions'. The Constitution specifically provides for the standing committee on cultural matters constituted by 'representatives of cultural interests'. The Constitution thus vests a discretion in the RA to establish other committees.[193]

The overall function of the standing committee on cultural matters is therefore 'culture' within a given region.[194] The phrase 'cultural matters' has a wide content under the Constitution. It includes the choice and installation of a traditional leader or cultural leaders; determination of matters relating to traditional or cultural leaders or royal lineage; the choice of clan leadership; funeral rites and customary inheritance; clan lands, shrines and installations; and cultural practices which are consistent with the Constitution.[195]

The standing committees on cultural matters must consult a traditional or cultural leader while executing their functions.[196] A decision by a committee on cultural matters is not effective until approved by a traditional or cultural leader, and in cases of the process of appointing a new traditional leader, a cultural or clan leaders' council.[197] The above provision does not state how such an approval should take place. Such a provision is open to manipulation in the absence of a proper mechanism for its enforcement. For instance, the absence of a clear criterion to be followed before a traditional or cultural leader or a cultural or clan leaders' council can approve a decision of a standing committee is problematic. Besides, it is not clear whether the decision of the standing committee should affect some or all members of the clans before it can be approved.

5.4.4.3 Election of the RG chairperson

The Fifth Schedule to the Constitution provides that a chairperson of the RG must be elected by every adult member of voting age in the area. The RG chairperson is also RG political head.[198] To qualify to be a candidate for an RG chairperson, a person must be:

- a citizen of Uganda by birth;[199]
- a member of an indigenous community, whose parent or grandparent is or was a resident in the region and a member of an indigenous community existing and residing within the borders of the region as at 1 February 1926;[200]

193 Paragraph 3(1) & (2) Fifth Schedule pursuant to Article 178 of the Constitution.
194 Paragraph 3(3) Fifth Schedule pursuant to Article 178 of the Constitution.
195 See Paragraph 3(4) Fifth Schedule pursuant to Article 178 of the Constitution.
196 See Paragraph 3(5) Fifth Schedule pursuant to Article 178 of the Constitution.
197 See Paragraph 3(6) Fifth Schedule pursuant to Article 178 of the Constitution.
198 See Paragraph 4(1) & 4(3)(a) & (d) Fifth Schedule pursuant to Article 178 of the Constitution.
199 Article 10 of the Constitution.
200 See Paragraph 1(2)(a) Fifth Schedule pursuant to Article 178 of the Constitution.

- qualified to be a Member of Parliament;[201]
- not be less than 35 years of age;[202] and
- 'willing and able, where applicable, to adhere to and perform the cultural and traditional functions and rites required by his or her office'.[203]

Parliament is empowered to determine the manner in which a chairperson of an RG can be removed.[204] Provision is also made for the appointment of RG ministers with the approval of the RA.[205] In 2009, a bill was published to implement the provisions of Article 178 of the Constitution. However, the bill was never discussed in Parliament and is not going anywhere near the floor of the House.[206] I propose not to discuss the details of the bill given its date of publication and the current debate that surrounds its dubious nature.

5.4.4.4 Assessment

Uganda has been relatively stable for the last two decades.[207] The only challenge has been the civil war in the northern parts of the country.[208] Of late, however, there has been some kind of latent anger and frustration in the southern parts of the country.[209] Varied reasons can be given for this anger, including cases of

201 Paragraph 4(2)(b) Fifth Schedule pursuant to Article 178 of the Constitution.
202 Paragraph 4(2)(c) Fifth Schedule pursuant to Article 178 of the Constitution.
203 Paragraph 4(3)(b) Fifth Schedule pursuant to Article 178 of the Constitution.
204 Paragraph 4(4) Fifth Schedule pursuant to Article 178 of the Constitution.
205 Paragraph 5(1) Fifth Schedule pursuant to Article 178 of the Constitution.
206 See the Regional Government Bill, 2009 No. 20/2009. The memorandum of the Bill states that: The object of this Bill is to provide for the establishment of the Regional Governments in accordance with the Constitution as amended by the Constitutional (Amendment) (No.2) ct, 2005 (Act No. 21 of 2005); to provide for the functions and services of the Regional Governments; to provide for the formation by Regional Governments of regional assemblies and the composition, functions, services, speaker, and committees of regional assemblies; to provide for headship of Regional Governments and for Ministers of Regional Governments; to require co-operation of the Regional Governments with Central Government; to provide for the Chief executive officer and staff of Regional Governments and for districts which do not form Regional Governments; and to make provisions for the elections in respect of Regional Governments; to provide for the takeover of the administration of Regional Governments by the President in special circumstances and related matters.
207 Siegle & O'Mahony 2006: 47.
208 The northern part of the country, in political terms, is predominantly Luo-speaking, although it has other ethnic subgroups, such as the Acholi and the Lango-speaking peoples. In geographical terms, however, the northern part of the country also includes parts of the West Nile Region. From 1986 to 2009, the northern region witnessed one of the most horrific civil conflicts in Uganda that involved Uganda government forces (formerly the National Resistance Army (NRA), now the Uganda Peoples Defence Forces (UPDF)) and the Lord's Resistance Army (LRA) under Joseph Kony. The war, although fought mainly in the Acholi region, equally affected the entire northern region. For details on the northern Uganda conflict, see generally Dolan (2009).
209 See 'Deaths in Uganda forest protest' *BBC*, available at http://news.bbc.co.uk/2/hi/af rica/6548107.stm. 'Uganda MPs angry at forest plan' *BBC*, available at http://news.bbc.co.uk/2/hi/africa/6478829.stm. State Department report on Uganda avail-

corruption, political violence and intolerance.[210] All these have fomented some resistance against the government. Thus, from 2001 to 2008, there have been an unprecedented number of protests against the government.[211] For instance in 2010, clashes between supporters of the Buganda Kingdom and military and police led to injuries and loss of life.[212] This anger is in part the result of the poor institutional design of local government that has alienated an important pillar of local governance – traditional leadership. Even if the provision for the RG was intended to specifically address the Buganda Kingdom's special federal status, there is still active discontent on this issue.

The provision for RGs and governance structures thereunder is an attempt to address simmering ethnic questions within the nation state.[213] Key to the establishment of the RGs is the requirement to comply with constitutional principles relating to democracy.[214] The establishment of RGs seems to have stalled after a serious political confrontation with the Buganda Kingdom.

It is also noted that it is procedurally difficult to establish an RG given that all district and sub-county councils and councillors must, by a two-thirds majority vote, approve the proposal to join. Thus RAs are not realistic forums for ethnic groups that may wish to take up the offer as a watered-down version of asymmetrical federalism.[215] It is maintained that the provision for the RGs does not address the inadequacies in decentralisation, given the RGs' main focus on cultural matters.[216] Moreover, the apparent constitutional protection of the indigenous people's cultural rights subject to the existence of a traditional or cultural leader, assumes that every ethnic minority group necessarily must have a leader.[217]

---

able at http://www.scribd.com/doc/30655494/Clinton-Report-42710#about. 'Chogm debate flops again', *Daily Monitor*, available at http://www.monitor.co.ug/News/National/-/688334/917286/-/wymahm/-/index. 'Museveni an obstacle to democracy' *The Independent*, available at http://www.independent.co.ug/index.php/cover-story/cover-story/82-cover-story/2824-museveni-an-obstacle-to-democracy-. See also *Esrom William Alenyo vs. The Electoral Commission and Another* Court of Appeal Election Petit Appeal No. 9 of 2007; *Kirunda Kivejinja Ali v Katuntu Abdu* Court of Appeal Election Petit Appeal No. 24 of 2006.

210 See State Department report on Uganda, available at http://www.scribd.com/doc/30655494/Clinton-Report-42710#about; 'Chogm debate flops again' *Daily Monitor*, available at http://www.monitor.co.ug/News/National/-/688334/917286/-/wymahm/-/index.

211 See 'Museveni an obstacle to democracy' *The Independent*, available at http://www.independent.co.ug/index.php/cover-story/cover-story/82-cover-story/2824-museveni-an-obstacle-to-democracy-.

212 'The riots were not about Kabaka Mutebi and Kayunga' *The New Vision*, available at http://www.newvision.co.ug/D/8/20/695436; 'Deaths in riot after Uganda fire' *Aljazeera*, available at http://english.aljazeera.net/news/africa/2010/03/20103183262 6 4 9981.

213 See Article 178 of the Constitution.

214 See Article 178(1)(a) of the Constitution.

215 Siegle & O'Mahony 2006: 45.

216 Paragraph 3(2) and (3) Fifth Schedule pursuant to Article 178 of the Constitution. Paragraph 4(3)(b) Fifth Schedule pursuant to Article 178 of the Constitution.

217 See Paragraph 2(1)(d) Fifth Schedule pursuant to Article 178 of the Constitution

Thus, in cases where no leadership structures exist among certain indigenous peoples, there is no constitutional protection extended to them from an RG.[218]

Since RGs are only limited to cultural aspects of the regions, they ignore the legitimate demands of certain communities, like the Buganda, who demand a special federal status within Uganda.[219]As argued by Kaplan, the protection of unique identity groups through greater political autonomy is a credible way to fix the political fragility if the state fragility is linked to ethnic strife that exists in many less developed countries.[220]

The Buganda Kingdom's quest for a special federal status poses subtle problems in protecting the rights of minorities that exist within it.[221] Some ethnic groups, with a culture distinct from that of the Buganda, have historically existed within it. In addition, many other ethnic groups from other parts of the country have settled in the Buganda Kingdom as a result of migration. The key test for a successful quest for and configuration of the Buganda Kingdom's special federal status would be the manner in which such a federal arrangement protects and integrates minorities that have historically existed within Buganda, such as through stronger local governments.[222]

The constitutional promise to protect marginalised groups as a right[223] presupposes that some ethnic groups, like the Batwa,[224] demand special attention and protection. Recognition of cultural diversity should not have been the only constitutional precondition for the establishment of an RG.[225]

5.5 Conclusion

The discussion in this chapter has traced the promulgation of the 1995 Constitution to the repealed unitary Constitution of 1967. As highlighted in Chapter Four, the 1967 Constitution not only provided for a highly centralised state but had also abolished the territorial autonomy of the Buganda Kingdom that was provided for under the 1962 Constitution.[226] The chapter examined the role of the Odoki Commission under the 1995 Constitution and argued that to a large extent, the recommendations by the Commission were adopted by the Constituency Assembly.

218 Jjemba 2009: 1–17.
219 Singiza & De Visser 2011: 10.
220 Kaplan 2008: 32–3.
221 For example, the 'Banyala', the 'Baluli' and the 'Bakoki' have traditionally existed within the Buganda Kingdom.
222 Singiza 2010: 9.
223 See NODPSP No.III of the Constitution.
224 The Batwa are an indigenous people in the great lakes region and are found in Burundi, Rwanda Democratic Republic of Congo and Uganda.
225 See Article 12(1) of the Constitution. See also 'MPs oppose autonomy for minority tribes' *The New Vision*, available at http://www.newvision.co.ug/D/8/13/699607 (accessed 30 October 2009).
226 Chapter Four § 4.8.2.

The chapter described the different local government institutional structures in Uganda, but maintained that only district and sub-county councils enjoy legal personality, with the exception of the municipal council, which takes the form of a hybrid rural-urban council. The chapter discussed the legal and policy background to the creation of many districts and argued that the process has been open to abuse by the central government for the sake of politics, rather than sound economics. The creation of many districts was also discussed together with the centralisation of Kampala City to highlight the extent of the abuse of the process of creating or altering local government boundaries in Uganda. The chapter argued that there is evidence to suggest that the creation of many districts serves as a reward for political support and, in part, to weaken strong ethnic groups. An economically stronger and/or more populous district can compete politically with the central government better than an economically weaker or less populous one. Ultimately the chapter pointed out that the object of decentralisation as identified in Chapter Two has been deliberately undermined by the central government.[227] Using the newly established KCCA as an example, the chapter explained that the centralisation of Kampala City was carried out, in part, to punish local communities for continuously voting for the opposition parties, and not necessarily to improve the quality of service delivery to Kampala City residents.

While evaluating the 1995 constitutional amendment that provides for RGs, the chapter made the point that RGs are in fact a response to the Buganda Kingdom's demand for special federal status. The chapter concluded that the rejection of the RG offer from the central government by the Buganda Kingdom calls for immediate legal reform of Uganda's decentralisation programme. The preceding two chapters have examined the historical context of decentralisation, and the reforms introduced after the promulgation of the 1995 Constitution. They have laid the ground for the next two chapters that analyse the governance structures and the powers and functions that are devolved to district councils.

227 Chapter Two § 2.3.1.

6 District council government

6.1 Introduction

This chapter presents evidence that Uganda's legal framework is a major causal variable for the intrusive top-down decentralisation. The chapter also highlights the role of political parties, ethnicity, national identity, educational background, the power of elites, political patronage and clientalism, corruption and traditional leadership in accentuating the intrusive nature of Uganda's district council governing structures.

The Constitution of Uganda calls for the protection of the right to public participation of all citizens in the democratic process. Consequently, access to leadership positions at all levels and the ability of citizens to freely elect their leaders are projected as core to democracy.[1] It is for this reason that the right to vote is guaranteed under the Constitution.[2] The Odoki Commission took the view that:

> [f]rom the pre-colonial period to the present, people became increasingly marginalised in deciding on matters which affect them, and grew apathetic about government. Yet it is at the local level that the citizens have the fullest opportunity to participate directly in their own governance ... The emasculation of local governments meant fewer opportunities to exercise political power. Many Ugandans believe that this partly accounts for the intense and sometimes violent competition for political and public offices at the national level.[3]

According to the Odoki Commission, districts should be controlled by elected representatives of the people, who must remain answerable to the electorate at all times.[4] Adopting the Odoki Commission recommendation, Article 80(2) of the Constitution vests Parliament with the power to prescribe, among others, the election and composition of the members of the district councils.

1 See NODPSP No II para. (ii) of the Constitution.
2 Section 59(1) of the Constitution.
3 See Odoki Constitution Commission 1993: 491 para. 18.56–18.57.
4 See Odoki Constitution Commission 1993: 498 para. 18.9.

Chapter Two linked the role of local elections in a decentralised system in fostering transparency and accountability in subnational governments.[5] In Chapter Three a point was made that an electoral system, particularly in fragmented societies, can only produce legitimate electoral outcomes if it is (a) representative, (b) accessible, (c) accountable, (d) promotes inclusive political mobilisation and (e) creates stability of governments.[6]

6.2 Features of Uganda's district council electoral system

In the discussion below, five salient features of the district council's electoral system are identified. In turn, these features are examined to assess whether the criteria (a) –(e) above are met. The major focus in this part of the chapter is on the choice between proportional representation and constituency voting on the one hand, and the universal adult suffrage, secret ballot and 'lining behind ones preferred candidate' on the other. The dominance of the ruling party in district council politics and the exclusion of ethnic minority representation are also presented as problematic for local democracy.

6.2.1 The choice between proportional representation and constituency voting

The Constitution does not specify a particular electoral system for district council elections. Instead, the Constitution provides that in every election, at the closure of the poll, the presiding officer must count and record the number of votes obtained by each candidate. Every candidate or his or her representatives or polling agents must verify that vote counting at the polling station was accurate. The results are then announced.[7] In the words of section 135(1) of the LGA: 'Each returning officer shall, immediately after the addition of all the votes for each candidate or after any recount, declare elected a candidate who has obtained the largest number of votes by completing a return in a prescribed form'.

The person who obtains the highest number of votes wins the electoral seat or area. The practical effect that flows from section 135(1) of the LGA is that once a winning person in any electoral area has been declared, the losing party or supporters thereof are not represented.[8] Section 135(1) of the LGA adopts the 'winner-takes-all' electoral system.

5 Chapter Two § 2.3.1.2.
6 Chapter Three § 3.4.3.
7 Articles 68(2), (3) and (4) of the Constitution.
8 For example, the UK winner-takes-all system has been criticised by the United Kingdom's Electoral Commission Chairwoman, Jenny Watson, as 'Victorian, antiquated, left over from an era when less people had to vote'.

6.2.2 *The choice between universal adult suffrage, secret ballot and line voting*

As discussed in Chapter Five, the debate on district council elections in the Odoki Commission revolved around three main methods of voting: a secret ballot; lining up behind a person's preferred candidate; and electing district council leaders using electoral colleges.[9] Article 176 of the Constitution provides universal adult suffrage for district council elections. There is no particular injunction that district council elections (other than those of the district council chairperson) should be by a secret vote. The only injunction is that district council elections should be in accordance with Article 181(4) of the Constitution, which makes reference to a five-year term of office. In any case, Parliament has the discretion to exempt district council chairperson elections from the secret ballot requirement.[10] Thus, the method of physically standing behind one's preferred candidate is constitutionally valid.[11] Currently, the LGA adopts a secret ballot and universal adult suffrage for all district council elected officials.[12] Against this background, the discussion below examines whether the adoption of a constituency-based system, in which three methods of voting are provided for, counters the inadequacies of the winner-takes-all system.

6.3 District council constituencies

The right to vote is a key criterion for the demarcation of electoral areas under Article 181 of the Constitution.[13] The Constitution vests the obligation in the

9 Chapter Five § 5.1.2.4.

10 Article 68(1) of the Constitution

11 See the repealed section (2) 111 of the LGA. See also Makara 2009: 9.

12 Section 111(1) of the LGA. Until recently, only the election of the district council chairperson was by universal adult suffrage and by a secret ballot. The election of sub-county and municipal, town and county local government chairpersons was conducted differently. Voters would physically line up behind their preferred candidate, who would have been nominated for the office, or his or her representative, or portrait. See the repealed section (2) 111 of the LGA. See also Makara 2009: 9. Article 68 (6) of the Constitution provides: 'Parliament may by law exempt any public election, other than a presidential or parliamentary election, from the requirements of clause (1) that it shall be held by secret ballot'. Thus, the method of electing candidates by physically standing behind them remains and is constitutionally valid.

13 Article 181 of the Constitution provides that for elections of local government councils: '(1) A district shall be divided by the Electoral Commission into electoral areas which shall be demarcated in such a way that the number of inhabitants in the electoral areas are as nearly as possible equal. (2) The number of inhabitants in an electoral area may be greater or less than other electoral areas in order to take account of means of communication, geographical features and density of population. (3) The demarcation of electoral areas shall ensure that a sub-county, a town council or an equivalent part of a municipality is represented at the district council by at least one person. (4) All local government councils shall be elected every five years. (5) Subject to article 61 of this Constitution, elections of all local government councils shall take place on such date as the Electoral Commission shall determine in accordance with the law'.

Electoral Commission to demarcate districts into equal electoral areas according to the number of inhabitants.[14] However, the number of electoral areas may differ depending on logistical considerations, such as communication, geographical features and population density.[15] To ensure full participation of people in every district, demarcation of the electoral areas must ensure that at least one person represents a sub-county or a town.[16]

The LGA provides that the process of demarcation of electoral areas is required to ensure that every sub-county or municipal division is represented in the district council.[17] Thus, a district as an electoral area may be subdivided into sub-counties and/or municipal divisions. The LGA provides that a district electoral area should have about 30,000 inhabitants.[18]

According to the LGA, the population quotas notwithstanding, the demarcation of the electoral areas for female representatives should ensure that women constitute at least one-third of the district council.[19]

As stated in Chapter Five, a sub-county (or LCIII) is a constituency for electing district council councillors.[20] The Constitution enjoins Parliament to determine districts and sub-counties as political institutional structures.[21] At the same time the Constitution mandates the Electoral Commission to create district council constituencies.[22] In principle, the criteria for creating districts and sub-counties are similar to those for creating district council electoral constituencies.[23] All district council councillors' and chairpersons' elections are organised, conducted and supervised by the Uganda Electoral Commission. The Electoral Commission is specifically mandated to 'compile, maintain, revise and update the voter's register'.[24]

What the above means is that should the population quota in a given district result in less than the minimum number of female councillors in any district council, then the electoral areas would have to be increased to meet the minimum requirements.

14 Article 181(1) of the Constitution.
15 Article 181(2) of the Constitution.
16 Article 181(3) of the Constitution.
17 Section 109(1)(a) of the LGA.
18 Section 108(1)(c) of the LGA.
19 Section 108(3) of the LGA.
20 See Chapter Five § 5.3.1
21 Article 179 of the Constitution.
22 Article 181(1) of the Constitution.
23 Article 181(2) of the Constitution. See detailed discussion in Chapter Five § 5.3.1.1.
24 Article 61(2) of the Constitution. See also section 101 of the LGA. Where there are fewer women's seats than what all lower councils in a district can provide, the electoral areas for female councillors under section 110(e) are permitted by themselves to co-opt two or more female councillors from the lower councils. The electoral areas for female councillors must, in co-opting more female councillors, use a population quota that is determined by the Electoral Commission.

6.4 The role of political parties

In Chapter Two, the role of political pluralism was highlighted as crucial for local democracy.[25] In Chapters Four and Five, the history of political pluralism was also given.[26] As noted earlier, when the present ruling party captured state power in 1986, political parties and their activities were *de facto* banned. It was in this environment of restricted political party activities that the process of devolution of powers to district councils began.[27] Makara argues that

> although the NRM (until 2005) had claimed to be a movement and not a one-party state, it did operate like the latter. The reality of the politics of decentralisation in Uganda tends to vindicate Manor's argument that the real reason why national politicians accept decentralisation is because they wish to use decentralisation to connect their regime with social groups and to sustain or revive their party organisations.[28]

Indeed, at the inception of decentralisation in 1986, district councils, then known as the Resistance Committees Five (RC5), were intertwined with the ruling party's security apparatus, and hence undermined their democratic credentials.[29]

6.4.1 The Movement Political System

The Constitution provides for two main political systems, namely the non-party political system (or the Movement Political System) and the pluralistic political system (or the Multiparty Political System).[30] Either of the two political systems is subject to the voters' 'choice', expressed either by an election or a referendum. In addition, the Constitution provides that either of the two political systems can be adopted through a majority vote of the elected representatives in Parliament. However, their decision has to be supported by a resolution of the majority of each of the district councillors. At least 50% of the district councils in the whole country must support such a resolution.[31]

The 1995 Constitution defined the Movement Political System by listing its four basic principles: (i) ensuring that every citizen was involved in the decision-making process; (ii) promoting transparency in that every decision taken had to be justified and explained to the citizens; (iii) ensuring that every citizen had an opportunity to access any leadership position; and (iv) ensuring a

25 Chapter Two § 2.3.2.4.
26 Chapter Four § 4.6 and Chapter Five § 5.1.2.5.
27 Oloka-Onyango 2007: 11.
28 Makara 2009: 64.
29 Makara 2009: 135.
30 See Articles 69–71 of the Constitution.
31 See Article 74 of the Constitution.

candidate's individual merit.[32] The Constitution specifically prohibited political parties from performing any activities that would 'interfere with the Movement Political System'.[33] The Movement Act (MA) was enacted to give effect to the Movement Political System.[34] It provided for a National Executive Committee, its Secretariat and district council committees. The MA also provided for the National Conference as the body corporate of the Movement Political System.[35] The National Conference was also the executive organ of the Movement Political System.[36]

According to the MA, the National Conference consisted of a Chairperson, a National Political Commissar and all members of Parliament.[37] Importantly, it also included all members of executive committees of district councils and all district council chairpersons.[38] The Chairperson of the National Conference was the head of the Movement Political System and chaired the National Conference and the National Executive Committee. He or she convened and presided over National Conference and National Executive Committee meetings. The Chairperson implemented the 'policies and principles of the movement'.[39] He or she was also the chief spokesperson of the Movement Political System and the overall source of guidance to the organs of the Movement Political System and could 'do any other thing necessary for the good of the Movement'.[40]

There was arguably very little distinction between the government of the day and the Movement Political System. Thus, the structures of the Movement Political System were for all intents and purposes a 'rival' and not a 'shadow' government.[41] Makara argues that 'although the NRM (until 2005) had claimed to be a movement and not a one-party state, it did operate like the latter'.[42]

In this part of the chapter, the main focus is on the re-introduction of political pluralism in 2005, following the 2005 constitutional amendment. The Constitution, in its amended form, adopts the multiparty political system. Political parties can compete for political office in district councils.[43] A candidate

32 See Article 70 of the Constitution.
33 See Article 269 of the Constitution and Lambright 2011: 28.
34 The long title to the Movement Act, Cap 261 provided: 'an Act to make provision for the movement political system pursuant to article 70 of the Constitution and for related matters'.
35 Section 3(3) of the MA.
36 Section 5 of the MA.
37 Section 4 of the MA.
38 Sections 3(1) and (2)4 of the MA.
39 Section 6 of the MA.
40 Section 6 of the MA.
41 Singiza & De Visser 2015: 115.
42 Makara 2009: 64.
43 See generally the Constitution (Amendment) Act No 11 2005. The case of *Rubaramira Ruranga v Electoral Commission and Another*, Constitution Petition No. 21 of 2006, was the first to test the notion of multiparty politics in district elections after the constitutional amendment that allowed for the return of multiparty politics. The case dealt with the composition of electoral colleges of LCI, II and IV. The Constitutional Court held that in a

may also be nominated as an independent without the sponsorship of any political organisation or political party.[44] The Constitution in its current form places numerous injunctions on the formation and participation of political parties. The Constitution obliges every political party in a multiparty political system to be of a 'national character'[45] and not one based on 'sex, ethnicity, religion or other sectional division'.[46]

The framework for political parties is regulated by the Political Parties and Organisations Act of 2005 (PPOA).[47] The PPOA, while adopting the provisions of Article 71(1)(b) of the Constitution, prohibits the formation of political parties 'based on sex, race, colour, or ethnic origin, tribe, creed or religions or other similar division'.[48] Further, the PPOA prohibits the use of words, slogans or symbols which might arouse any of the divisions prohibited above.[49] In other words, Parliament on the instruction of the Constitution restricts the expression of ethnic identity in a multiparty political system.

This principle is also followed through in local government. Local government elections are regulated, in the main, by the Local Governments Act (LGA).[50] This act, too, prohibits the use of any colours or symbols that have a tribal or religious affiliation or 'any other sectarian connotation' as a basis for one's candidature for election or in support of one's campaign.[51] Under the LGA, individual candidates who violate this provision not only put their candidature at risk but also risk the imposition of a fine of 48 currency points or two years imprisonment. In other words, the government of Uganda did not want the reintroduction of multiparty politics to open the door for ethnic mobilisation. In fact, it imposed an outright ban on party political campaigning around ethnic, religious or cultural matters.[52]

Before the introduction of multiparty politics, the one-party political system emphasised the 'individual merit' of an individual candidate.[53] Under the Movement Political System a person was elected to a political office based on his or her ability to perform. Under the pluralistic political system, however, emphasis is placed on the internal democratic organisation of an individual political

multiparty system it is not an individual that is nominated, but rather a party flag-bearer. The Court nullified elections of all LCI, II and IV local administrative unit councils throughout the country on account of non-compliance with the constitutional guarantees of political pluralism. According to the Constitutional Court, an electoral collegial system that did not provide for parties to nominate candidates was unconstitutional. Thus, a person could not be validly nominated as a candidate unless provision was made for different parties to nominate candidates in a collegial system for LCI, II and IV elections.

44 Section 119A of the LGA.
45 Article 71(1)(a) of the Constitution.
46 Article 71(1)(b) of the Constitution.
47 Section 3 of the PPOA.
48 Section 5(a) of the PPOA.
49 Section 5(b) of the PPOA.
50 See the Local Governments Act Cap, 243, as amended.
51 The LGAs 125(2).
52 The LGAs 125(4). See also Singiza & De Visser 2015: 118.
53 Article 70 of the Constitution.

party. Thus, under a multiparty political system, an individual candidate, as a party flag-bearer, is selected first by the party members (through a system of party primaries), and then voted into a political office by the majority of the voters in an electoral area.[54]

6.5 Rules for candidacy

That local governments have the ability to identify local priorities and development needs better than the central government is by now very clear. Emphasis was placed on the consensus-building attributes for traditional institutions; the leaders of these institutions supplement local democracy rather than hinder it.[55] As already noted, an adequate local government electoral model should be representative, accessible, foster political competition and accountability, be competitive, inclusive and create stable government.[56] The Constitution does not exclude any category of person from participating in district council elections and therefore accords with the above arguments.

The LGA provides specific grounds that may disqualify a person to be elected as a district councillor. These are either:

- insanity;[57]
- holding any office relating to the conduct of an election under the LGA;[58]
- being a traditional or cultural leader;[59]
- being under sentence of death, or serving a term of imprisonment exceeding six months without the option of a fine;[60]or
- employment by a district council for which a person seeks to stand.[61]

The discussion below will highlight two issues, namely (1) the absence of educational qualification and (2) the banning of traditional leaders from politics.

The Odoki Commission did not recommend the exclusion of candidates for district council councillors on account of his or her level of educational qualification. The Commission reasoned:

> Many people have given views on qualifications for a person to be elected to the district council. On the whole, people want candidates with a reasonable

54 Article 71 of the Constitution. In practice, there is a fine line between the Movement Political System and the 'multiparty political system' since both emphasise party discipline and internal cohesion.
55 Chapter Two § 2.3.2.4.
56 Chapter Three § 3.4.3.
57 Section 116(2)(a) of the LGA.
58 Section 116(1)(b) of the LGA.
59 Section 116(1)(c) of the LGA.
60 Section 116(1)(d) of the LGA.
61 Section 116(1)(e) of the LGA.

> standard of education and a clean record in the community. ... In our view, there is no need to prescribe any formal education standard. Any person who can read and write and speak the local language reasonably fluently should qualify to be elected. We must trust that the electoral process itself will weed out incompetent people and produce the right councillors for the district.[62]

It should be noted that this recommendation covered all members of a district council. In the CA, attempts to set higher education standards were resisted on the grounds that the majority of district politicians had a lower level educational background.[63] Hence a higher educational qualification might disenfranchise the electorate of their freedom to choose.[64]

It is arguable that the absence of educational qualifications for councillors accords with what the majority of the CA delegates wanted. To the extent that the Commission considered a higher educational qualification as an unjustified limitation is in accord with the arguments advanced for an inclusive and accessible local government electoral model. The Constitution adopted the stance of the Commission. Thus, under the Constitution, the only condition that a person must fulfil is that he or she must be a citizen of Uganda.[65] However, under Article 180(2) of the Constitution, Parliament is vested with powers to provide, among others, for additional qualifications. The additional qualifications are discussed below.

The provisions of the Constitution, the LGA and the newly enacted Institutions of Traditional or Cultural Leaders Act (ITCA)[66] explain the rules of candidacy for district council councillors. Article 246 of the Constitution provides for the existence of traditional institutions.[67] Article 246(2)(e) of the Constitution provides that 'a person shall not, while remaining a traditional leader or cultural leader, join or participate in partisan politics'. Article 246(2)(e) of the Constitution, on which basis section 116(2)(c) of the LGA and section 13(1) of the ITCA are enacted, clearly bars traditional and cultural leaders from local government politics.[68] Section 116(e)(1)(c) of the LGA provides: 'A person shall not be elected a local government councillor if that person ... is a traditional or cultural leader as defined in article 246(6) of the Constitution'. It is noted that the Constitution only prohibits traditional or cultural leaders from

62 Odoki Commission 1993: 499.

63 See CA debates 1994: 3755 per Okalebo Ephrahim.

64 See CA debates 1994: 3755 per Lt. Col. Sserwanga Lwanga.

65 Article 180(3) of the Constitution.

66 Cited as The Institutions of Traditional or Cultural Leaders Act (ITCA).

67 Article 246(6) of the Constitution defines a 'traditional leader or cultural leader' as 'a king or similar traditional leader or cultural leader by whatever name called, who derives allegiance from the fact of birth or descent in accordance with the customs, traditions, usage or consent of the people led by that traditional or cultural leader'.

68 See also sections 13(1) and (2) of the ITCA. Section 13(2) of the ITCA provides that any traditional or cultural leader that joins or participates in partisan politics must abdicate his position not less than 90 days before the date of the nomination.

joining or participating in 'partisan politics'.[69] It may difficult for a traditional leader, who is elected to a district council, to remain neutral, if he or has been sponsored by a political party. However, it is possible for a traditional leader, who is elected to a district council on an independent ticket, to remain neutral. The LGA blanket provision that bars traditional and cultural leaders from district councils is therefore unconstitutional.

6.6 Special representation

6.6.1 Introduction

An adequate electoral model should be representative, accessible and capable of promoting reconciliation, accountability and inclusive political mobilisation. These features are necessary for creating stable local governments.[70] Against the background of the above norm, the section below assesses the elections of minority social groups to determine if the electoral process is capable of producing legitimate outcomes necessary for democratic local government.

6.7 Electoral approach

It is the duty of the Electoral Commission to help establish the different bodies that form the electoral colleges.[71] The Electoral Commission must engage with the associations of social minorities and political parties to elect their representatives by appointing returning officers and presiding officers for the purposes of conducting elections of representatives of each special interest group.[72] As noted earlier, only adult members of voting age of these associations (electoral colleges) qualify to vote by a secret ballot for candidates representing social minorities.[73] The Constitution provides for special interest group representation in the district councils and instructs Parliament to make provision for representation of social minorities in the district councils.[74] The LGA provides for electing special interest groups such as women, the youth and persons with disabilities. The manner in which the LGA provides for their special presentation is problematic. The LGA mandates the Electoral Commission to reach out to social minorities in electing district council special interest group councillors.[75] The Electoral Commission,

69 Article 178 of the Constitution defines the term 'partisan' only in relation to the RA deliberations and provides: 'A matter shall be considered to be of a partisan nature if in the course of its being tabled or debated in a regional assembly it is declared by a majority vote of the directly elected representatives to be partisan'.

70 See Chapter Three § 3.4.3.

71 Section 118(2B) of the LGA.

72 Section 118(3) of the LGA.

73 Section 111(1) of the LGA. See also *Rubaramira Ruranga*.

74 Article 180(2)(b), (c) and (d) of the Constitution.

75 Section 117(1) of the LGA.

on the instruction of the LGA,[76] considers only youth, persons with disabilities[77] and elderly persons as social minorities that require special representation.[78] Whereas the first two associations are statutory, the latter one, on whose basis district council councillors representing the elderly are elected, is not.[79] Yet ethnic minority groups in Uganda, even those affiliated to the Minority Rights Group International,[80] are not accommodated. The mechanism for electing social minorities in district councils is not representative, does not foster inclusive political mobilisation and therefore contradicts the norm established in Chapter Three.[81]

6.7.1 Women

The LGA specifically requires that at least one-third of district council councillors must be females.[82] A Member of Parliament (every district has a female MP representing women) is an *ex officio* member of a district council in his or her constituency but has no voting right in the council.[83]

The procedure for the election of female councillors is subject to such alterations as may be deemed necessary by the Electoral Commission.[84] The women councillors in district councils are elected by universal adult suffrage.[85] What this means is that whereas a person must be a woman to stand as a councillor to occupy the special seats for women in a district council, she has to be voted for by both men and women of voting age in an electoral area.

6.7.2 Youth

The LGA provides for the election of two councillors representing the youth (the members of the executive committee of the National Council of Youth in the district acting as the electoral college), one of whom must be female.[86] The respective youth councils are provided for under section 5 of the National Youth

76 Section 118(2B) of the LGA.
77 See the National Youth Council Act Cap. 319 and the National Council for Disability Act (No. 14), 2003.
78 Article 80(2) of the Constitution on affirmative action.
79 The Uganda Reach the Aged Association (URTAA) is a voluntary, non-profit Non-Governmental Organisation (NGO) whose main focus is to improve the quality of life and preserve the dignity of older people in Uganda.
80 See the World Directory of Minorities and Indigenous Peoples, available at http://www.minorityrights.org/744/directory/world-directory-of-minorities-and-indigenous-peoples.html#sthash.L7bU5rY2.dpuf (accessed 10 March 2014).
81 See Chapter Three § 3.4.3.
82 Section 10(1)(e) of the LGA.
83 Section 10(2) of the LGA.
84 Section 117(1) of the LGA. For instance, the Electoral Commission may make regulations relating to the procedure of electing special interest groups councillors.
85 Section 117(2) of the LGA.
86 Sections 10(1)(c) and 118 (1)(a) of the LGA.

Council Act (NYCA) Cap. 319.[87] Provision is also made under the NYCA for the composition and hierarchy of youth councils.[88]

6.7.3 Persons with disabilities

The LGA provides for the election of two councillors representing persons with disabilities (the members of the executive committee of the National Council of Persons with Disability in the district acting as the electoral college), one of whom must be female.[89]

The National Council for Disability Act 1 of 2003 (NCDA) provides for the National Council of Disability,[90] whose functions include, among others, 'to assist the Electoral Commission to ensure the conducting of free and fair elections of representatives of persons with disability to Parliament and District Councils'.[91] The NCDA establishes district and sub-county councils for disabled persons.[92] The LGA provides that councillors representing persons with disabili-

87 Section 1 of the NYCA provides that a '"district", "county", "sub-county", "division", "town", "parish", "ward", and "village" have the meanings ascribed to them under the Local Governments Act'. Section 5 of the NYCA provides:'The following youth councils are established in each district – village youth councils; parish or ward youth councils; sub-county, division or town youth councils; county youth councils; and a district youth council'.

88 Section 6 of the NYCA provides: 'A village youth council shall consist of every person who has attained the age of eighteen years but is below the age of thirty years and is a resident of the village. A parish or ward youth council shall consist of all the members of the village youth committees in the parish or ward. A sub-county, division or town youth council shall consist of all the members of the parish youth committees in the sub-county, division or town. A county youth council shall consist of all the members of the sub-county, division or town youth committees in the county. A district youth council shall consist of – the chairperson, vice chairperson, secretary, publicity secretary and finance secretary of each county youth committee in the district; and one male representative and one female representative of each sub-county youth council in the district elected by the sub-county youth council'.

89 Section 10(1)(d) of the LGA.

90 Sections 2 and 3 of the NCDA. Section 2 of the NCDA defines 'disability' as a 'substantial functional limitation of daily life activities of an individual caused by physical, sensory or mental impairment and environmental barriers'.

91 Section 6(1)(i) of the NCDA.

92 Sections 18(2) and 21(1) of the NCDA. Under section 18 of the NCDA, the district council for the disabled consists of the following: a district rehabilitation officer, a district finance officer, a district education officer, the district director of medical services, two district councillors with disability and the chairperson of the district committee responsible for disability affairs or social services. These members are *ex officio* members. In addition, the district council for disability consists of two other persons with disability in the district, one of whom must be female. Further, a representative of the parents of children with disabilities appointed in consultation with the organisations of persons with disability in the district and one representative of the Non-Governmental Organisations (NGOs) working with persons with disability in the district are also members. A youth representative of persons with disability on the district local government council, and a person of proven integrity with knowledge of disability who is involved in the advocacy of disability matters appointed in consultation with the organisation of persons with disability in the district, are

ties are elected by the electoral college formed by all the members of the district executive committee and sub-county executive committee of the National Union of Disabled People of Uganda (NUDPU).[93]

6.7.4 The elderly

In every district council, two councillors representing the elderly are elected by an association of the elderly forming an electoral college.[94] The two councillors representing the elderly are elected by the electoral college formed by all the members of the district executive committee and sub-county executive committee of the National Association of Elderly Persons.[95]

6.8 Recalling a councillor

The Constitution provides for the revocation of the mandate of any member of the district council by the electorate.[96] Parliament is vested with powers to prescribe the procedure for revocation of the elected members of the district council.[97] Regulation 7 of the Local Government Council Regulations (LGCR)[98] provides for the grounds upon which the mandate of an elected councillor can be revoked. These grounds are: failure by the councillor to declare his or her assets within three months after assuming office; neglect of a councillor's duty; and commission of acts incompatible with his or her position as a member of the council.

Thus, the criteria for revoking a district councillor's mandate relate to the link between decentralisation and accountability.[99] The detailed discussion on the relationship between decentralisation and accountability was made in Chapter Two.[100]

A councillor's mandate is revoked by the electorate if one-third of the registered voters in a district councillor's electoral area sign a petition and lodge

---

also members. The district council for disability has a chairperson and a vice-chairperson who have to be elected from amongst persons with disability of the district council of disability. At least the chairperson or the vice-chairperson has to be female.

93 Section 118(2)(a) of the LGA. Section 118(2) of the LGA. Although the LGA does not provide that a councillor representing disabled persons has to be disabled, the fact that the criteria for membership of the National Union of Disabled Persons of Uganda is disability implies that a councillor representing disabled persons has to be disabled.

94 Section 118(2A) of the LGA.

95 Section 118(2A)(a) of the LGA. The Uganda Reach the Aged Association (URTAA) is the main organisation that represents elderly persons in Uganda.

96 Article 182(1) of the Constitution.

97 Article 182(2) of the Constitution.

98 See LGCR 7(a) and (b) under Part II of the Third Schedule to the LGA.

99 See the Ministry of Local Government *Decentralisation Policy Strategic Framework* 2006: 19.

100 See Chapter Two § 2.3.1.2.

it with the Electoral Commission. Once the authenticity of the petitioners and the validity of the petition is ascertained by the Electoral Commission, a district councillor's seat is declared vacant.[101]

6.9 Assessment of the electoral system of district councillors

6.9.1 Determining constituencies based on the number of inhabitants

The demarcation process which depends on estimates of population numbers is open to manipulation and statistical errors, given the absence of a credible voters' register.[102] In the absence of a credible centralised national identification system,[103] it is difficult to precisely determine persons of voting age or whether in fact a voter is dead. Thus, under-age voters and 'ghost voters' continue to fraudulently take part in the voting process.[104] Furthermore, the determination of electoral areas based on the number of inhabitants and not on that of voters is misleading. Usually, the exercise of the right to vote is based on universal adult suffrage only. In addition, it should not have been for the Electoral Commission to determine the political boundaries in district councils but an independent boundary demarcation body.[105]

6.9.2 The dominance of the Movement Political System

The change from the Movement Political System to the Multiparty Political System of government was adopted in 1995 after a constitutional amendment.[106] The change from a de facto one-party system to multiparty politics was not a genuine one. Rather, it was a political compromise after persistent pressure from different stakeholders, including the donor community, to re-introduce multi-party politics. As part of the compromise, the constitutional amendment catered for the extension of the Presidential term limits, a political move described as the 'purification of the Movement'.[107]

101 LGCR 7(2) and (3) under Part II of the Third Schedule to the LGA.

102 See Save the Children, 'Lack of Birth Certificate Fuelling Child Abuse - Save the Children' *The Observer*, 26 November 2009. See also sections 15–18 of the Births and Deaths Registration Act 1973 Cap 309, which provides for an onerous procedure of registering deaths. It is difficult to register the death of person when his or her birth particulars are unknown.

103 See Ojwee D 'Aronda warns ID project staff against arrogance' *The New Vision*, available at http://www.newvision.co.ug/news/654665-aronda-warns-id-project-staff-against-arrogance (accessed 19 April 2014).

104 *Col. Dr. Besigye Kiiza v Museveni Yoweri Kaguta, Electoral Commission* (Election Petition No.1 Of 2001) [2001] UGSC 3 (21 April 2001).

105 See Chapter Three § 3.3.3.3.

106 See generally the Constitution (Amendment) Act No. 11 2005 Act.

107 Oloka-Onyango 2007: 24. The removal of presidential term limits in 2005 essentially allowed President Museveni, in power since 1986, to seek another term or terms in office

Consequently, the transition to multiparty politics in 2005 was not a genuine political and legal reform measure. It was, as Oloka-Onyango observes, a means by which dissidents in the ruling party could be 'purged', pleasing Western donors, without undermining the ruling party's political dominance of the district council structures.[108] Moreover, the legal provision that prohibits the use of ethnicity as a rallying force in the formation of political parties attests to the unproven fear that multiparty politics are unsuitable for multi-ethnic countries such as Uganda.[109] The most common argument against multiparty politics has been that it is unsuitable for Ugandan district council politics, as Uganda has no strong middle class.[110]

In a true sense, political pluralism is merely tolerated, not totally favoured in district council elections for councillors.[111] Thus, notwithstanding the introduction of political pluralism, the philosophy and political dominance of the *de facto* one-party state remain intact.[112]

6.9.3 Electoral outcomes

The electoral outcomes of district councils show an overwhelming dominance of the ruling party. For example, as of 2005, only three out of 70 district councils were controlled by opposition-leaning chairpersons, while in the 2006 local government elections, only 15 out of 84 district council chairperson seats were won by opposition parties, despite the fact that the ruling party's share of the national vote had statistically declined.[113] In the 2011 Local Government Elections, out of a total of 112 district council seats, 85 were won by the ruling party while the remaining seats were shared between the opposition parties and independent candidates.[114] The former Kampala City Council was among the few district councils that had not been fully dominated by the ruling party.[115]

after serving for the two constitutional terms from when the 1995 Constitution was promulgated. In fact, he had then served for five terms from 1986.

108 Oloka-Onyango 2007: 24–5.

109 Museveni 2000: 15.

110 Oloka-Onyango 2007: 25.

111 For example, Lambright 2011: 201 documents evidence of political intimidation where the former Vice-President warned voters against electing opposition-leaning district political leaders in the 2011 local council elections. Citing another instance, the same author explains that in 2006 when the Pallisa district elected a member of the opposition party as the district chair, the chair-elect could not form an executive committee until he 'signed a memorandum of understanding with the NRM'.

112 See Lambright 2011: 28.

113 Lambright 2011: 28.

114 See the *Uganda Electoral Commission, District Council Elections*, 2011. It is noted that some of the independent candidates lean towards the ruling party.

115 See Chapter Five § 5.3.11, on the relationship between voting trends at national level and the proliferation of districts in Uganda. See also Singiza & De Visser 2010.

Table 6.1 Electoral outcomes of district council chairpersons

Election year	*NRM*	*Others*	*No. of districts*	*Female district chair persons*	*PWDs district chairpersons*
2001	70	3	73	1	0
2006	69	15	84	1	1
2011	85	27	112	1	0

Source: Adopted from the Uganda Electoral Commission District Council Elections results from 2001 to 2011

Table 6.1 illustrates the evidence of the domination of the district councils by the ruling party.[116] This hegemony can be explained by the history of devolution in Uganda.

6.9.4 Exclusion of ethnic minorities

Chapter Three made a point that a proportional representation electoral system may suit local democracy in fragmented societies, given proportional representation's inclusive nature. The proportional representation electoral system contributes to stability, which ultimately translates into stable local government institutions.[117]

The adoption of the 'winner-takes-all' model is not only risky for local democracy, but excludes ethnic minorities. The local government electoral system does not provide for the special representation of ethnic minorities. Four special interest categories of councillors were discussed: councillors representing women, the youth, persons with disability and the elderly.

Article 80(2)(c) of the Constitution specifically provides that 'any law enacted by virtue of this article shall provide for affirmative action for all marginalised groups referred to in article 32 of this Constitution'. Article 32(1) of the Constitution bestows an obligation on the state to 'take affirmative action in favour of groups marginalised on the basis of gender, age, disability or any other reason created by history, tradition or custom, for the purpose of redressing imbalances which exist against them'. From the above provision, although 'gender', 'age' and 'disability' are the prominent criteria on which the state may take affirmative action, the criteria are widened by the phrase 'or any other reason created by history, tradition or custom'. Categories of people such as the Batwa, the Ik and the Nubians, have historically been discriminated against and treated as inferior to other ethnic groups. The Batwa have their unique traditions and customs with a special attachment to their ancestral land. The Nubians, likewise, although culturally considered as Luos from northern Uganda, have a strong

116 See for instance Tusasirwe 2007: 36, who discusses voters' cynicism in the country's electoral process.

117 See Chapter Three § 3.4.3.

Islamic culture that is distinct from the majority of the Luo ethnic communities.[118] The examples of these two ethnic groups are what Article 80(2)(c) of the Constitution envisages.

The provision for the election in district councils of representatives of minority social groups accords with the constitutional vision of affirmative action under Article 32 of the Constitution and the guiding principles of State Policy.[119] The existing constitutional and legislative framework for the representation of women, the youth, persons with disabilities and the elderly in the district councils has not translated into them competing for the highest political offices in a district. In a way, affirmative action through special representation has confined these social groups to less powerful political positions in districts.[120] Thus many special interest groups in district councils just as in Parliament consider their seats as favours from the ruling party, rather than as a right.[121] The absence of minority groups, such as the Batwa, the Ik and the Nubians from special representation in the district councils remains a big gap in the legislation and is a clear contradiction of the Constitution,[122] not to mention the indignity, shame and outrage that ethnic minorities inevitably must suffer as a result of this unfairness. The manner in which the Constitution and the LGA provide for a district council therefore falls short of the standard of accessibility and inclusiveness that was discussed in Chapters Two and Three.[123]

Ayele, writing on intra-regional territorial political representations within the Ethiopian federal system, identifies four major advantages for ethnic-based political representation: it allows minority ethnic groups to participate in the democratic process without feeling alienated by the majority ethnic groups; it gives the minority ethnic groups the necessary political space within which to operate; it acts as a buffer against the cultural domination of the minority ethnic groups by the majority; and it has the overall effect of restoring a group's 'dignity and pride' and hence its peace-building potential within a broader political scheme.[124]

The third criticism deals with the low participation levels of women in district councils. Byamukama remarks rather sadly that once women have their allotted seats of one-third, few have the courage to compete for the remaining slots that are open to men as well. The author explains that the cumbersome existing

118 Singiza & De Visser 2011: 27.

119 See NODPSP No. XIV and XV of the Constitution.

120 Tusasirwe 2007: 32.

121 Bainomugisha & Mushemeza 2006: 31.

122 According to the Election Commission, Local Government Election Results 2011, there was not a single councillor from the Batwa ethnic group in the Kanungu and Kisolo district councils, districts that are inhabited by the Batwa ethnic group. Besides, Kaabong district, in Karamoja region, with a population of about 11,272, has only two Ik councillors (male and female) in the district council. The two councillors in fact represent Kamion sub-county, an area populated by the Ik people.

123 See Chapter Two § 4.3.6 and Chapter Four § 4.5.

124 Ayele 2014: 69.

electoral system makes it more difficult for women to compete with men on the same footing.[125] Ultimately, as Tusasirwe points out,

> [t]he reservation of special seats for women under sections 10, 16 and 47 of the LGA were clearly a good starting point for ensuring the participation of women. But how come [sic] women still minimally participate in civic matters? It is therefore clear the people still minimally participate in their own governance despite rather than because of the provisions of the Act.[126]

6.9.5 Educational qualification

The disqualification of a person who wishes to stand as a councillor on the grounds of insanity, or of being under a sentence to death, or of serving an extended term of imprisonment is a justifiable limitation to the right to participate in district council elections. In addition, the disqualification of a person on the grounds of employment by a district council, and/or a candidate's role in the elections under the LGA are reasonable and justifiable limitations to ensure free and fair elections. However, the absence of educational qualifications for councillors, and the exclusion of the traditional or cultural leaders are more questionable, and will be examined now.

The LGA outlines the following, irrespective of the level of local council, as mandatory duties of a district councillor:

- to maintain close contact with the electoral area and consult the people in matters to be discussed in the council;
- to present views, opinions and proposals in the district council;
- to attend sessions of the district council and meetings of the district council's committees and subcommittees of which he or she is a member;
- to appoint a day in a given period so as to meet people in his or her electoral area;
- to report to the electorate on decisions made by the council and actions taken to resolve problems raised by residents in the electoral area;
- to 'bring to bear on any discussion in the council the benefit of his or her skill, profession, experience or specialised knowledge'; and
- to take part in communal and development activities in his or her electoral area and the district.[127]

From Table 6.2, it is clear that a district councillor plays an important role in promoting the right to public participation in the district council. In addition, it can be inferred that a district councillor must possess a certain level of skill and

125 Byamukama 2000: 6.
126 Tusasirwe 2007: 32
127 Regulation 8(1) of the LGCR of part I of the Third Schedule to the LGA.

Table 6.2 Distribution of district council seats across social groups for 2011

Political processes	*Directly elected district council seats*	*Women councillors*	*Special interest groups*
No. of seats	1,339	921	448

Source: Adopted from the Uganda Electoral Commission District Council Elections results 2011

professional expertise in order to execute his or her duties.[128] The argument here is that the district councillors should be literate. They should be knowledgeable in simple arithmetic, computer literate and able to analyse complicated documents, such as budgets and financial statements. This position finds support in the fact that a district councillor has a duty to 'bring to bear on any discussion in the council the benefit of his or her skill, profession, experience or specialised knowledge', if any.[129]

Two studies on Uganda district human resource capacity present conflicting findings on the level of human resource skills at all levels of district councils. One study by Ts'oele and Goldman shows that most districts' staff are highly qualified.[130] Steiner, on the other hand, finds a shortage of educated and skilled human resources both at the political level and civil service level, with high deficiency levels in areas such as accounts, planning, engineering, teaching and health.[131] If the findings of Ts'oele and Goldman are accurate, the high levels of education are not reflected in the political leadership. Taking the findings of Steiner as more representative of the reality on the ground, the absence of a large number of skilled civil servants in many districts makes a compelling case for a reasonably skilled political leadership. Kanyeihamba bemoans the lack of skills for the majority of political office-holders in the country.[132]

On the other hand, it may be argued that such a provision would amount to unlawful discrimination under Article 21(2) of the Constitution.[133] This view is supported by the fact that the Odoki Commission had in fact merely recommended the 'ability to read and write' as the minimum educational qualification for all members of the district councils. The academic qualification as a condition for candidacy might have been rejected by the majority of the CA delegates on account of the prevailing conditions then. There is now evidence that districts such as Bushenyi, Mbararaa and Gulu, which had highly academically qualified district political leaders, performed better in accordance with major governance

128 Singiza & De Visser 2011: 12. See also CLGF 2005: 8 Principle no 8 para. 3.

129 Regulation 8(1)(f) of the LGCR of part I of the Third Schedule to the LGA.

130 Ts'oele & Goldman 2006: 6.

131 Steiner 2006: 14.

132 Kanyeihamba 2002: 265–6, cited in Singiza & De Visser 2011: 12.

133 Article 21(2) of the Constitution provides: 'Without prejudice to clause (1) of this article, a person shall not be discriminated against on the ground of sex, race, colour, ethnic origin, tribe, birth, creed or religion, social or economic standing, political opinion or disability'.

criteria than other districts whose district councils were populated with councillors with modest education levels.[134]

6.9.6 Limitations on the recall of councillors

In Chapter Three, two models of democracy were highlighted: direct democracy and representative democracy. The conclusion was that even if none of the democratic systems are purely direct or representative, direct democracy ensures that citizens are more engaged in the decision-making process than in representative democracy. Hence, a recall process such as one under Article 182(1) of the Constitution and Regulation 7(a) and (b) under Part II of the Third Schedule to the LGA is a direct means through which the electorate express their approval or disapproval of their representatives.[135] In theory a recall process may make local councils more democratic in that district councillors must constantly demonstrate to local citizens that the decisions they make accord with the community's priorities. In practice, however, there is a real danger of a backlash from the national government. For instance, a recall process may lead to conflict between districts and the central government in cases of revoking the mandate of the central government's preferred councillors, resulting in the risk of withdrawal of state privileges and resources.[136] Thus, the provision for the revocation of the mandate of district council councillors poses some practical challenges.

Tusasirwe, citing Burkey, argues that it is practically impossible to revoke the mandate of the district's elected councillors in Uganda. His argument is that the fear of the central government's reprisal against local communities (should the recalled councillor happen to be a member of the ruling party), outweighs possible dividends that may come from the revocation of the district councillor's mandate.[137] It is noted that Burkey's view, on whose authority Tusasirwe relies, dealt with the pre-1997 district council constitutional and legal regime, where district councillors were not directly elected by universal adult suffrage.[138]

Lambright's study finds districts that overwhelmingly support the ruling party demonstrate higher performance levels than districts that support opposition parties. In addition, those districts that overwhelmingly support the ruling party show higher levels of political autonomy than districts that support the opposition.[139] The author argues: 'Popular and elite support for the ruling party *directly* influences councils' ability to effectively translate policy into outputs and to respond to the needs of their constituents' (emphasis in original).[140] The above analysis,

134 See the Annual Assessment of Minimum Conditions and Performance Measures for Local Governments 2009: Synthesis Report March 2010: 9.
135 See Chapter Three § 2.3.2.
136 Tusasirwe 2007: 15.
137 Tusasirwe 2007: 15.
138 Burkey 1991, cited in Tusasirwe 2007: 15
139 Lambright 2011: 139–44.
140 Lambright 2011: 140–1.

while difficult to challenge, may lend credence to the erroneous view that voters' support of the opposition parties in district councils has no political dividends at all and illustrates the economic risk associated with recalling a ruling party councillor.

Thus, although in the past revocation of a district councillor's mandate was difficult, it is now possible, given that most councillors (except those councillors that represent special categories) are elected by universal adult suffrage. However, the above argument is simplistic, given that no district councillor's mandate has ever been revoked by the electorate in the entire country. Invariably the practical importance of the provisions of Articles 182(1) and (2) of the Constitution is questionable. The fact that no councillor's mandate has been revoked since 1997 suggests that the fear of a backlash from the central government remains.

6.9.7 Exclusion of traditional leaders

Traditional leadership in Uganda is hereditary and male-dominated.[141] Traditional leadership does not fit into the modern definition of democracy. The argument would then be that if district councils as deliberative assemblies are to play any democratic role, undemocratically chosen rulers should be excluded from them. Moreover, traditional leaders might have a greater advantage over their political opponents given their high profile in local communities.

Yet the exclusion of traditional or cultural leaders poses a number of human rights and constitutional challenges. Disqualifying an individual to stand as a candidate for a district council on the basis of his or her traditional leadership role counters the notion of the right to public participation without any reasonable justification. Moreover, excluding traditional or cultural leaders from district councils undermines the possibility of incorporating traditional democratic values into a democratic decentralised system. It is misleading to assume that 'elderly persons' with no voting rights in a district council, can represent an ethnic group on traditional and cultural matters. Even if there may be a reason for excluding traditional institutions from district council politics, provision should have been made for an Assembly of Traditional Leaders (or an 'Assembly of Clan Leaders') separate from district councils. Such an assembly should have the power to veto district council laws or policies that may undermine the cultures and customs of a given ethnic community.[142]

6.10 The district chairperson

6.10.1 Introduction

In Chapter Two, the argument was that the notion of local democratic autonomy is grounded in the ability of the local population to elect their own leaders.[143] In this part of the book, the district council chairperson's functions are examined.

141 See Tamale 1999: 272.
142 See Chapter Three § 3.5.3.
143 See Chapter Two § 2.3.2.4.

In turn, an assessment is made to determine whether, in light of his or her functions, the approach adopted by both the Constitution and the LGA in electing the district council chairperson produces legitimate political outcomes necessary for a developmental and democratic local government.

6.10.2 Executive functions of the chairperson

The district chairperson is mandated by the Constitution to preside over the district council executive committee meetings[144] and to oversee the general administration of the district council. Further, the district council is obliged to coordinate the activities of the urban and rural councils within a district council. In addition, the district council chairperson must coordinate and monitor the central government functions within the district council. He or she may also perform any other functions assigned by Parliament.[145]

The LGA repeats the provision of the Constitution on the functions of the district council chairperson.[146] The only addition is that the district council chairperson must abide, uphold and safeguard the Constitution and the district laws and other laws of Uganda, and 'shall endeavour to promote the welfare of the citizens in the district'.[147]

The district council chairperson is subject to the decisions of, and answerable to, the district council's authority.[148] Arguably, both the district council and the district council chairperson seem to have a separate democratic legitimacy, with a potential of conflict in cases of serious political disagreements between the two. It is noted that a district chairperson is the executive head of a district given he or she is the head of the district council executive committee[149] and that members of the district council executive committee serve at his or her pleasure.[150]

The discussion below examines the elaborate procedure of electing the district council chairperson. The system of electing the chairperson is assessed from the criteria adopted in Chapter Three, namely (a) representativeness, (b) accessibility, (c) accountability, (d) inclusive political mobilisation and (e) stability of governments.[151]

6.10.3 The electoral system

Similar to the electoral system of district council councillors, the Constitution does not specify an electoral system that is uniquely tailored to district council

144 See the discussion on the composition and role of the district council executive committees in § 6.11 of this chapter.
145 Article 183(1)(b) of the Constitution.
146 Section 13(1) of the LGA.
147 Section 13(2) of the LGA.
148 Article 183(1)(b) of the Constitution.
149 Article 186(2)(c) of the Constitution.
150 Section 20(1)(a) of the LGA.
151 See Chapter Three § 3.4.3.

chairperson elections. Instead, it provides that in every election, at the closure of the poll, the presiding officer must count and record the number of votes obtained by each candidate. The same procedure is adopted for electing the district council chairpersons. It is emphasised that the term of office of the district chairperson is five years.[152]

Under the Constitution, every person is permitted to have access to leadership positions in local district councils. However, there are parameters set before one can run for the office of district chairperson. The Constitution lists three crucial conditions: (a) a person must be qualified to stand as a Member of Parliament; (b) a person should be between 30 and 75 years of age; and (c) a person should be ordinarily resident in the district.[153]

Section 111(3) of the LGA expands the three conditions under Article 183(2) of the Constitution to ten. Thus, a candidate for a district chairperson must fulfill the following conditions:

- possess Ugandan citizenship;
- be a proven resident in the district;
- be aged between 30 and 75 years;
- be a registered voter;
- have a minimum education of advanced level or its equivalent; [154]
- have submitted his or her nomination papers on the nomination day;
- have attached to his or her nomination paper a list of 50 registered voters from at least two-thirds of the electoral area with each of their signatures appended;
- have paid a non-refundable fee of five currency points;
- during the time when Parliament adopts the multiparty political system,[155] a public officer has to resign his or her office at least 30 days before nomination day;[156] and
- when Parliament has adopted a multiparty political system, a district candidate may be nominated by a political organisation or political party sponsoring him or her. He or she may also be nominated as an independent without the sponsorship of any political organisation or political party.[157]

152 Article 181(4) of the Constitution.

153 Article 183(2) of the Constitution.

154 Section 111(3A) of the LGA. The LGA caters for situations in which a person obtains his or her academic qualification in Uganda or outside Uganda, and then claims that his or her academic qualifications are equivalent to the Advanced Level standard of education. He or she may also have obtained his or her academic degrees from outside Uganda. See Sections 111(3B), (3C) and (3D) of the LGA.

155 See the detailed discussion on change from either of political systems in § 6.3.1 of this chapter.

156 Section 116(3), (4) and (5) of the LGA.

157 Section 119A of the LGA.

It is noted the LGA requires that district council candidates must be nominated by a certain number of registered voters even after he or she has been nominated as a flag-bearer of a political party. Consequently, a candidate nominated by a particular party may be disqualified if he or she fails to raise the required number of registered voters to nominate him or her.[158]

Article 80(1) of the Constitution, a provision that deals with educational qualifications of Members of Parliament (essentially similar to the provisions of section 111(3) of the LGA[159]) has been subject to comment by the courts in Uganda. In the words of Justice Twinomujuni, 'This is a clear and mandatory provision of the Constitution. You either have these qualifications and you qualify for the election to Parliament or you don't and you are not qualified'.[160]

Courts have been consistent as to what amounts to an equivalent advanced certificate of education. The common view has been that where a candidate's academic qualifications have been challenged, then the challenged candidate should have the burden to prove that in fact he or she does have the qualifications.[161] In fact, a number of candidates for the position of district council chairpersons have had their nominations declared invalid because either all or one of the qualifications under subsection 3 of section 111 of the LGA had not been satisfied.[162]

6.10.4 Vacation of office

Both the Constitution and the LGA provide for the removal of the district council chairperson from office.[163] In Chapter Three, the argument was that local government institutions should be constitutionally protected.[164] The Constitution outlines four instances in which the district chairperson may have to vacate office. These are:

- abuse of office;
- misconduct or misbehaviour;
- physical or mental incapacity;[165] and
- change of party affiliation.

158 Section 111(3) of the LGA.
159 Article 80(1) of the Constitution provides in part that a candidate must have 'completed a minimum formal education of advanced level standard or its equivalent'.
160 See *Lubya iddi Kasiki v Kagimu Maurice Peter* Election Petition Appeal No. 6 of 2002 per Twinomujuni, JA.
161 See *Abdul Balingira Nakendo vs. Patrick Mwonda* Court of appeal Election Appeal No. 23 of 2006; *Lubya iddi Kasiki v Kagimu Maurice Peter* Election Petition Appeal No. 6 of 2002.
162 See *Lubya iddi Kasiki v Kagimu Maurice Peter* Election Petition Appeal No. 6 of 2002.
163 See Article 185 of the Constitution. Section 14 of the LGA.
164 Chapter Three § 3.2.1.
165 Article 185(1) of the Constitution.

Parliament is vested with powers to make provision for any other grounds on which the district chairperson may vacate office.[166] The LGA thus adds seven more instances for which a district chairperson may vacate his or her office. These are:

- resignation;[167]
- violation of the leadership code (the discussion of the leadership code will follow);[168]
- failure to attend four consecutive meetings of the council;[169]
- death sentence or a sentence of more than six months;[170]
- acceptance of a public office appointment;[171]
- conviction on an offence of moral turpitude, within the preceding six years;[172] and
- when circumstances arise under any law which disqualify him or her.[173]

The constitutional and legal frameworks that provide for vacation of office of the political head of district councils under clearly and legally stated circumstances, strengthens those very institutions.

6.10.4.1 Procedure

There are two separate procedures for the removal of the chairperson of a district, both of which are initiated by the district council. The procedure depends on the reasons for removing him or her. Where the intention to remove the chairperson depends on any of the grounds other than his or her mental illness, a tribunal is constituted to determine his or her removal.[174] Where the intention to remove the district chairperson is based on mental illness, a medical board has to be constituted to determine his or her removal.[175]

166 Article 185(2) of the Constitution. See also sections 14(1)(a), (b), (c) and (d) of the LGA.
167 Section 14(1A)(a) of the LGA.
168 Section 14(1A)(c) of the LGA. See also 'Kayunga LC5 reinstated', *The New Vision*, available at http://www.newvision.co.ug/D/8/19/718582 (accessed 3 March 2011). The Leadership Code Act 2002 is an Act of Parliament that provides 'for a minimum standard of behaviour and conduct for leaders; to require leaders to declare their incomes, assets and liabilities; to put in place an effective enforcement mechanism and to provide for other related matters'. See the detailed discussion of the leadership code in § 6.10.4.4 of this chapter.
169 Section 14(1)(e) of the LGA.
170 Section 14(1A)(e) of the LGA. See also 'For killing his opponent, Mayuge LCV boss to hang', *The Daily Monitor*, available at http://www.monitor.co.ug/News/-/688324/824790/-/c5ne17/-/index.html (accessed 4 June 2010).
171 Section 14(1A)(d) of the LGA.
172 Section 14(1A)(f) of the LGA. Section 14(1A)(f) of the LGA. Kavanagh 2000: 1267 defines the word 'turpitude' in terms of depravity and wickedness.
173 Section 14(1A)(g) of the LGA.
174 See section 14(1) of the LGA.
175 Section 14(7) of the LGA.

The major safety net against the abuse of the tribunal or medical board procedure is that the process to remove the chairperson must be preceded by a resolution by district council supported by a two-thirds majority.[176]

6.10.4.2 Dismissal on grounds other than mental illness

The LGA provides that a motion to recall a district chairperson commences with a notice signed by not less than one-third of the members of the council and submitted to the Speaker.[177] The notice must state the intention to remove the chairperson and the reasons on which the intended notice is based. In other words, the chairperson must be informed beforehand of the charges he or she faces.[178] This provision minimises the possibility of abuse of the process. For instance, the majority of councillors can unilaterally resolve to remove a district council chairperson and choose to inform the chairperson of the impeachable offences preferred at the time of the tribunal hearing. This means that she or he will not adequately prepare for her or his defense at the hearing stage. Under such circumstances, the district council chairperson can be condemned without a fair hearing.

Once a notice of intention to remove the chairperson has been submitted to the Speaker, no member of the council who had signed it may withdraw his or her signature.[179] Within 24 hours of the receipt of the notice, the Speaker shall inform the chairperson and the Minister.[180] From the wording of section 14(3) of the LGA, it is within the Minister's discretion, in consultation with the Attorney General, to refer the notice to remove the chairperson to the tribunal.[181] This implies that the central government could decide to make any purported notice to remove the chairperson ineffective.

Once the Minister is satisfied that sufficient grounds exist for removing the chairperson, he or she must constitute a tribunal within 21 days from the date of the notice. The tribunal is composed of a judge of the High Court or a person qualified to be a High Court judge and two other members, all of whom are appointed by the Minister in consultation with the Chief Justice. The LGA provides that only persons of high moral character and proven integrity, considerable experience, demonstrated competency and high calibre in the conduct of public affairs are eligible to be appointed to the tribunal.[182] At all times the chairperson has a right to appear at the proceedings, with legal representation or any other expert of his or her choice.[183]

176 See section 14(1) of the LGA.
177 Section 14(2) of the LGA.
178 Sections 14(2)(a) and (b) of the LGA.
179 Section 14(2A) of the LGA.
180 Section 14(3) of the LGA.
181 Section 14(4) of the LGA.
182 Section 14(4) of the LGA.
183 Section 14(5) of the LGA.

The purpose of the tribunal is to investigate the allegations against the chairperson and not to determine if he or she should cease to be in office.[184]

Upon a determination of the *prima facie* case against the chairperson by the tribunal, the district council by a resolution, supported by a vote of not less than two-thirds majority of all members of the council, must approve the findings of the tribunal before the chairperson vacates the office.[185]

Even if a tribunal determined that a *prima facie* case existed against the chairperson, the ultimate arbiters are the members of the district council. Notwithstanding the central government's influential role at the commencement of the procedure to remove a chairperson, the final decision to remove a chairperson lies with the district council. It is noted here that the central government to some extent controls the procedure to remove the chairperson from office. However, given the level of independence of the tribunal, whatever interference in the process to remove the district chairperson by the central government is minimal.

6.10.4.3 Dismissal on medical grounds

Under subsection 1(e) of section 14 of the LGA a chairperson of a district may be removed on the basis of his or her physical or mental incapacity. The procedure commences with a notice in writing signed by not less than one-third of all members of the council and submitted to the Speaker.[186] The notice has to state the intention to remove the chairperson on grounds of physical or mental incapacity and the particulars of the alleged incapacity.[187] The Speaker must, within seven days of the receipt of the notice, ensure that a copy of the notice is served on the district chairperson and the Chief Justice.[188]

Should the district chairperson fail or refuse to appear before the medical board 14 days after it has been constituted, then he or she ceases to hold office, as long as the district council has passed a resolution supported by not less than two-thirds of all members of the council to that effect.[189]

It is noted that throughout the procedure for the removal of the chairperson, time is of the essence given the possibility of a political vacuum in the district should any delays occur. Thus a motion for a resolution for the removal of the chairperson has to be moved within 14 days from the date the Speaker

184 Section 14(4) of the LGA. See also 'Local govt probing disappearance of Masindi boss', *The New Vision*, 2 June 2010, available at http://www.newvision.co.ug/D/8/18/721549 (accessed 2 June 2010).

185 Section 14(6) of the LGA. The requirement for a vote to be supported by not less than a two-thirds majority of all members of the council refers to the majority of members of the council present at the meeting of the council, which is quorate.

186 Section 14(7) of the LGA.

187 Sections 14(7)(a) and (b) of the LGA.

188 Section 14(8) of the LGA.

189 Section 14(14) of the LGA.

receives the report from the medical board. Consequently, where a resolution is not passed within 14 days, the resolution will be invalid.[190] Implicitly, a person who is unfit to perform the functions of the chairperson of a district can remain in office on a mere technicality. The LGA provides for adherence to the principle of legality at all times during the procedure to remove the district chairperson.[191]

6.10.4.4 Violation of the leadership code

As explained earlier, the violation of the leadership code is possible grounds for dismissal of the district council chairperson.[192] In the discussion below, the consequence of the violation of the leadership code is discussed. In Chapter Two a distinction was drawn between the narrow sense of the term 'accountability' as control, sanctions and punishment, and a broader sense of the legal constraints on public officials' exercise of power and discretion.[193] The Leadership Code (LCA) generally provides for the minimum standard of behaviour of conduct for leaders, and[194] defines a 'leader' as 'a person holding any of the offices specified in the Second Schedule to this Code'.[195] The LCA also defines 'Government' to include a district council.[196] The Constitution provides for the IGG and deputy IGG who are appointed by the President with the approval of Parliament. The IGG must be qualified to be appointed as a High Court judge. The IGG must be a Ugandan, of high moral character, proven integrity, considerable experience, demonstrated competence and high calibre in the conduct of public affairs.[197] The Inspectorate of Government Act (IGA) provides for the Inspectorate of Government (IG) consisting of the IGG and two Deputy Inspectors General.[198] The IGA repeats the provisions of Article 233(5) of the Constitution in relation

190 Section 14(16) of the LGA.
191 Section 14(17) of the LGA.
192 See § 6.9.3 of this chapter.
193 Chapter Two § 3.1.2.
194 See the long title of the Act cited as Act 17 of 2002.
195 Section 2(1) of the LCA. Part A of the Second Schedule to the LCA lists the President, the Vice President, the Speaker and the Deputy Speaker of Parliament; the Chairperson and the Vice Chairman of the National Conference under the Movement Political System; the Prime Minister and Deputy Prime Minister; the National Political Commissar under the Movement Political System; the Attorney General; Ministers; Ministers of State and Deputy Ministers; the Members of Parliament; the Director and the Deputy Director of Movement Political System; a member of the National Executive of any political party or organisation; the Chairpersons and Vice Chairpersons of district councils; members of district executive committees; district council councillors; and Speakers and Deputy Speakers of district councils.
196 Section 2(1) of the LCA.
197 Article 223(5) of the Constitution.
198 Section 3(1) of the Inspectorate of Government Act (IGA) cited as Act 5 of 2002.

to the qualifications, appointment and term of office of the IGG.[199] The IGA provides for ten functions of the IGG.[200]

The relevant functions are:

- promotion and fostering of the rule of law and principles of natural justice in administration;[201]
- elimination of corruption and abuse of authority;[202]
- promotion of fair, efficient and good governance in public office;[203] and
- enforcement of the Leadership Code of Conduct.[204]

The IGA also vests the IGG with the power to investigate on his or her own initiative or upon a complaint by any person against any leader.[205]

The obligation to enforce the Leadership Code vests in the IGG, whose functions are to receive and examine declarations, to examine instances of corrupt practices and breaches of the Leadership Code and to investigate and report on any alleged 'high handed, outrageous and infamous or disgraceful conduct' of a leader, determination of which is made by the Minister.[206]

6.10.4.5 The role of the IGG under the Leadership Code Act

Under the LCA, the IGG is empowered to receive complaints relating to the breach of the leadership Code.[207] The IGG is mandated to 'inquire into, or cause the complaint to be inquired into'[208] once he or she makes a finding that the complaint is not baseless, and that the matter is within his or her mandate.[209] The LCA provides that once the inquiry is completed, the IGG is obliged to communicate his or her decision in a report to the authorised person.[210] The authorised person is then obliged to implement his or her decision.[211] The legal limits of the IGG role in the enforcement of the leadership role is discussed in Figure 6.1.

199 Sections 3(3), (4) and (5) and 4(3) of the IGA.
200 Section 8(1) of the IGA.
201 Section 8(1)(a) of the IGA.
202 Section 8(1)(b) of the IGA.
203 Section 8(1)(c) of the IGA.
204 Section 8(1)(d) of the IGA.
205 Section 8(2) and (3) of the IGA.
206 Section 3 of the LCA. Section 2(1) of the LCA defines a 'Minister' as 'responsible for ethics and integrity'.
207 Section 18(1) of the LCA.
208 Section 18(2) of the LCA.
209 Section 18(2) of the LCA.
210 Section 19(1) of the LCA. Section 2(1) defines the term 'authorised person' as 'a person or body authorised by law to discipline the leader in relation to whom the expression is used'.
211 Section 20(1) of the LCA. *John Ken-Lukyamuzi v AG and the Electoral Commission*, Constitutional Petition No. 19/2006 was the first case to test the consequences of the violation of the Leadership Code by elected leaders dealt with a Member of Parliament. Article 83(1) of the Constitution (the equivalent of section 14(1A)(c) of the LGA) has been subject to

Figure 6.1 The IGG's investigative powers in district councils.

6.10.4.6 Limits to the IGG's oversight role

In this section, the jurisprudence emerging from the courts on the legal limits of the IGG in removing elected district council political leaders from office is discussed.

In the case of *Hajji Mohammed Baswari Kezaala v The Inspector General of Government and Others*,[212] Mr Kezaala applied to set aside the Jinja Municipal Council's resolution which adopted the IGG's report that recommended his interdiction/suspension from the mayoral office of Jinja municipal council. The main grounds of the application were that Mr Hajji Kezaala had been impeached from office despite the existence of two court orders restraining them from effecting the recommendations of the IGG. There was evidence that the IGG in fact

interpretation by both the Constitutional Court and the Supreme Court. The Constitutional Court took the view that once a violation of the Leadership Code has been determined by the Inspector General of Government (IGG), a Member of Parliament has to vacate his seat. Overruling the decision of the Constitutional Court, the Supreme Court in *John Ken-Lukyamuzi v The Attorney-General and Another*, and Constitutional appeal NO. 02 OF 2007 arising out of the Constitutional Petition No. 19 of 2006, held that the IGG cannot order a Member of Parliament to vacate his or her seat unless an independent tribunal has made the determination. See also *Hajji Mohammed Baswari Kezaala v The Inspector General of Government and Others* Miscellaneous application No.28 of 2009 which appear to adopt the Supreme Court position.

212 *Hajji Mohammed Baswari Kezaala v The Inspector General of Government and others* Miscellaneous application No.28 of 2009.

pressurised Jinja Municipal Council to implement her recommendations.[213] The High Court restated the oversight role of the IGG in its investigative and inquiry powers in relation to public bodies such as district councils.

The High Court concluded that it was inappropriate, illegal and oppressive by the IGG to pressurise Jinja Municipal Council to implement her decision to remove the Mayor from officer in defiance of a court order.[214] The High Court also distinguished between the IGG's investigative powers and powers of inquiry. The High Court took the view that proceedings of the IGG commence with investigations, in which case he or she may gather information through interviews. During that stage, the IGG may not be required to comply with the rules of natural justice.

Two main issues emerged: first, the distinction between the IGG's power to investigate and carry out an inquiry, and second, whether the IGG could force any elected leader from office after merely conducting an inquiry. According to the High Court's reasoning, when the IGG forms an opinion, from the findings of the investigations, under sections 19, 23 and 26 of the LCA, he or she must carry out an inquiry, a process that is judicial or quasi-judicial in nature. In which case, Article 44(c) of the Constitution relating to natural justice has to be complied with.[215]

The High Court was of the view that the IGG treated the completion of an investigation as if it were a completion of an inquiry, in terms of sections 18, 19 and 20 of the LCA. Ultimately, the recommendation to the Jinja Municipal Council to remove the Mayor from office on the basis of an 'investigation', and not an 'inquiry', was erroneous. As a result, the Mayor's right to be heard, as required of any inquiry, was violated.[216]

The High Court nullified the resolution by the Jinja Municipal Council to remove the Mayor and set aside the report of the IGG.[217] This case clarifies the correct procedure to be adopted before district council elected leaders are removed from office on account of abuse of office. The case also illustrates the incidence of the central government seeking to exercise control over the removal of local government political leaders from office.

Even if the district council chairperson violated any of the provisions of the Leadership Code, he or she has to be tried by an independent tribunal of competent jurisdiction. He or she cannot simply be removed from office on an allegation of the violation of any of the legal provisions. Evidence must be adduced, a fair hearing must take place and then an order must be made by an independent tribunal of competent jurisdiction.

213 *Hajji Mohammed Baswari Kezaala* 10.
214 *Hajji Mohammed Baswari Kezaala* 16.
215 *Hajji Mohammed Baswari Kezaala* 21–2.
216 *Hajji Mohammed Baswari Kezaala* 25–6.
217 *Hajji Mohammed Baswari Kezaala* 27.

6.11 District council executive committees

In Chapter Three, the point was made that local government executive powers are important for initiating and enforcing local government policies.[218] The description below examines the role of the district council executive committees in initiating and executing district council policies. As the sections below will show, their powers do not compare with the views expressed in Chapter Three.

The Constitution provides for the district council executive committee to 'perform the executive functions of council'.[219] According to the Constitution, the district executive committee has to be composed of the district chairperson, the district vice-chairperson and such number of secretaries as the council may decide.[220] According to the Constitution the secretaries have to be nominated by the chairperson of the district council from members of the district council and approved by a majority of all the members of the district council.[221]

6.11.1 Composition and size

The LGA further provides that the district council executive committee must not exceed one-third of the district council.[222] The LGA provides that the number of secretaries should not exceed three.[223] In addition, the LGA provides that one of the secretaries of the executive committee must be a female.[224]

Parliament has no powers to limit the number of secretaries since a district council has a discretion under the Constitution to decide on the number.[225] The district council has the discretion to determine any number of secretaries as may be necessary. Hence, the provision of the LGA which limits the number of the secretaries to three is invalid in the face of Article 186(2)(c) of the Constitution.

218 Chapter Three § 3.6.2.1.
219 Article 186(1) of the Constitution. See also Section 16(1) of the LGA.
220 Article 186(2)(c) of the Constitution.
221 Article 186(4) of the Constitution.
222 Section 16(2) of the LGA.
223 Section 16(2)(c) of the LGA.
224 Section 16(3) of the LGA.
225 Article 186(2)(c) of the Constitution. See also the Odoki Commission 1993: 505 para. 18.119(b). The Odoki Commission had in fact recommended a long list of portfolios of secretaries and covered areas, such as finance and development, security, social services, land use, environment, agriculture, youth and women. Thus, the role of secretaries, according to the Odoki Commission, related to the social and economic development functions of a district council which may be inexhaustible.

6.11.2 Functions

The key role of a district council executive committee is to initiate and formulate policies for council's approval.[226] In addition, the district council executive committee monitors the implementation of district council programmes. The district executive committee may then correct any errors in those programmes.[227] This committee also recommends persons to the district council to be appointed to the district service commission, the district public accounts committee, the district contract's committee board (then referred to as the district tender board), the district land board(s) and any other commissions or committees that may be created.[228] It is also a dispute resolution forum for any conflict involving lower councils.[229] Lastly, the district council executive committee considers and evaluates the council's performance with regard to approved workplans and programmes.[230] The district council may also authorise the district executive committee to perform any other function.[231]

The role of secretaries is to perform the district council executive committee duties as assigned to them by the district council chairperson.[232] For example, the LGA provides that the district council chairperson must assign at least two of the secretaries to the health and child welfare portfolio and the persons with disabilities and the elderly portfolio. The district vice-chairperson and secretaries act as avenues through which the assignment of portfolios to secretaries may take place. [233]

6.11.3 Remuneration

The offices of the members of a district council executive committee, including the offices of the chairperson, vice-chairperson and secretaries, are full-time jobs,[234] whose emoluments are specified in the First Schedule of the LGA.[235] The LGA prohibits any member of the district executive committee to hold any profitable position likely to compromise his or her office.[236]

226 Section 17(a) of the LGA.
227 Section 17(c) of the LGA.
228 Section 17(d) of the LGA.
229 Section 17(e) of the LGA.
230 Section 17(f) of the LGA.
231 Section 17(g) of the LGA.
232 Article 186(7) of the Constitution.
233 Section 16(4) of the LGA.
234 See section 19(2) of the LGA.
235 Section 19(2) of the LGA. Lambright's study finds that in 1999, a district council chairperson earned approximately $494, while a vice-chairperson earned $327. The study also finds that each of the executive committee members earned $275. In comparison, the study finds that the annual district council expenditure per person was approximately $13 dollars, illustrating the financial burden of the district council politicians on local tax payers. See Lambright 2011: 52.
236 Section 19(3) of the LGA.

6.11.4 Termination of membership

6.11.4.1 Reasons for termination of membership

Membership of the district executive committee terminates under certain circumstances:

- revocation by the chairperson;
- election of a member as a district council Speaker or deputy Speaker;
- resignation;
- disqualification from the council;
- physical or mental disability;
- death;
- censure; or
- assumption of office by the new district chairperson.[237]

Other than the procedure of censure, all the other listed circumstances seem to be obvious and therefore no special procedure is needed. For instance, revocation of a member's mandate, election of a member as a district council Speaker's or deputy Speaker, resignation from office and/or death requires a simple official letter and/or a copy of the death certificate. In the discussion below the process of censure of a member of the district council executive committee is discussed.

6.11.4.2 Procedure for censure

The section below assesses the procedure of ensure against the backdrop of the discussion on local democracy and accountability.[238] The word 'censure' means to 'express severe disapproval of'.[239] The power to censure a member of the district council executive committee emanates from the district council's power to determine the composition of the district executive committee, under subsection 1(c) of section 16 of the LGA.

The process of censure starts with a petition to the chairperson of the district council through the Speaker of the district council. The petition of censure must be signed by not less than one-third of the members of the district council and must state the grounds for dissatisfaction 'with the conduct or performance of the member of the district executive committee'.[240] Upon receipt of the petition, the chairperson of the district council is required to ensure that the district council executive committee member is given a copy of the petition of censure.[241] The

237 Section 20(1)(a), (b), (c)(i), (c)(ii), (c)(iv) and (c)(v) of the LGA.
238 Chapter Two § 2.3.1.1.
239 Kavanagh *et al.* 2000: 184.
240 Section 21(2) of the LGA.
241 Section 21(3) of the LGA.

motion of resolution of censure cannot be debated until after 14 days from the date the petition was sent to the chairperson.[242]

The LGA provides for the right to be heard during the process of censure, although no specific aspects of this right are mentioned, thus creating a legal uncertainty on the true meaning of the right to be heard. [243]

6.12 Challenging electoral outcomes

Challenging electoral outcomes refers to the ability of the voters or candidates to contest the declared district council election results before an independent arbiter to determine its validity and/or fairness.

In Chapter Two local democracy was shown to be at work in elections that privilege the following rights and freedoms: freedom to form and join organisations; freedom of expression; the universal right to vote; eligibility for public office; the right to compete for support and votes; alternative sources of information; and the expression of other preferences.[244] It was noted that irrespective of a person's political or ethnic affiliations, local elections ultimately 'force' all political players to work together under the broad umbrella of the nation state. The consensus-building nature of local elections therefore promotes co-operation and respect across the political spectrum.[245] The above views are only true if the elections are conducted under an adequate electoral model necessary for local democracy.[246] Because it is important that electoral outcomes can be challenged in an open and democratic way, the discussion below tests whether the provisions on challenging the district council electoral outcomes accord with the views expressed in Chapters Two and Three.

The election results of a district councillor can be challenged by a candidate who loses an election.[247] Second, they can be challenged by an individual registered voter. For an individual registered voter to challenge the election result of a councillor, he or she has to be supported by not less than 500 registered voters in the constituency.[248] This must be done within 14 days from the time of declaration of the results by the Electoral Commission.[249]

The LGA lists four grounds upon which a petition challenging election results of a district councillor can be based. These are:

- a failure to comply with the provisions of the LGA, non-compliance with which would have affected the results in 'a substantial manner';[250]

242 Section 21(5) of the LGA.
243 Section 21(5) of the LGA.
244 Chapter Two § 2.3.2.
245 Chapter Two § 2.3.2.4.
246 Chapter Three § 3.4.
247 Section 138(3)(a) of the LGA.
248 Section 138(3)(b) of the LGA.
249 Section 138(3)(c) of the LGA.
250 Section 139(a) of the LGA. See also *Kakooza John Baptist v Electoral Commission and Another* Supreme Court Election Petit Appeal No. 11 of 2007. One example of non-

- declaration of a person as elected that actually did not win the elections;[251]
- commission of illegal practices, or any other offence under the LGA, in connection with the election by the candidate personally or indirectly through his agents;[252] or
- that the candidate at the time of the election was not qualified or was disqualified as a candidate.[253]

The LGA also provides that only an aggrieved candidate may petition against the election of a district council chairperson and seek an order that the person declared as elected was not validly elected.[254] The opening lines of section 138(1) are: 'An aggrieved candidate for chairperson may petition'.[255]

The LGA provides that a notice of the presentation of the petition, together with the petition, must be served by the person challenging the election results 'on the respondent or respondents as the case may be'.[256] This provision does not clearly state exactly against whom a petition challenging the election of the chairperson of a district may lie. It is noted that the district elections are organised, conducted and supervised by the Uganda Electoral Commission.[257]

A reading of section 139(1) of the LGA shows that a petition that challenges the validity of the election results is against 'a candidate declared elected as a chairperson'. Thus a person who has been declared by the Electoral Commission as a winner under section 137 of the LGA must be the first person against whom a petition challenging the validity of his or her election lies. Under section 2 of the Uganda Electoral Commission Act (UECA), the Electoral Commission is a corporate body which can sue or be sued in its own name. The Electoral Commission has the duty to conduct and organise district elections.[258] Should the Electoral Commission fail to conduct free and fair district council elections then it becomes a ground in any petition challenging the election of the chairperson of a district.

compliance with the electoral laws is ballot stuffing. In *Kirunda Kivejinja Ali v Katuntu Abdu* Court of Appeal Election Petit Appeal No. 24 of 2006, proven evidence of bribery of voters was also ground to nullify the election result.

251 Section 139(b) of the LGA.

252 Section 139(c) of the LGA.

253 Section 139(d) of the LGA.

254 Section 138(1) of the LGA. *See also Ndahura Roanald v Hajji Nadduli Abdul* Election Petition Appeal No. 20 of 2006 (unreported). In this case, the Court took the view that in order to challenge the election results of an LC5 chairperson under section 138 (1) of the LGA, a person must have been a candidate. In other words, a person who was not a candidate cannot be 'aggrieved' by an invalid election result.

255 See *Ndahura Roanald v Hajji Nadduli Abdul* Election Petition Appeal No. 20 of 2006 (unreported) per Justice L.E.M Mukaza-Kikonyogo 7. In *Ndahura Roanald v Hajji Nadduli Abdul*, a petition to challenge the election results of the district chairperson was dismissed for want of *locus standi*.

256 Section 141 of the LGA.

257 Section 101 of the LGA.

258 Section 101 of the LGA.

The LGA provides instances upon which a petition challenging the election results of the district chairperson may be based. These grounds are similar to those of challenging the election results of district council councillors. The essential test is the failure to comply with the provisions of the LGA, non-compliance with which affected the results in 'a substantial manner'.[259] Three examples of non-compliance with the electoral laws are ballot stuffing,[260] proven evidence of bribery of voters and 'forced open' voting as opposed to secret ballot.[261]

The Supreme Court in the case of *Col. Dr. Besigye Kiiza v Museveni Yoweri Kaguta, Electoral Commission*[262] took the view that before any election results can be invalidated on the grounds of non-compliance with any of the legal provisions, the effect of non-compliance therewith should be 'substantial'. Ordinarily, acts such as vote-rigging, bribery, violence, bias of electoral officials, an inflated voters' register or falsification of the electoral results should have had a substantial effect on the entire election. In this case the Supreme Court based its argument on the Presidential Elections Act 2000 and the evidential burden in Presidential Petitions,[263] the provisions of which are similar in wording to that of section 139(a) of the LGA that provides for challenging district council elections. In the Supreme Court's view, a person can still be declared a 'winner' of a rigged election (even when any of the four grounds have been proven), on account to failure to substantially discharge the burden of proof. This view has in turn been adopted by the Court of Appeal and the High Courts in all cases dealing with district election petitions.[264]

6.12.1 Assessment

Chapter Two discusses the ability of decentralisation to promote local development, local democracy and accommodation of ethnic diversity.[265] The assessment

259 Section 139(a) of the LGA.

260 See *Kakooza John Baptist vs. Electoral Commission and Another* Supreme Court Election Petit Appeal No. 11 of 2007.

261 See *Kirunda Kivejinja Ali vs. Katuntu Abdu* Court of Appeal Election Petit Appeal No. 24 of 2006.

262 *Col. Dr. Besigye Kiiza v Museveni Yoweri Kaguta, Electoral Commission* (Election Petition No. 1 of 2001) [2001] UGSC 3 (21 April 2001); See also Rtd. Col. Dr. Kizza Besigye v Electoral Commission, Yoweri Kaguta Museveni (Election Petition No. 1 Of 2006) [2007] UGSC 24 (31 January 2007)

263 Section 58(6)(a) of the Presidential Elections Act 2000 provides: 'The election of a candidate as a President shall only be annulled on any of the following grounds if proved to be satisfaction of the Court – (a) non-compliance with the provisions of this Act, if the Court is satisfied that the election was not conducted in accordance with the principles laid down in those provisions and that the noncompliance affected the result of the election in a substantial manner'.

264 Although a large number of district elections have been nullified by the courts, many district election petitions have failed because the petitioners did not adduce enough evidence to substantially demonstrate non-compliance with the legal provisions.

265 See Chapter Two § 2.3.

below examines the debate that surrounds the educational qualifications of district council elected leaders, the procedure for removing district council elected leaders from office and the erroneous rules of challenging the electoral outcomes of district council elections against the backdrop of the principles of Chapter Two.

6.12.1.1 Academic qualifications

The provision for academic qualifications for a district council chairperson may amount to unlawful discrimination under Article 21(2) of the Constitution.[266] However, the academic qualifications of a district chairperson may promote innovation and creativity in a district given that a more educated person is expected to adopt better and more efficient methods of leadership than a less educated person. Arguably an innovative and creative district council elected political leadership supports the thesis that links decentralisation to efficiency as argued in Chapter Two.[267] It may be less cumbersome to train a person with an advanced level of education or similar qualification than to train a completely illiterate person in areas such as information technology or elementary accounting. Secondly, the provision for an academic qualification guards against 'mediocrity' in district politics.[268]

In fact, the provision for an 'equivalent' academic qualification may be circumvented by presenting academic certificates that are hard to verify.[269] The qualification for a district chairperson should be specified such that if a person does not possess an advanced level education certificate then, he does not qualify at all even if he or she may have some other equivalent educational qualifications.

6.12.1.2 Infringement of voters' mandate

Arguably the two separate tribunal procedures for removing a district council chairperson ensure political accountability of district council chairpersons to local representatives. The two procedures underpin the importance of political accountability as an integral part of local democracy. However, the two procedures seem to infringe on the political authority of the electorate from whom the district council chairperson derives the political power to govern because he or she is directly elected by local citizens.

The question then becomes: why should a district council, with a narrow electoral mandate, move to remove a district chairperson with a wider electoral

266 Article 21(2) of the Constitution provides: 'Without prejudice to clause (1) of this article, a person shall not be discriminated against on the ground of sex, race, colour, ethnic origin, tribe, birth, creed or religion, social or economic standing, political opinion or disability'. See the detailed discussion on arguments for and against educational qualification for district political leaders in § 6.1 of this chapter.

267 See Chapter Two § 2.3.1.1.

268 Kanyeihamba 2002: 265–6.

269 Kanyeihamba 2002: 265–6.

mandate?[270] Arguably, in a presidential system, the legislature can only impeach a directly elected executive. The explanation here is that both the Constitution and the LGA adopt a hybrid system that incorporates both the presidential and the parliamentary systems. The two procedures may promote 'vertical and downward accountability', where central government and district councils keep the district council elected leaders under constant scrutiny.[271]

In this context, 'downward' accountability relates to the political risk that district elected politicians face should they not respond to local needs. On the other hand, 'vertical' accountability relates to the central government's and district council's institutional capacity to check on the excesses of district political leaders. The provision for the removal of the district chairperson does not threaten the institutional integrity of local government. Instead, the procedure is an indicator of a democratic and accountable governance system. The fact that the voters may elect the head of the district council and remove him or her through their elected representatives in the district council is a good indicator of a responsive democratic system that emphasises performance.

Earlier in this part of the chapter, the executive powers of the district council chairperson were discussed.[272] The executive powers of the district council chairperson are so narrow and only limited to IGR and social welfare aspirations, with a limited political mandate. For instance, other than the fact that the district council chairperson presides over the district council executive meetings, he or she is very much limited to the oversight role of the general administration in the district council. It is not clear how the chairperson can, only his or her own, protect the Constitution or promote the welfare of the citizens in the district.

The process of censure of the members of the district executive committee potentially leads to conflict between two district organs, each with its own electoral mandate. On the one hand, the members of the district executive committee serve at the pleasure of the district chairperson. On the other hand, members of the district executive committee can be censured by the district council.[273] In cases where the district council chairperson is from a different political party than the one that controls the majority of seats in the district council, there is a real possibility of a political stalemate in the appointment of new members of the district council executive committee,[274] hence limiting their potential to initiate and execute district council policies.

270 The chairperson of a district council is directly elected by all voters, whereas some of the councillors of the district council are elected by the electoral colleges.

271 See the Ministry of Local Government *Decentralisation Policy Strategic Framework* 2006: 19.

272 See § 6.9 of this chapter.

273 See sections 20(1)(a), (b), (c)(i), (c)(ii), (c)(iv) and (c)(v) of the LGA on the criteria for the motion of censure of the members of the district executive committee.

274 For instance, Lambright 2011: 201 cites press reports where an opposition district chairperson failed to form a district executive committee until he signed a 'memorandum of understanding' with the ruling party and hence not only limited the executive and political

6.12.1.3 The role of the IGG

It is also noted that faced with numerous complaints by members of the public,[275] the IGG has tended to be overzealous in its monitoring mandate with regard to district councils. In its most controversial recommendation, the IGG directed a municipal council to dismiss an elected political official, a decision that the High Court considered highly arbitrary. It is noted that the experience of the IGG in enforcing the Leadership Code for district councils' elected leaders resembles the kind of control exercised by the central government.[276] Ultimately, its role in ensuring that district council chairpersons are accountable to their electorate remains very limited. However, when a broader understanding of the term 'accountability' is adopted, the provision for the Leadership Code, insofar as it aims at enforcing political accountability, become relevant. The provisions on the leadership code, insofar as they call for district council chairperson to comply with the minimum standards of leadership, mirror the views expressed in Chapters Two and Three that link the ability of decentralisation force local leaders to offer explanations and justifications of their decisions to the local electorates.[277]

6.12.1.4 The future of political pluralism in district councils

The importance attached to local governments in nurturing political pluralism was discussed in Chapter Two, where the argument ran that local governments were hatcheries for multiparty democracy. The chapter disputes the unproven assertions that political pluralism was unsuitable for local governments in multi-ethnic societies on account of the fact that multiparty politics exacerbates ethnic conflicts.[278] The existing jurisprudence on loss of a political seat due to a change in political affiliation is problematic and informs the larger debate on political pluralism in Uganda. In my view, such jurisprudence should only be confined to national political leaders.[279]

As already noted, section 119A of the LGA only provides for a candidate's nomination for any district council elections. It was within the powers of Parliament to state that once a district political office-bearer changes his or her

authority of the chairperson in the district executive committee but also 'muted' the voters' preference in the district.

275 The Inspectorate of Government Report to Parliament July–December 2007: 8.

276 Kakumba & Fourie 2008: 122. In South Africa, for instance, the government Ombudsman's recommendations are merely advisory. Because the Ombudsman's office remains largely neutral and outside the fray of politics, its opinions are generally highly respected.

277 Chapter Two § 2.3.1.1, 2.3.1.4 and 3.4.2.3.

278 Singiza & De Visser 2014.

279 For example in the case of *George Owor v Attorney General & Another* ((Constitutional Petition No. 038 of 2010) February 2011), the Constitutional Court held that an MP elected on a political party ticket or affiliation loses his or her seat the moment he or she joins another political party. This decision has been confirmed by the Supreme Court, in the case of *Attorney General v George Owor* Constitutional Appeal No. 1 of 2011.

political affiliation, he or she must automatically vacate his or her seat. A district council political office-bearer should never vacate his or her office on a change of political party affiliation, in the absence of any specific constitutional or statutory provision.

6.12.1.5 Onerous rules of challenging electoral outcomes

The grounds upon which an aggrieved candidate may challenge the election of a district council councillor and chairperson may on the face of it appear sufficient for a free and fair election. One controversy, however, emanates from the substantive test under section 139(a) of the LGA, which provides that non-compliance with any of the provisions of the LGA should have affected the results in 'a substantial manner'. The question then becomes: should a district election result be validated or invalidated by adopting a qualitative or quantitative test for a free and fair election? Should non-compliance with any of the legal provisions relate to the number of illegal acts or to the nature and quality of the elections? It is conceded that it is wrong for any court to strike down the whole elections for minor irregularities. The argument is that only 'major' but not necessarily 'substantially major' irregularities should be condemned.[280]

Chapter Three makes the point that a local government electoral system should be capable of producing legitimate electoral outcomes that fairly represent the consent of local communities.[281] An electoral system that makes it difficult to reasonably challenge a fraudulent electoral outcome impedes the electorate from producing a legitimate council. The above assessment fundamentally affects the importance attached to local elections as expressed in Chapter Two.[282] Moreover, given the evidence of political interference in districts' elections,[283] the above jurisprudence is problematic to local government democracy as expressed through local elections. Lambright's study, on the one hand, finds that 'voter buying' and political patronage of a district council weaken the ability of local politicians to question the central government's political excesses. Ultimately, the political patronage through interference in the district electoral process not only weakens the integrity of the district institutions, but also limits their ability to perform their tasks.[284] On the other hand, according to Lambright, the political

280 For instance, in the Unites States of America case of *Bush v. Gore*, 531 U.S. 98 , the issue revolved around whether it was just and equitable to count all votes, including the so called 'dimpled' ones. By majority vote, the Supreme Court declined grant an order to count the 'dimpled' votes arguing that counting such votes amounted to using a different standard of counting votes in different counties, an order that could have violated section 1 of the Fourteenth Amendment to the United States Constitution on the equal protection of laws.
281 See Chapter Three § 3.4.3.
282 See Chapter Two § 2.3.2.4.
283 See Lambright 2011: 200, who finds that voter interference occurs at the selection stage of candidates, the provision of campaign resources, especially the privileged access to state resources for the ruling party-leaning candidates and voter intimidation.
284 Lambright 2011: 148.

interference in district council elections by the central government has had minimal effect on the overall election outcome.[285] In spite of Lambright's conclusion, it is very difficult to expect people in local communities to marshal sufficient resources to adduce evidence that is so substantial in order to overturn an invalid district council election result.

It may not be easy for an individual to get the endorsement of not less than 500 registered voters within the 14-day period before his or her petition becomes valid. The first criticism deals with the provision for a large number of registered voters required in order to validate one's candidature. The above provision may be open to ethnic, religious or gender biases. For example, the majority of the voters from an ethnic group with historical prejudices against a candidate from an ethnic minority group may refuse to nominate a candidate on account of his or her ethnic origin. Second, the possibility for an individual to challenge election results is practically almost non-existent.

Consequently, an invalid councillor's election result may remain legally unchallenged. Furthermore, some of the alleged electoral malpractices such as 'forced open voting' relate to inclusion of voting by lining behind a person's preferred candidate under the LGA,[286] a valid voting method that is easy to manipulate. The practice of political parties whipping their party-faithful to vote in a certain way is not uncommon in Uganda. Thus, where a controversial bill is pending a vote, parliamentary rules of procedure dealing with a secret ballot may either be suspended or altered to ensure that individual party members' votes are known.[287] It is tantamount to electoral fraud, and therefore unusual, for any political party to enforce the same party discipline even at a polling station or in the voting booth.

In the last part of this chapter, the district councils' deliberation and decision making-process is examined.

285 Lambright 2011: 201–9.

286 See § 6.2.2 of this chapter.

287 Bainomugisha & Mushemeza 2006: 27. See also *Paul Ssemogerere and Another v The Attorney General* Constitutional Petition No. 3 2000 where the one of the issues revolved around whether parliamentary rules that allowed voting by voice was constitutional. The Constitutional Court ruled it was not. In the South African case of Breede Valley Onafhanklike and Others *v Municipal Manager: Breede Valley Municipality* case no. 3390/006 Cape High Court (unreported), the dispute arose after two parties in a municipal council coalition agreed to monitor their members' votes during the election of office bearers. As part of the monitoring, not only would councillors belonging to different parties sit next to each other but also show their ballot papers to their neighbours to ensure that they voted according to the coalition agreement. The High Court, while examining whether the coalition agreement was valid, considered the adoption of the fundamental right to vote under section 19 of the Constitution to mean that such a right has to be exercised in secrecy. Thus, the coalition agreement which took away the right to a secret ballot was invalid. Further, the waver of secrecy in voting had the ability to exert pressure to vote in a specific way. Steytler and De Visser argue that the above decision did not distinguish the right to a secret ballot while electing legislative assemblies and the voting process in municipal council meetings. See Steytler & De Visser 2013: 3–11.

6.13 Council deliberation and decision making

6.13.1 Introduction

This part of the chapter deals with the manner in which district council meetings are regulated. As already noted in Chapter Two, a proper decentralised system must provide appropriate institutions for public participation for all categories of local communities.[288] Public participation may take the form of either representative democracy or direct democracy.[289] A local council is therefore one of the institutions through which citizens may participate meaningfully, though indirectly, through their local representatives. As Makara notes, the combination of attributes of both direct democracy and representative democracy ensures that citizens' voices at grassroots levels can be heard.[290]

A local council meeting is primarily a forum where the elected representatives make decisions. A local council meeting is a platform where the local council can engage with outside stakeholders. Arguably, a local council meeting as a vehicle for community participation must conform to the need to recognise diversity, reconcile differences and stimulate collaboration amongst different political and social groups. Thus, the insistence on consensus-seeking is a positive democratic attribute. The question then becomes: does the regulation of district council meetings promote the right to public participation of the different political and social groups as a consensus-seeking measure? In answering this question, the role of the district council Speaker and his or her functions, the convening of district council meetings and the role of the district council standing committees must be examined.

6.13.2 Speaker

The Constitution merely provides that there be a Speaker for each district council to perform the functions similar to those of the Speaker of Parliament; it does not provide for the position of the deputy Speaker.[291] The Odoki Commission took this view:

> In order to have an in-built system of checks and balances between the district executive and the district legislature, the district chief executive should not chair the meetings of the district council. It is proposed that there should be a chairman for each district council, elected in the same way as district executive [sic] from among the elected members of the district council. His or her role is to chair meetings of the council; in essence, it will be a position similar to that of the speaker of the national parliament.[292]

288 Chapter Two § 2.4.
289 See Chapter Two § 2.3.2.
290 Makara 2009: 9.
291 See Article 184 of the Constitution.
292 See the Odoki Commission 1993: 502 para. 18.116.

The LGA clearly spells out the Speaker's role. The Speaker's primary role is to preside over all meetings of the district council.[293] He or she has the overall authority over and supervision of order in the district council meetings. He or she ensures enforcement of rules of procedure.[294] The functions of the Speaker of the district council are similar to those of the Speaker of Parliament.[295] Thus, no business can be transacted in the district council until the Speaker of the district council has been elected.[296] The Speaker of the district council presides at the election of the deputy Speaker.[297]

There is as yet no jurisprudence in Uganda that has interpreted the role of a Speaker of a district council. Instead, the Constitutional Court has dealt with the powers and role of the Speaker of Parliament. The Constitutional Court takes the view that although the powers of the Speaker of Parliament are discretionary, he or she is subject to the direction of the Constitution. For instance, the Speaker of Parliament cannot override constitutional rules relating to the procedure of lawmaking.[298]

It follows that the powers of the Speaker of a district council have to be exercised subject to the Constitution.

The LGA provides for the election of a Speaker and a deputy Speaker from the members of the district council by a vote of more than 50% and by secret ballot.[299] The chief magistrate is mandated to preside at the first election of the Speaker, following the general election of the district local council.[300]

A district council Speaker holds a full-time position.[301] He or she is paid emoluments and allowances. A Speaker of the district council may not hold any office of profit or emolument likely to compromise his or her office.[302]

The Speaker and deputy Speaker of a district council, just like any other elected official, can vacate office under certain instances. There are different instances when a district Speaker and deputy Speaker must leave office. These include:

- a conviction for abuse of office;
- proven incompetence;
- proven misbehaviour;
- physical or mental incapacity;[303]
- resignation;

293 Section 11(9)(a) of the LGA
294 Section 11(9)(b) of the LGA.
295 Section 11(9)(c) of the LGA.
296 Section 11(10)(b) of the LGA.
297 Section 11(8A) of the LGA.
298 See *Paul Ssemogerere and Another v The Attorney General* Constitutional Petition No. 3 2000 per Twinomujuni, JA.
299 Section 11(3) of the LGA.
300 Section 11(8)(a) of the LGA.
301 Section 11(11) of the LGA.
302 Section 11(12) of the LGA.
303 Sections 11(6)(a), (b), (c) and (d) of the LGA.

- acceptance of another appointment to public office; and
- death.[304]

The LGA vests the district council with the power to remove the Speaker or deputy Speaker from office by resolution.[305]

The procedure for the removal of the Speaker and the deputy Speaker of the district local council commences with a notice in writing signed by at least one-third of all the members of the council, which is submitted to the district chairperson. The notice must state the grounds for removal and the intention to pass a resolution to remove him or her.[306] Once a councillor has appended his or her signature to the notice for the purposes of the resolution to remove the speaker, he or she may not remove it.[307] Although the LGA provides that the Speaker has to preside at the council meeting for the removal of a deputy Speaker,[308] there is no mention of who presides at the council meeting for the removal of the Speaker. It is suggested that a Chief Magistrate should preside at the district council meetings to remove the Speaker. Rather than submit the notice of the motion to remove a district council Speaker to the district council chairperson, it should be submitted to the Minister of Local Government in order to limit the possibility of conflicts of interest.[309] For example, where the district council Speaker and district council chairperson come from different political parties, accusations of bias may arise resulting in political paralysis in the district.

6.13.3 Council meetings

According to the regulations made under section 28 of the LGA, the district council meetings must take place 'at least' once every two months, at a place and time determined by either the Speaker or the chairperson of a district council.[310] The number of times that district council meetings may take place may be increased to more than once in two months where necessary.

Clearly, the above provision conflates the roles of the two political offices, with potential for conflict. Arguably, the above provision ensures that neither the district council Speaker, nor the district council chairperson, is able to forestall the process of convening district council meetings by deliberately refusing to convene meetings.[311] The regulations provide for a seven-day notice period

304 Section 11(7) of the LGA.
305 Section 11(6) of the LGA.
306 Section 11(6A) of the LGA.
307 Section 11(6B) of the LGA.
308 Section 11(8A) of the LGA.
309 Lambright 2011: 145.
310 See Regulation 9(1) of Part III of the Third Schedule of the LGA.
311 For instance, in Bushenyi district council, a petition of censure against the district council Speaker was signed by the majority of the councillors and supported by the district chairperson on grounds of 'misconduct, abuse of office and failure to conduct council meetings in an impartial manner'. The allegation against the Speaker emanated from the Speaker's

before the commencement of a district council meeting. The notice of the meeting must state the agenda, and has to be circulated to all members of the district council and, if necessary, followed up by public announcements.[312] No court case in Uganda has examined the importance of having a district council agenda.

It is submitted that the requirement for the notice of a district council meeting to state the agenda is to ensure an informed debate in the district council meeting. Generally, district council meetings are open to the public unless, in the view of the Speaker or by resolution of district council, it should be held in camera for reasons of confidentiality.[313] While the regulations do not specify the language to be used, any record of proceedings has to be in English.[314]

A district council presents a forum through which communities' priorities may be assessed and deliberated upon. Thus, district council meetings are important for debating local development issues. In addition, district council meetings are forums through which actual public participation at lower orders of government may take place. It is important that the rules of conduct of district council meetings under the LGA foster orderliness in their deliberations.

Ordinarily, the rules of conduct should promote the culture of consensus-building and civility through deliberative debates in the district councils. For example, the regulations require that 50% of the district council members shall form a quorum.[315] Further, the determination of matters of the district council has to be by consensus, and if not, then by simple majority of the present members.[316] It is noted that the fact that a district council decision must be determined by consensus or by a simple majority has a consensus seeking attribute and suggests inclusivity. It is probable that the provision for a '50%' attendance as the minimum quorum for the council meetings ensures that district council meetings are easy to convene and ultimately promote the consensus-seeking character of district councils' deliberations. In cases where a district council is not controlled by a single political party, it may still be possible to raise the necessary quorum for a district council meeting to convene. A district council meeting that is easily convened ultimately helps to legitimatise the district council decision-making process.[317]

Nonetheless, the fact that the district council's records are in English makes it difficult for other linguistic groups to readily access the debates of a district

---

ruling against the Minister of Local Government to leave the council chambers for showing disrespect to the office of the Speaker. The chairperson later wrote to the same Minister to help in ensuring that the Speaker was removed from office. See Lambright 2011: 145.

312 See Regulation 9(1) of Part III of the Third Schedule of the LGA.

313 See Regulation 9(3) of Part III of the Third Schedule of the LGA.

314 See Regulation 10(2) of Part III of the Third Schedule of the LGA.

315 See Regulation 9(5) of Part III of the Third Schedule of the LGA.

316 See Regulation 9(6) of Part III of the Third Schedule of the LGA.

317 This view is supported by evidence of political polarisation between the ruling party and other party members in the Bushenyi district council, where a good proposal is usually rejected by the ruling party council members simply because such a proposal may have been moved by members of the opposition parties. See Lambright 2011: 219.

council. Moreover, the manner in which district council meetings take place (and their minimal frequency) indicates that they are incapable of promoting local democracy and communitarian voices. For instance, other than the provision that district councils must meet once every two months,[318] Lambright's study covering the three districts of Bushenyi, Mpigi and Lira also notes poor attendance levels at council meetings.[319] It is suggested that a district council councillor who misses two consecutive district council meetings should be suspended and not be paid any allowances for the rest of the year. It is further suggested that the frequency with which a district council may meet or the language in which district council business should be conducted should be determined by the district council itself and not regulated by Parliament.

6.13.4 Standing committees

In the discussion below, district council standing committees are examined from two angles: first, as a technical committee that may guide the district council legislative process, and second as necessary fora for ordinary citizens to engage with the district councils' deliberative processes.

The Constitution provides for the establishment of district standing committees and other committees, whose chairpersons and members are elected from members of the district council.[320] The district chairperson, his or her vice chairperson and a secretary may take part in the district council standing committee's meeting but have no voting rights.[321] Section 22(2) of the LGA provides for election of the chairpersons and members of district standing committees by secret ballot and by a simple majority of members of the district council. In order to avoid any conflict of interest, members of the district executive committee are not eligible to vote.[322]

The LGA provides that the number of district council standing committees should be equal to the number of district council secretaries.[323] The LGA vests the district council with the discretion to determine the number of standing committees.[324] However, no member of a district standing committee may belong to more than one committee.[325] The reason may be that since district council standing committees must independently give technical advice to the district council, they should not be influenced by internal political considerations and biases.

318 See Regulation 9(1) of Part III of the Third Schedule of the LGA.
319 Lambright 2011: 228.
320 Article 186(8) of the Constitution.
321 Article 186(9)(a) and (b) of the Constitution. Section 22(4) of the LGA.
322 Section 22(2) of the LGA.
323 Section 22(1) of the LGA.
324 See the opening line of section 22(1) of the LGA.
325 Section 22(3) of the LGA.

Although the LGA provides that the functions of these committees relate to the efficient performance of the functions of the district council,[326] no specific functions are mentioned for these committees. Hence, their exact mandate and role are not clear. However, since district standing committees support the district councils and perform duties that are only assigned to them, the district council must exercise discretion in determining their exact roles. During the CA debates, the role of district council standing committees was compared to the central government cabinet portfolios and district heads of department.[327] This comparison is, however, narrow and only correct when a district council is viewed as an executive authority.

When a district council is also viewed as a legislative authority, the role of district council standing committees is more accurately comparable to the standing committees of Parliament under Article 90(1) of the Constitution.[328]

In the *Paul Ssemogerere* case, the bill, which was passed into law without going through the committee of Parliament that should have dealt with the subject matter, was invalidated as unconstitutional. The Court held:

> Article 90(1) makes it mandatory for Parliament, during its first session, to appoint standing committees and other committees necessary for the efficient discharge of its functions. It is noteworthy that members of the standing committees are elected from among members of Parliament, and are not elected during the first session of Parliament, 2(a). The 1995 Constitution does not name a committee of the whole house or spell out its functions. Some of the functions of the standing committee as specified under [sic] 90(3) are to discuss, scrutinize, carry out research and make recommendations on all the Bills laid before Parliament, carry out relevant research in their respective fields, and report to Parliament on their functions. In a nutshell the main function of a standing committee is to consider Bills in the minute details and depth [sic], thus doing what *the house as a whole could not easily do if it had time.* (emphasis added)[329]

326 Section 22(1) of the LGA.

327 See CA debates 3776–82.

328 Article 90 of the Constitution provides for Committees of Parliament that: '(1) Parliament shall appoint committees necessary for the efficient discharge of its functions. (2) Parliament shall, by its rules of procedure, prescribe the powers, composition and functions of its committees. (3) In the exercise of their functions under this article, committees of Parliament – (a) may call any Minister or any person holding public office and private individuals to submit memoranda or appear before them to give evidence; (b) may co-opt any member of Parliament or employ qualified persons to assist them in the discharge of their functions; (c) shall have the powers of the High Court for – (i) enforcing the attendance of witnesses and examining them on oath, affirmation or otherwise; (ii) compelling the production of documents; and (iii) issuing a commission or request to examine witnesses abroad'.

329 See *Paul Ssemogerere and another v the Attorney General* Constitutional Petition No. 3 of 2002 per A.E.N. Mpagi-Bahigeine, JA. (Judgment unpaginated.)

Whenever the district council exercises its legislative function, the role of the district council standing committees should be similar to those of the standing committees of Parliament, namely to scrutinise bills of the district council before they are passed into ordinances. Arguably, the district council standing committees play an oversight role to ensure that ordinances enacted by the district council comply with the Constitution, government policy and any other relevant legislation.

Azfar, Livingston and Meagher, while generally commenting on all of the district committee system in Uganda, take the view that the system of committees under the LGA is problematic for the following reasons. First, district council committees are seen as tools of local political class hegemony in which the local politicians and the elite groups determine who participates in these committees. This hegemony undermines the very essence of public participation in district councils. Second, in most cases these committees serve as avenues through which local resources are diverted for personal use in the form of unjustified sitting allowances, and hence these committees promote corruption and political patronage in district councils. Third, the fact that these committees rarely meet means that the members of the public are never afforded an opportunity to air their views.[330]

6.14 Conclusion

In Chapter Two the point was made that local elections are the means through which local communities may participate in their own affairs by determining through a vote who is to lead them.[331] The assumption was that even when local elections may result in different outcomes, after elections local politicians must agree to work together under the umbrella of a nation state. The chapter called for an adequate local government electoral system, which should be competitive and inclusive.[332]

The discussion in this chapter finds that the district councils' elections are exclusionary to certain social and political groups, such as ethnic minorities and political parties. The discussion also reveals the following: that the procedure for challenging the election outcomes of the political office-bearers and the criteria under which those office-bearers may vacate office have a negative bearing on their overall political legitimacy. While examining the district council's committee system, the discussion finds that rather than serve as an avenue for public participation, the district committee system is open to political abuse and manipulation. Ultimately, the district council's governance structures are not accessible to all, contradicting the view that decentralised systems of government are good 'hatcheries' of democracy.

330 Azfar, Livingston & Meagher 2006: 234.
331 See Chapter Two § 2.3.2.1
332 Chapter Three § 3.4.3.

The above views are supported by Lambright's study which reveals a correlation between local economic conditions and district electoral outcomes. For instance, according to the author, there is evidence that more incumbent district chairpersons lost elections in 'slow developing districts' than 'in rapid developers' after the reintroduction of multiparty politics.[333] This is evidence that local elections can enforce accountability in district councils. Thus, in spite of the criticism of district councils' electoral system, elections remain one of the best avenues through which local communities can democratically express their voices.[334]

Oloka-Onyango, however, argues that the numerous district elections in Uganda have not translated into actual community participation, where local people's inputs, as voters, are considered by local politicians.[335] Tusasirwe's study also reveals the dissatisfaction of local communities with local elections because of the absence of tangible results for local communities.[336]

The main problem is that the legal regime and the emerging jurisprudence on elections generally in Uganda do not address vigorously the 'plague' of election rigging. In my view, it would have been better if the legislation barred a 'guilty party' in an election petition from standing again in a fresh election, as a deterrent against electoral malpractice. Second, it would have been better if the courts offered clearer guidance on how to curb the problem of rigged elections. The discussion in the next chapter focuses on the interpretation of the powers and functions of district councils.

333 Lambright 2011: 206. This view is supported by Lambright 2011: 207, who finds a relationship between improved political competition and electoral outcomes especially after the return of multiparty politics.

334 Kabwegyere 2000: 71.

335 Oloka-Onyango 2007: 17.

336 Tusasirwe 2007: 36.

7 District councils' powers and functions

7.1 Introduction

In this chapter further evidence of the intrusive, 'hard edged' top-down centralism is presented in the allocation of district council competences. The sharing of power and functions between the central government and local governments is a cornerstone of a good decentralised system, and an expression of developmental and democratic autonomy.[1] Chapter Three emphasises the point that local governments should be vested with clear functions. The central government's limitation of local governments' discretion to initiate and execute their functions must be legally justified, and only limited when local governments cannot efficiently perform certain tasks.[2] Clarification of local governments' powers and functions not only helps in delineating competencies amongst the various orders of government,[3] but also fosters co-operative governance.[4]

7.1.1 Historical context

Before the 1995 Constitution, as discussed in Chapter Four, district councils (which were known as district local administrations) had no powers or functions constitutionally entrenched. Their powers to make laws came from an act of Parliament. District local administrations' powers and functions were delegated by Parliament which could be varied or withheld at any time. District local administrations had no executive powers, only administrative responsibilities as agents of the central government.[5]

The division of powers and functions between the central government and local governments in Uganda was, in the past, ill-defined. As discussed in Chapter Four, what existed was the delegation of administrative functions in a prescriptive manner.[6] Decentralisation as a state reform measure, introduced in 1993

1 Chapter Two § 2.3.
2 Chapter Three § 3.6.
3 Steytler 2006: 8. See also Young 2006: 19.
4 Quieroz, De Ribeiro & Garson 2006: 17.
5 See Chapter Four § 4.7.6.
6 See Chapter Four § 4.7.6.

in Uganda and constitutionally protected under the 1995 Constitution, created new modes of sharing power between the central government and district councils in a manner that is often practised in federal systems of government.[7] The power-sharing arrangements that were finally adopted under the Constitution show that the debates by the CA delegates on the devolution of powers and function to district councils were influenced by power-sharing systems of federal and decentralised Constitutions in Europe, North America and East Asia.[8] Moreover, as described in Chapter Four, federal power-sharing schemes existed under the 1962 Constitution.[9] Uganda was thus no stranger to the federal power-sharing arrangement and hence carried these debates forward through the CA.

7.1.2 *Absence of a policy context*

It is difficult to interpret the precise powers and functions that devolve to district councils in Uganda given that the decision to devolve powers and functions to them was never informed by a comprehensive policy. Rather, the decision was initiated through a presidential speech.[10] This means that the existing constitutional and legislative framework on district councils did not proceed from any coherent central government policy.[11] In countries that have devolved powers and functions to lower orders of government, such as South Africa, the objects of the local governments are provided for.[12] The absence of the object of the district councils in the Constitution complicates the determination of the nature of district council powers and functions.

7.1.3 *The mandate of district councils under the LGA*

The relationship between the National Objectives and Directive Principles of State Policy (NODPSP) and the functions that devolve to district councils have

7 See Chapter Five § 5.1.2.9.

8 Some CA delegates argued for power-sharing based on those of Nigeria, Germany and the United States of America. Although it is conceded that conceptually the district council power-sharing scheme was based on that of the Nordic countries, given the influence of the Nordic consultancy group, the influence of federal power-sharing systems on the CA delegates cannot be disputed.

9 Chapter Four § 4.7.4.

10 See President Yoweri Museveni's address when launching the Local Government Decentralisation Programme on 2 October 1992, p.6. See also *Decentralisation in Uganda: The Policy and its Philosophy*, Decentralisation Secretariat, 1993.

11 Oloka-Onyango 2007: 21. See also the Ministry of Local Government *Decentralisation Policy Strategic Framework* 2006: 3 para. 1.1

12 Section 152 of the Constitution of the Republic of South Africa provides: '1. The objects of local governments are (a) to provide democratic and accountable governments for local communities; (b) to ensure the provision of services to communities; (c) to promote social and economic development; (d) to promote a safe and healthy environment; and (e) to encourage the involvement of communities and community organisation in the matters of local government. 2. A municipality must strive, within its financial and administrative capacity, to achieve the set of objectives set out in subsection (1)'.

been examined by some writers on decentralisation in Uganda.[13] The above relationship is restated in Uganda's Decentralisation Policy Strategic Framework.[14] This policy was published in 2006, 11 years after the promulgation of the 1995 Constitution that provides for decentralisation.

The LGA lays down three parameters for district councils in the exercise of their legislative mandate:

- district councils are obliged to protect the Constitution.[15] District councils' functions should be interpreted with the overall objective of protecting the Constitution;
- district councils have a responsibility to promote democratic governance. Hence, an interpretation of the district council powers and functions must be of such a nature that they promote public participation, openness, accountability and good governance;[16] and
- district councils are vested with the responsibility to implement and comply with government policy.[17]

On the one hand, the LGA recognise the role of district councils as important in the promotion of constitutional and democratic rule, but on the other hand they are inclined towards central government control, given the obligation to 'comply' with the central government's policy.[18] It is against the above objective standard and its legislative mandate that the powers of district council are interpreted.

7.2 Constitutional framework for interpreting district powers

It is important to purposefully interpret the Constitution in order to understand precisely which particular powers and functions devolve to district councils. Where relevant and appropriate, the framework discussed in Chapter Two will be adopted to interpret the transfer of powers and functions to district councils.

7.2.1 Constitutional interpretation in Uganda

Even though there have been very few cases interpreting powers and functions of district councils in Uganda,[19] an examination of certain rules of constitutional interpretation has been made elsewhere and they require no further detailed

13 Singiza & De Visser 2011: 28.
14 See the Decentralisation Strategic Policy Framework the Ministry of Local Government 2006: 4–8.
15 Section 30(1)(c) of the LGA.
16 Section 30(1)(c) of the LGA.
17 Section 30(1)(d) of the LGA.
18 Soanes *et al.* 2004: 293 define 'comply' as 'act in accordance with the wish or command'.
19 See *Victor Juliet Mukasa Yvonneoyo v A.G* Miscellaneous Cause No. 247/06 p 17.

discussion here.[20] The Constitutional Court acknowledges, quite rightly and firmly, the supremacy of the Constitution. Invariably, any practice or law which contradicts the Constitution is null and void.[21]

The various cases[22] in which the rules of constitutional interpretation were adopted by the Ugandan courts are briefly summarised as follows:

- first, the principles which govern construction of a statute are the same as those which govern the interpretation of the Constitution. According to the Constitutional Court, constitutional provisions should be given the widest possible interpretation;[23]
- second, the interpretation of the Constitution should be dynamic, progressive and flexible, so as to keep pace with ever-changing ideals of a society;[24] and
- third, the Constitution should be interpreted as a whole with no single provision to be relied on to negate any other.[25] No single provision should be separated from the rest, but that all the provisions should be brought within the perspective of the entire constitutional scheme.[26]

As argued in Chapter Three, in order for the transfer of local government powers to serve the purpose of decentralisation, these powers should be clearly defined. Further, the central government legislative control of the local government's functional areas should be supportive and not defeat the object of decentralisation.[27] Given the specific content of rules of constitutional interpretation, the cumulative effect of these rules means that the district council's functions and powers must be progressively interpreted so as to promote the application of new emerging legal concepts without destroying the original text and meaning of the Constitution.[28] Thus the use of the word 'dynamic'[29] calls for the interpretation of local government powers informed by the emerging trends on local governments manifested through a range of statements on decentralisation in Africa.

20 Singiza 2007: 8–9. Although the author's examination of the rules of constitutional interpretation was in the context of the right to non-discrimination on grounds of sexual orientation, the same rules apply in interpreting the powers and functions of district councils.
21 *Susan Kigula & 416 others v the AG* Constitutional Petition No. 6 of 2003 (unreported) rule f.
22 *Charles Onyango Obbo Andrew Mujuni Mwenda v AG* Constitutional Petition No. 15 of 1997 (unreported).
23 *Susan Kigula* rule a.
24 *Susan Kigula* rule b.
25 *Susan Kigula* rule c.
26 *Susan Kigula* rule f.
27 Chapter Three § 3.6.5 and 3.6.4. See also President Yoweri Museveni's address when launching the Local Government Decentralisation Programme on 2 October 1992, p. 6.
28 Oloka-Onyango 1996: 144.
29 Soanes 2004: defines 'dynamic' to mean 'of a process or system characterized by constant change or activity'.

It is also noted that the rules of constitutional interpretation as adopted by the Constitutional Court call for a careful balancing of competing values and interests. For example, the phrase 'dynamic, progressive and flexible' as used by Constitutional Court in the *Kigura* case,[30] presupposes that in certain cases the judges may be confronted with two competing interests. The judges must address, on the one hand, the interests of the central government, and on the other, the interests of the district council.

In such cases the determination of which interest outweighs the other demands, as Aleinikoff argues, 'the development of a scale of values external to the Justices' personal preferences'.[31] Thus depending on which order of government is best suited for the performance of a task, the scale would have to tilt in favour of the constitutional purpose of decentralisation. Clearly, there is no hard and fast rule in determining which of two interests should give way to the other. The discussion below examines the appropriateness of district councils' powers and functions vis-à-vis their constitutional mandate.

7.2.2 The district council role in the state's directive principles

If the whole constitutional scheme has to be read together, then the directive principles must therefore be relevant to the interpretation of the district powers. In the absence of any Constitutional object of district councils, this part of the chapter examines the link between decentralisation and the directive principles. Eight directive principles are singled out: democracy; human rights; economic growth; distribution of income; environment; protection of disabled persons; and education.

7.2.2.1 Democracy

One of the most important directive principles of state policy is the promotion of democracy. This includes empowering and encouraging citizens' active participation, access to leadership positions at all levels and decentralisation and devolution of governmental powers and functions.[32] As argued in Chapter Two, notwithstanding the possibility that in some cases local government structures may be prone to capture by elite groups, local communities learn about the essence of democracy (trade-offs and compromises) at local level better than at national level.[33] This means that when interpreting district council powers and functions, regard must be had for the constitutional purpose of democratic district councils. Such an interpretation should test whether district councils are vested powers that are relevant and truly connected to democracy. For instance, the power to

30 *Susan Kigula*, 2006.
31 Aleinikoff 1987: 973.
32 NODPSP no. II of Uganda Constitution.
33 Chapter Two § 2.3.2.3.

make laws is connected to the right to public participation, itself an essential feature of a constitutional democracy, without which the broader constitutional and democratic scheme of decentralisation would be limited.

7.2.2.2 Human rights

In Chapter Two, the theory of decentralisation was predicated on good governance, the essential features of which include the promotion of human rights.[34] One of the fundamental roles of a state is to promote human rights. Thus, the directive principles oblige the state to ensure that institutions which are charged with the responsibility to protect and promote human rights are adequately resourced.[35] If the state is serious about promoting human rights, it must do so by promoting the right to political participation.[36] The right to political participation is best realised and exercised at local levels of the state.

7.2.2.3 Economic growth

The Constitution directs the state to become the pillar of growth in the areas of agriculture, industrial technology and scientific development.[37] The role of district councils in economic development is based on the assumption that smaller orders of government can be more responsive and efficient than the central government. In this regard, the role of district councils in the promotion of economic growth through certain essential sectors, such as agriculture, is critical in interpreting district council powers and functions.

7.2.2.4 Distribution of income

The Constitutional directive principles envisage balanced development as a means of narrowing the income inequality between rural and urban areas. District councils in this regard are not symbols of development per se but transformational tools for rural development.[38] In Chapter Two, it was conceded that redistribution is generally better performed at national government level. However, this does not imply that decentralisation cannot foster redistribution of income, especially where discretion is vested in local governments in the determination of how they spend equalisation grants.[39] The discretion over equalisation grants does not automatically result in income distribution in a district, but merely produces the district council's autonomy. However, a district council can play a very important role in interpersonal redistribution of incomes, such as taking into consideration

34 Chapter Two § 2.3.
35 NODPSP no. V of Uganda Constitution.
36 NODPSP no. VII of Uganda Constitution.
37 NODPSP no. XI of Uganda Constitution.
38 NODPSP no. XII of Uganda Constitution.
39 Chapter Two § 2.3.1.3.

the ability to pay in the provision of basic services. The interpretation of the role of district councils in income distribution should take into account this ability to narrow the gap between the rich and poor through equalisation grants.

7.2.2.5 Environment

The Constitution places an obligation on the state to protect and sustainably manage natural resources.[40] The Constitution also requires the state to promote and implement clean energy policies.[41] Natural resource management and clean energy, among other things, refer to good water and fuel management policies. Thus, the interpretation of district council powers should also bear in mind the essential role of lower orders of government in managing and protecting the local environment.

7.2.2.6 Women and persons with a disability

The recognition of the rights of persons with disabilities and of women as directive principles is helpful in interpreting which functions vest in the district council. Persons with disabilities in the past were discriminated against in Uganda. Equally, in the past, women in Uganda were legally discriminated against.[42] Recognition of the rights of persons with disabilities and the rights of women reinforces the idea that in order to achieve real participatory democracy at grassroots level, vulnerable groups in a society, particularly those previously discriminated against, must be recognised and their interests protected. In this regard the role of district councils in the promotion of gender-sensitive policies and the protection of people with disabilities cannot be underestimated.[43]

For example, the provision of basic services such as agricultural extension services, rural ambulance services and the control of contagious diseases, should vest in the district council. The role of district councils in the provision of these services impacts directly on households. Since women run most households and provide the essential labour in the agricultural production sector, the powers of district councils should be interpreted bearing in mind the immediate impact on women.

In addition, physical infrastructure, such as rural roads, is delivered by district councils. The type of physical infrastructure has a direct impact on persons with disabilities. The type of physical infrastructure either empowers or impairs persons with disabilities, depending on how accommodative it is of persons with disabilities. Thus, the interpretation of district council powers should consider

40 NODPSP no. XIII of Uganda Constitution.
41 NODPSP no. XXVII of Uganda Constitution.
42 For instance, under Article 20 of the 1967 Constitution, sex and disability were not prohibited grounds of discrimination.
43 NODPSP no. XV and XVI of Uganda Constitution.

the essential role of district councils in providing physical infrastructure that reasonably accommodates persons with disabilities.

7.2.2.7 Education and health services

The Constitution directs the state to promote compulsory basic education by obliging it to take appropriate measures to afford every citizen an equal opportunity to attain the highest education standard.[44] The Constitution also directs the state to take all practical measures to ensure the provision of basic medical services to the population.[45]

District councils occupy unique spaces in the promotion of compulsory basic education. District councils may promote the use of local languages as the medium of instruction in primary schools. The promotion of local languages in schools may be linked to the realisation of compulsory basic education. It also grants an opportunity to minority groups, such as indigenous peoples, to access the highest standard of education. The use of local languages in the provision of medical services is a practical measure in the promotion of basic medical services to the local populations. For districts councils to promote access to education by enabling use of local languages, they need the authority/power to determine the language of instruction in primary schools.

7.3 The principle of subsidiarity in interpreting district council powers

Chapter Two of the book discussed in detail some of the compelling notions for decentralisation. An articulation of the international normative framework for decentralisation was primarily located in the principle of subsidiarity. For example, emerging international soft law calls for the transfer of functions to local governments on the basis of the local government's ability to more effectively match goods to local preferences than the central government.[46] It is reiterated that the manifestations of subsidiarity in emerging international soft law on decentralisation call for the vesting of clear powers and functions to local governments.[47]

Subsidiarity as a principle is prevalent in Uganda in two ways: under the Constitution's directive principles and under Article 176(2)(b) of the Constitution. First, the directive principles of state policy provide that '[t]he State shall be guided by the principle of decentralisation and devolution of governmental functions and powers to the people at appropriate levels where they can best manage and direct their own affairs'. Second, Article 176(2)(b) of the Constitution provides that 'decentralisation shall be a principle applying to all

44 NODPSP no. XVIII of Uganda Constitution.
45 NODPSP no. XX of Uganda Constitution.
46 Chapter Two § 2.8. De Visser 2010: 114.
47 See Article (4)(3) of the ECLSG & CLGF 2005: 6 Principle no 4 *para.* 1. See Chapter § 2.8.

levels of local government and, in particular, from higher to lower local government units to ensure people's participation and democratic control in decision making'. The key phrases here are 'at appropriate levels where they can best manage and direct their own affairs' and 'from higher to lower local government units'. The Constitution thus directs that decentralisation and devolution of powers should favour lower orders of government as a means through which local communities can best manage their affairs.

Thus, the drive towards subsidiarity as expressed in the Constitution becomes a criterion for transfer of powers.

According to the Decentralisation Policy Strategic Framework, 'Current development thinking is that programmes that impact on people are better implemented through decentralisation of functions and powers and responsibilities to local levels'. [48]

According to the Strategic Framework, decentralisation is efficient and effective in that local communities are able to determine their needs and priorities on a sustainable basis.[49] In essence, according to the Strategic Framework, those powers where community input is of limited import should not be transferred.[50]

The process of assignment of roles to district councils should be examined against the background of the principle of subsidiarity. Ultimately, the district council powers and functions under the Constitution should be interpreted in a manner that prefers smaller orders of government.

7.4 Functional areas over which district councils have authority

7.4.1 Examining the lists

In the section below, the approach adopted by the Constitution in the transfer of powers and functions to the district councils is examined against the backdrop of the arguments for decentralisation made in Chapters Two and Three and the principles and rules of constitutional interpretation stated above.

Article 189(1) of the Constitution provides that 'subject to the provisions of this Constitution, the functions and services specified in the Sixth Schedule to this Constitution shall be the responsibility of the Government'. Article 189(3) of the Constitution provides that '[d]istrict councils shall have responsibility for any functions and services not specified in the Sixth Schedule to this Constitution'. The Sixth Schedule of the Constitution provides for 28 areas of competency for which the central government is responsible.

In summary, the Constitution lists 28 exclusive powers of the central government. Implicitly, all other public powers are residual powers of the district councils.

48 *Decentralisation Policy Strategic Framework Ministry of Local Government*, 2006: 14 para. 30.
49 *Decentralisation Policy Strategic Framework Ministry of Local Government*, 2006: 14 para. 30.
50 *Decentralisation Policy Strategic Framework Ministry of Local Government*, 2006: 18 para. 3.4.

Section 30(1) of the LGA provides for functions that vest in the district councils.[51] District councils have the discretion to exercise all the functions except those listed under Part I of the Second Schedule of the LGA.[52] Part I of the Second Schedule to the LGA is similar in wording to the Sixth Schedule of the Constitution. The LGA proceeds to define district council authority by providing that district councils can exercise their authority within their area on any of the listed competencies under Part II of the Second Schedule of the LGA.

Under Part II, the district council is vested with the provision of services such as education; 'medical and health services' [sic] such as primary health care services; water; roads (except those under the responsibility of the central government); and the provision of all decentralised services (27 areas of services). These includes areas such as the aiding and supporting of schools; preservation of public decency; undertaking private works and services; selling of all by-products from district-related works or services; promotion of district council publicity; promotion of health schemes; provision of sports and social welfare; and vehicular parking services.[53] Lastly, the district council has the obligation to register births and deaths and to help the central government in environment-related activities.[54]

The list of exclusive central government powers as described in Schedule 6 to the Constitution and Part I of the Schedule 2 to the LGA is so long and detailed that nothing remains for the district councils. The long list makes it difficult to determine precisely which areas of competency remain for the district council. In addition to the long list, the Sixth Schedule has an item 29 which provides that '[a]ny matter incidental to or connected with the functions and services mentioned in this Schedule'. In my view, when Parliament enacted section 30(1) of the LGA resulting in 18 areas of competency listed under Table 7.1, it overlooked that in terms of item 29 of the Sixth Schedule of the Constitution almost no powers remained to be vested in the district councils.

The delineation of the district council functions under Part II of the Second Schedule of the LGA, read within the context of the Sixth Schedule of the Constitution, suggests, as will be explained in Table 7.2, a concurrency of powers. The apparent concurrency of powers has its origins in the way the Constitutions treats the allocation of powers to the central government and the district councils, namely by:

- defining so many central powers that nothing remains for the district council;
- including item 29, which suggests that, despite the residual functions of district council, they revert back to central government; and
- suggesting that Parliament will prescribe and detail the residual functions of the district council.

51 Section 30(1)(a) of the LGA.
52 Section 30(1)(b) of the LGA.
53 Section 30(2) of the LGA and Part II para 1–18 of the Second Schedule to the LGA.
54 Ibid.

Table 7.1 Twenty-nine exclusive competencies of central government

1.	Arms, ammunition and explosives.	13.	National elections.	25.	National research policy.
2.	Defence, security and maintenance of law and order.	14.	Energy policy.	26.	Control and management of epidemics and disasters.
3.	Banks and banking.	15.	Transport and communications policy.	27.	Health policy.
4.	Taxation and taxation policy.	16.	Development and upgrading of national roads.	28.	Agricultural policy.
5.	Citizenship, immigration and emigration.	17.	National censuses and statistics.	29.	Any matter incidental to or connected with the functions and services mentioned in this Schedule.
6.	Copyrights, patents and trademarks.	18.	Public services of Uganda.		
7.	Land, mines, mineral and water resources and the environment.	19.	The judiciary.		
8.	National parks.	20.	National standards.		
9.	Public holidays.	21.	Education policy.		
10.	National monuments and antiquities.	22.	National surveys and mapping.		
11.	Regulation of trade and commerce.	23.	Industrial policy.		
12.	National plans and coordinating plans made by local governments.	24.	Forest and wildlife reserve policy and management.		

Table 7.2 District councils' functions under Part II of Second Schedule of LGA

1. Education services
   a) nursery
   b) primary
   c) secondary
   d) trade
   e) special education
   f) technical education
2. Medical and health services
   a) hospitals other than those providing referral and medical training
   b) health centres, dispensaries, sub-dispensaries and first-aid posts
   c) maternity and child welfare services
   d) control of communicable diseases, such as HIV/AIDS, leprosy and tuberculosis
   e) control of spread of diseases in the district
   f) rural ambulance services
   g) primary health care services
   h) vector control
   i) environmental sanitation
   j) health education
3. Water services
   a) maintenance of water supplies in liaison with the line ministry
4. Road services
   a) construction
   b) rehabilitation
   c) maintenance of roads not under the responsibility of government
5. Preventing damage to property of the central government and the council.
6. Undertaking private works and services
7. Selling all by-products resulting from carrying out any works or services
8. Promoting publicity for the council and the district
9. Promoting schemes of health, education and road safety sensitisation.
10. Providing and managing
    a) sports and recreation
    b) social work development
    c) remedial social welfare programs
    d) welfare of children and the elderly
    e) public vehicles
11. Registration of marriages, birth and deaths for transmission to the Registrar-General.
12. Assisting the central government in environment preservation and protection.
13. Upon delegation by the central government, identification and preservation of sites and objects or buildings of historical and architectural value.
14. Payment of salaries of all established staff (this function cannot devolve to sub-counties).
15. Regulation, control, management, administration promotion and licensing of council functions and services
16. Aiding and supporting the establishment and maintenance of schools, hospitals, libraries, art galleries, museums, tourist centres, homes for the aged, destitute or infirm or for orphans; providing bursaries to assist children residing in the district; making donations to charitable and philanthropic bodies, welfare, youth, persons with disabilities, women and sport organisations
17. Preserving public decency and preventing offences against public order in public places
18. All decentralised services, such as:
    a) crop, animal and fisheries husbandry extension services
    b) entomological services and vermin control
    c) human resource management and development
    d) recurrent and development budget
    e) district statistical services
    f) district project identification
    g) district planning
    h) local government development planning
    i) land administration
    j) land surveying
    k) physical planning
    l) forests and wetlands
    m) licensing of produce buying
    n) trade buying
    o) trade development
    p) commercial inspectorate
    q) co-operative development
    r) industrial relations
    s) social rehabilitation
    t) labour matters
    u) probation and welfare
    v) street children and orphans
    w) women in development
    x) community development
    y) youth affairs
    z) cultural affairs
19. Any other service or function which is not specified in this schedule.

The adoption of a concurrency of powers by Parliament under section 30 of the LGA is in fact what the CA delegates were keen to avoid.[55] During the CA debates, the terms 'concurrent' and 'shared' powers were never favoured by the CA delegates. According to one CA delegate,

> the committee started with three lists, the Central Government, Concurrent and Local Government. Then ultimately we called in the technical advice not necessarily from the Ministry of Local Government but through the Ministry of Local Government to International Consultants. They advised that it is normal and advisable to specify the functions of the Central Government. Anything that is not specified as a function of the Central Government is automatically a function of the Local Government because it has been stated that before the responsibilities of the Local Government are inexhaustible.[56]

Had the CA delegates considered district council powers as inexhaustible, it would have given district council powers a wider scope. An initial reading of the Sixth Schedule without item 29 suggests that anything that is not included in the Schedule vests in the district council as a residual power. However, item 29 of the Sixth Schedule introduces the doctrine of incidental powers. As a consequence, only if a function is not 'incidental or connected with' the central government then it reverts to the district council.[57] The long list of the central government competencies and item 29 of the Sixth Schedule of the Constitution contradict the intentions of the CA delegates.

7.4.2 Overlap of central government and district council functions

A reflection on the manner in which this delegation is carried out in section 32 of the LGA is indicative of the fact that it is more of an instance of power-sharing on the basis of subsidiarity than the classical delegation of roles by superiors. It is submitted that the delegation of functions from the Ministry of Local Government to a district council is intended to strengthen the core functions of district councils. The contrary interpretation would in fact defeat the purpose of decentralisation all together.

Table 7.3 shows the overlap of function between the central government and the district council. The right-hand column in bold lists 16 areas of competency that the author considers should be the exclusive competency of the central government. The left-hand column in italics lists 15 areas of district council competencies that overlap with the central government competencies.

55 CA debates pp. 3833–4346.

56 Odoki Commission Report 1993: 513.

57 See item 29 of the Sixth Schedule.

Table 7.3 Overlap of central government and district council functions

The district government delegated functions under Part II of the Second Schedule of the LGA	*The central government functions under the Sixth Schedule of the Constitution.*
• District information services	• Transport and communication
• Road services	• Development and upgrading of national roads
	• Taxation and taking policy
• Land administration • Land surveying • Physical planning • Wetlands • Assisting the central government in environment preservation and protection	• Land, minerals, water resources and environment
• Human resource management and development. Payment of salaries of all established staff (this function cannot devolve to sub-counties)	• Public service
• Registration of marriages, births and deaths for transmission to the Registrar-General	• National census and statistics
• Education services	• Education policy
• Industrial relations • Social rehabilitation • Labour matters	• Industrial policy
• Forests	• Forest and wildlife reserve policy and management
• Control of communicable diseases, such as HIV/ AIDS, leprosy and tuberculosis • Control of spread of diseases in the district	• Control and management of epidemics and disasters
• Medical and health services such as hospitals other than those providing referral and medical training, health centres, dispensaries, sub-dispensaries and first-aid post-maternity and child welfare services • Water services	• Health policy
• Crop, animal and fisheries husbandry extension services • Entomological services and vermin control	• Agriculture policy
• Licensing of produce buying • Trade buying • Trade development • Commercial inspectorate • Co-operative development • Regulation, control, management, administration promotion and licensing of council functions and services a) Commercial inspectorate	• Regulation of trade and commerce
• District planning • Local government development planning • District statistical services • District project identification	• National planning
• Aiding and supporting tourist centres	• National parks
• Art galleries, museums, tourist centres, preservation of sites and objects or buildings of historical and architectural value	• National monuments, antiquities

Most of the functions under the Sixth Schedule of the Constitution and Part II of the Second Schedule of the LGA in fact offer little guidance. In any invent, a district council is not allowed to enact any laws on any matter that has been adequately provided for by the central government.[58]

What is 'incidental' in item 29 of the Sixth Schedule of the Constitution is not only what is auxiliary to the performance of the central government powers. The phrase 'or connected with' clarifies the intention of the entire scheme of devolution of powers and functions to the district councils. Thus, only if a matter is not 'incidental to or connected with' the Sixth Schedule does it become a district council function.[59] In Chapter Two, it was noted that the emerging soft law on local governments calls for the transfer of powers to local governments. Local governments tend to produce goods for which local communities express preference.[60] A clear and simple scheme of allocation of functions not only promotes efficiency and accountably, but is critical for the success of decentralisation.[61] The point is that the incidental powers of the central government must be interpreted restrictively.

Steytler and De Visser, writing in the context of power-sharing between local governments and the national government in South Africa, argue that the 'incidental powers doctrine' should be interpreted purposefully and restrictively.[62] The authors argue that there are functions which, when strictly interpreted, fall outside a local government core function but are in fact critical for the administration of a given local government function. The authors cite the example of the imposition of a fine in the enforcement of the by-laws. They argued that the imposition of fines, while not explicitly granted as a power, is incidental to other powers. The argument here is that incidental powers should not be used to increase the functional ambit of the central government.[63] Applying that reasoning to powers and functions of district councils in Uganda, the following can be argued:

> A liberal interpretation of item 29 of the Sixth Schedule of the Constitution may suggest that all residual powers of the district council powers revert to the central government, because all district council functions are connected to the central government. However, in light of the call for subsidiarity that was discussed in Chapter Two,[64] item 29 should be interpreted restrictively.

58 Section 42(2) of the LGA provides: 'For avoidance of doubt, no ordinance shall be made in respect of any matters that or issue for which adequate provision is made under the Constitution or any other law made by Parliament except for ease of reference, in which case the ordinance shall reproduce the provisions of article or law in its entirety'.

59 Garner 2004: 1288 defines the term 'incidental power' as 'a power that, although not expressly granted, must exist because it is necessary to the accomplishment of an express purpose'.

60 Chapter Two § 2.3.1.1.

61 Chapter Three § 3.6.6.

62 Steytler & De Visser 2013: 5–7

63 Steytler & De Visser 2013: 5–8

64 Chapter Two § 2.8.

For example, under the Sixth Schedule of the Constitution, national standards and health policy are competencies of the central government. In this regard, the Public Health Act is enacted to set standards in the manufacture, preparation, storage or transmission of any food article that is unfit for human consumption. The Act does not provide for all aspects of foods that may endanger human health. Against this framework the Local Government (Mbarara District) Brewing and Consumption of Native Beer Ordinance, Statutory Instrument No. 243–47 is enacted. Section 5 of the ordinance prohibits the supply of native beer to drunkards and young persons. In essence, the ordinance uses the legislative space afforded by the Constitution and the statutory framework to protect children and persons described as 'drunkards' from harmful native beers. Thus, the central government sets the standards for foods fit for human consumption, while the role of district council is to implement the framework using tailor-made ordinances to suit local circumstances. The legislative role of the district council is not subservient to the central government's legislative power, but rather supportive.

7.4.3 Validity of section 42(2) of the LGA

Section 42(2) of the LGA narrows the district council's power to make laws by excluding district councils from enacting any laws on any matter that has been 'adequately' legislated upon by Parliament. Given the arguments above, what is then the constitutionality of section 42(2) of the LGA given that it limits a district council's legislative power to matters which have not been legislated upon by Parliament?

A blanket limitation of district council legislative power on any matter that has already been legislated upon by Parliament is invalid in terms of Article 176(2) read together with Article 180(1) of the Constitution. Presumably, if Parliament chooses, it can legislate exhaustively on any given competency, leaving no room for the district council to perform its legislative role. Even if Parliament legislated on a competency that is shared with the district council, there is still room for the district council to exercise its devolved legislative power. All that Parliament is obliged to do is to ensure that the district council's legislative space that is created by Articles 180(1) and 176(2) of the Constitution is not unilaterally occupied by the central government.

7.4.4 Delegation of further powers

Article 189(2) of the Constitution creates room for the central government (on application by a district council) to allow a district council to exercise any of the competencies stated in the Sixth Schedule under a system of delegation.[65] The

65 Article 189(2) of the Constitution provides: 'District councils and the councils of lower local government units may, on request by them, be allowed to exercise the functions and services specified in the Sixth Schedule to this Constitution or if delegated to them by the Government or by Parliament by law'.

central government retains the power to 'assume responsibility for functions and services assigned to the district council'.[66]

Oloka-Onyango, while examining the nature of powers that devolve to district councils, argues that Article 189(2) of the Constitution manifests an inclination towards a highly centralised state.[67] The use of words and phrases such as 'may', 'be allowed' and 'if delegated' are pointed out by the author as evidence of the Constitution's centrist inclination.[68] The inclination towards a centrist state is buttressed by the fact that any additional functions that vest at the district councils are dependent on the pleasure of the central government. It is maintained that Subsidiarity should lead to central government allocating some of its powers to districts.

Section 32(1) of the LGA provides among other things for the delegation of the powers and functions and responsibilities that vest in the Ministry of Local Government to a district council.[69] In effect, section 32(1) adopts what Article 189(2) of the Constitution calls for. Before a delegation under section 32(1) of the LGA can take place, all the parties concerned must agree to the delegation. Secondly, there must be evidence that adequate resources have been made available to the district councils in order to fund the delegated mandates. Lastly, the delegation must be brought to the public's knowledge.[70]

Table 8 shows that most of the services that are decentralised to district councils are in fact connected to central government competencies as shown in the right column. What the three tables suggest is that neither the district councils, nor the central government have exclusive powers. There is such a high degree of overlap between the powers of the central government and the powers of the district council that it is perhaps better to speak of sharing powers.[71]

7.5 The district council's governance instruments

7.5.1 Introduction

In Chapter Three, three local government governance tools were discussed. These were: legislative, executive and administrative powers. The term 'legislative

66 Article 189(4) of the Constitution provides: 'Subject to the provisions of this Constitution, the Government may, on request by a district council, assume responsibility for functions and services assigned to the district council'.

67 Oloka-Onyango 2007: 15.

68 Oloka-Onyango 2007.

69 Section 32(1) of the LGA provides: 'A Minister responsible for a Government Ministry may, after consultation with the Minister, delegate functions, powers and responsibilities vested in that Ministry to a local government council'.

70 Section 32(2)(a), (b) and (c) of the LGA. In addition, the Minister of Local Government must send the instrument of delegation to the district council. The Minister must gazette or advertise the instrument of delegation in the local media at the expense of the Ministry of Local Government, and must affix a copy thereof in a conspicuous place on or near the outer door of the relevant district council's office.

71 Kabumba 2007: 33.

power' was defined with reference to local governments' ability to make laws so as to legally give effect to their functional mandate. The term 'executive powers' was defined with reference to the ability to initiate and to execute local government policies. Lastly, that local governments should be vested with administrative power and a discretionary power to choose whom to hire and to determine who manages the local governments' resources.[72] What follows is the examination of the district council's governance tools in executing their mandates against the backdrop of the above mentioned principles.

7.5.2 District council powers to make laws

Article 180(1) of the Constitution provides that a district council 'shall have legislative ... powers to be exercised in accordance with this Constitution'. In theory an institution that possesses the power to make laws also determines how executive powers are exercised and by whom.[73] Thus, Article 180(1) of the Constitution seeks to state the role of the council in a district and determines that the district council may exercise legislative authority in the district. The article implies that as long as the district council's laws do not contradict the Constitution, they are as valid as any national laws. A district council ordinance may apply to the whole district, or part thereof, or to a person practising a given profession in a district.[74]

A district council ordinance may create offences for breach of any of the regulations thereunder,[75] prescribe fines or a term of imprisonment,[76] forfeiture and destruction.[77] In addition, a district council ordinance may provide for the suspension or cancellation of a permit or licence,[78] and/or provide for recovery of a fine or expenses thereunder by way of a civil action.[79] Further, a district ordinance may provide for a fee or a charge or full cost recovery, under section 38 of the LGA.[80]

The district council power to make laws is a novel power that in fact evinces local autonomy. Indeed, as recommended by the Odoki Commission, '[t]he district council should be the *supreme political organ* in the district, *with powers to make policies, pass laws*' (emphasis added).[81] The Commission's recommendation is what in fact Article 180(1) of the Constitution adopted.

72 See Chapter Three § 3.6.
73 Lindseth 2004: 1354.
74 Section 42 of the LGA.
75 Section 40(a) of the LGA.
76 Section 40(b) of the LGA.
77 Section 40(c) of the LGA.
78 Section 40(d) of the LGA.
79 Section 40(e) of the LGA.
80 Section 41 of the LGA.
81 See the Odoki Commission Report para. 18.98: 499.

Article 79(2) of the Constitution,[82] read in isolation of Article 180(1) of the Constitution, may lead to the conclusion that the district council may not exercise its legislative authority on any of the delegated functions without its conferment by Parliament. Such a conclusion is misleading. Even if the district council's legislative role under Article 180(1) of the Constitution may be of a delegated kind, it is a unique power that must be interpreted to serve the purpose of decentralisation.[83]

Under the authority of Article 180(1) of the Constitution, the district council may exercise its legislative authority on any of the competencies under the Sixth Schedule of the Constitution, and Part I of the Second Schedule of the LGA. What this ultimately means is that under the Constitution, Parliament cannot legislate exhaustively on all shared competencies with a district council. The Constitution instructs Parliament to be cognisant of the principle of subsidiarity while exercising its legislative mandate.[84]

In addition to being limited to certain functional areas, the district council is limited by the requirement to obtain the Attorney-General's certification and by the prescripts with regard to procedures as set out in legislation.

7.5.2.1 Attorney-General's certification

The Constitution provides that the exercise of the district legislative powers has to be in conformity with the Constitution.[85] This means that the district council may only pass laws that do not violate any of the provisions of the Constitution.

Section 38(1) of the LGA repeats the constitutional provisions relating to the district councils' authority to make laws. The only addition made by the LGA is that in addition to conforming to the Constitution, the district council laws must conform to 'any laws made by Parliament'.[86] The LGA provides that an ordinance enacted by a district council must be certified by the AG. The role of the AG is to determine its compatibility with the Constitution or any other laws made by Parliament.[87] For instance, the AG is mandated to determine if the district council's proposed bill derogates from or contravenes the existing law or Constitution. In such instances, the proposed bill must be sent back to the district council within 90 days for modification or appropriate action.[88] Regulation 21 of Part IV of the Third Schedule of the LGA implies that the AG may suggest an amendment to a district council bill. In which case, the proposed amendment

82 Article 79(2) of the Constitution provides: 'Except as provided in this Constitution, no person or body other than Parliament shall have power to make provisions having the force of law in Uganda except under authority conferred by an Act of Parliament'.
83 See the detailed discussion of the distinction between the two terms in Chapter One.
84 Article 176(2)(b) of the Constitution.
85 Article 180(1) of the Constitution.
86 Section 38(1) of the LGA.
87 Section 38(2) of the LGA.
88 Section 38(3) of the LGA.

to the bill by the AG must then be effected before it can be signed into a district council ordinance and/or gazetted.[89]

The Constitution provides for the office of the Attorney-General as the principal legal advisor to the central government. He or she must be a person qualified to practice as an advocate of the High Court for ten years. The AG is a cabinet minister appointed by the President, with the approval of Parliament. Amongst his or her core functions are 'to give legal advice and legal services to the Government on any subject'. The AG is possessed of the requisite competency to determine whether a district council bill derogates from or contravenes the existing law or Constitution or not. His or her role is therefore technical in nature.

Despite the fact that the role of the Attorney-General in the exercise of the district council legislative power may be considered technical in nature, it amounts to an unjustified intrusion. The provision for the blanket intervention by the Attorney-General in all cases of the exercise of the district council's legislative power under Regulation 21 of Part IV of the Third Schedule of the LGA is invalid in light of the provisions of Article 180(1) of the Constitution that vests original legislative powers to the district council. In any case, it is not for the AG to determine whether a given district council ordinance is invalid or not. The only authority that is vested with the power to determine the validity or invalidity of any law, including a proposed district council ordinance, is the Constitutional Court.[90]

7.5.2.2 Procedural limitations

The LGA circumscribes the manner in which district councils should adopt laws. Every member of a district council has the discretion to introduce a bill for an ordinance.[91] Hence, before its publication, a bill for an ordinance must be introduced, debated and carried by way of motion.[92] In essence, before a motion for a district council bill can be carried, district councillors must deliberate on it. The bill is then signed into law and promulgated into the gazette (see Figure 7.1).

7.5.3 The district council's administrative powers

7.5.3.1 Introduction

In Chapter Three, three personnel systems for decentralisation were discussed. These were the separate, the unified and the integrated personnel systems. Whereas a separate personal system is preferred, in practice, a hybrid of both systems is usually adopted in order to mitigate the risks associated with a

89 See Regulation 21 of Part IV of the Third Schedule of the LGA.
90 Article 137(1) of the Constitution.
91 See Regulation 15 of Part IV of the Third Schedule of the LGA.
92 See Regulation 20 of Part IV of the Third Schedule of the LGA.

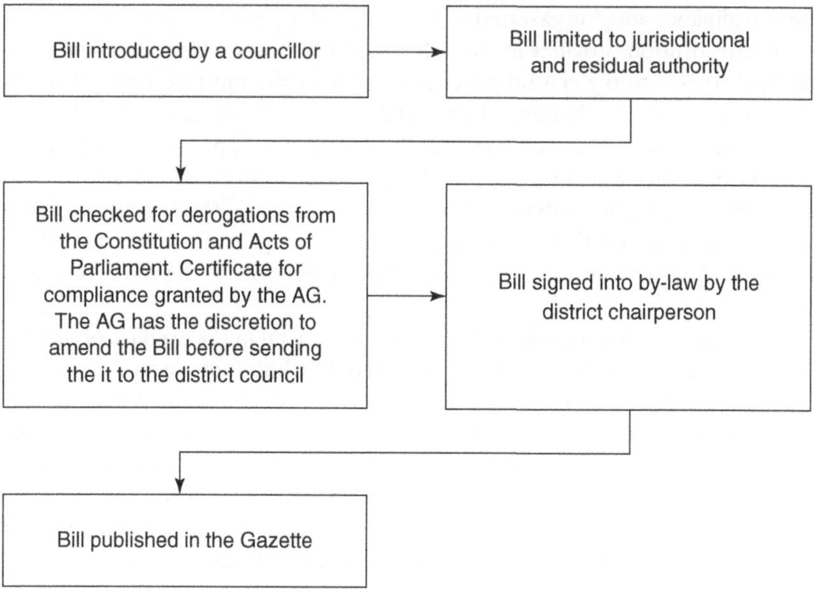

Figure 7.1 District council's legislative processes.

Source: Adopted from Article 180(1) of the Constitution, sections 30–42 of the LGA and Reg. 21 of Part IV to the Third Schedule to the LGA.

separate personnel system.[93] At the inception of decentralisation in Uganda, the discretion to make managerial decisions was vested in the Chief Administrative Officers (CAOs). The CAOs were subjected to district council political scrutiny and accountability.[94] However, in 2010, constitutional changes were adopted resulting in limited political control by the district council elected political leaders of the district staff. The constitutional changes have adopted a unified personnel system for all the senior managers in the district council.[95] As previously argued, accountability as a broader term incorporates legal constraints that minimise public administrators' discretion, as well as fiscal constraints that reflect fiduciary responsibility.[96] As distinguished from political accountability, which places emphasis on regular, free and fair elections for political leaders, administrative accountability is based on the discretion of the local council to hire, fire and discipline its own staff.[97]

93 See Chapter Three § 3.7.3.
94 Hubert & Andersen 1993: 10.
95 See Articles 188(2) and 200(4) of the Constitution.
96 Callahan 2007: 113.
97 Report on the Commission of Inquiry into the Local Government System 1987: 75.

The discussion below examines the extent of district council administrative autonomy against the backdrop of the theory discussed in Chapter Three which calls for local government's discretion to hire and control its own staff.[98]

7.5.3.2 *The district council Chief Administrative Officer*

The Constitution provides for the Chief Administrative Officer (CAO),[99] and vests a discretion in Parliament to determine, among other things, his or her functions.[100] In order to qualify to be appointed as a CAO, a person must have a university degree[101] and a diploma in public administration or development studies from a recognised institution.[102] He or she must have ten years working experience[103] and must be of a high moral calibre.[104]

7.5.3.3 *Functions of the CAO*

The functions and role of the CAO can be divided into five categories. These are: finance; staff administration; implementation of district council policies; advisory; and law and order.

7.5.3.4 *Finance*

The LGA provides that the CAO is the district council accounting officer.[105] The description of the CAO as the chief accounting officer of the district council presupposes that he or she has a duty to answer all questions relating to financial management in the district. This view finds support in the district council financial and accounting regulatory framework as provided for under the Local Government (Financial and Accounting) Regulations (LGFAR).[106] These Regulations are applicable to all financial transactions and business in every district council.[107] The CAO must ensure that there are proper systems in place for

98 Chapter Three § 3.7.4.1.
99 Article 188(1) of the Constitution.
100 Article 188(3) of the Constitution.
101 Section 63(2)(a) of the LGA.
102 Section 63(2)(b) of the LGA.
103 Section 63(2)(c) of the LGA.
104 Section 63(2)(d) of the LGA.
105 See sections 90(1) and 64(1) of the LGA. The term 'accounting officer' is defined under Regulation 3(1) of the LGFAR to mean 'the accounting officer under section 64 of the Act and in relations to an urban council means the accounting officer under section 65(2) of the Act'.
106 See generally the Local Government (Revenue Regulations) (LGFAR) Statutory Instrument No. 243-16, the Local Governments (Financial and Accounting) Regulations (LGFAR) Statutory Instrument No 2007 No. 25 and *The Local Governments Financial and Accounting Manual 2007* issued under sections 78(2) and 175 of the LGA.
107 Regulation 2 of the LGFAR.

efficient revenue generation that minimises financial loss. Hence, the CAO has the duty to maintain a budget desk which bolsters proper and efficient systems in budgeting and budgetary controls, revenue collection and accounting and financial control.[108]

Accounting officers in public administration 'have a special responsibility and leadership role in ensuring that the principles of compliance, prudence, and probity are observed in administration'.[109]

7.5.3.5 Staff administration

The LGA states that the CAO is the head of administration and public service in the district council.[110] This position involves determining when to recruit staff by declaring a position vacant; ensuring that only competent staff are recruited;[111] and establishing a framework for evaluating staff performance.[112]

The CAO is mandated to supervise, monitor and co-ordinate the activities of district councils' employees and departments to ensure accountability in the management of service delivery.[113] The CAO is equally tasked with the role of developing capacity for development and management of planning functions in a district.[114] This is done by supervising and co-ordinating activities of all delegated services and the officers charged with the performance of the delegated services.[115]

7.5.3.6 Implementation of lawful district council policies

The CAO is also responsible for the implementation of all lawful decisions of the district council.[116] The CAO's role here helps to separate the district council's policy-making process from the technocrats' translation of policies into action. The separation of policy-makers from policy implementers improves efficiency and reduces the possibility of conflict of interest. The question then becomes: must a CAO implement unlawful policies of the district council? In the South African case of *Manana v King Sabata Dalindyebo Municipality*, the court rejected the argument that only valid and lawful resolutions of the municipal council could be obeyed by its municipal manager. It held that once a municipal council has taken a decision it can only be challenged by its officials in courts of law. As an alternative, the court stated that an officer who disgrees with a municipal council's decision may apply to the council to either have the decision rescinded or

108 Regulation 7(1)(b) of the LGFAR.
109 Oliver 2009: 243.
110 Section 64(1) of the LGA.
111 Regulation 4(2) of the LGFAR.
112 Regulation 7(1)(c) of the LGFAR.
113 Section 64(2)(c) of the LGA.
114 Section 64(2)(d) of the LGA.
115 Section 64(2)(e) of the LGA.
116 Section 64(2)(a) of the LGA.

reconsidered.[117] According to the court, 'it would be conducive to disorderly public administration if officials were entitled to choose between executing or not executing a duly adopted resolution of the council depending upon their belief as to its validity – whether or not the belief is well-founded'.[118]

This case was therefore decided on the need to uphold the rule of law, rather the validity of law. Applying the reasoning used in the *Manana case* to section 64(2)(a) of the LGA, the CAO has the obligation to implement all district council policies without selection. He or she must implement all policies even if such policies ultimately discriminate against women, the elderly, people with disabilities or an ethnic minority group within a district. It is open to him or her to convince the district council to either rescind or alter its decision. It is also open to the CAO, as decided in *Manana* case, to challenge such a policy in a court of law.

7.5.3.7 Advisory role of the CAO

The CAO must give guidance to district councils and their departments on relevant laws and policies.[119] In addition, the CAO has an advisory administrative role to the district council.[120] The words 'guidance' and 'advisory' are a common feature. The assumption is that the CAO is highly skilled in financial management and public administration and able to give credible guidance to the district council. His or her guidance may relate, for instance, to how best to raise district council revenue.[121] The term 'guidance' denotes the supervision of an activity or duty for proper results.[122] In legal terms, it means that a person or an officer merely seeks advice from another highly skilled person or authority, whose advice the former is not obliged to take.[123]

The question may arise whether the CAO may become liable for giving poor or wrong advice. Under the law of tort, expert advice from especially skilled persons may give rise to a duty of care on the basis of which a civil action could result in case of harm. The test is: that a skilful person should give reasonable advice which persons with similar skills would ordinarily have given.[124] This may mean that a CAO, as an especially skilled person in public administration or accounting, should only give advice that is reasonably acceptable by other people in the same profession. Should the CAO give advice that is fundamentally erroneous he or she may be sued for negligence. This view finds favour in Regulation 10 of the

117 *Manana v King Sabata Dalindyebo Municipality* [2011] 3 All SA (SCA) para. 21.
118 Manana case para. 22.
119 Section 64(2)(b) of the LGA.
120 Section 64(2)(h) of the LGA.
121 Regulation 4(1) of the LGFAR.
122 Simon 2008: 1561.
123 See *Roland Kakooza Mutale v Attorney General* Application No. 665/2003 arising out of HCCA No. 40/2003.
124 Simon 2008: 1561.

LGFAR that calls on all public officers to adopt prudent financial and accounting measures while handling district council finances.[125]

7.5.3.8 Law and order

The CAO assists in the maintenance of law and order and security in the district.[126] The obligation to keep law and order suggests that the CAO should have instruments of coercion, such as district council police, courts and prisons. However, the police force, prison services and judiciary are centralised.[127] In the absence of these three instruments of coercion, it may be difficult for the CAO to fulfil the above obligations. It is recommended that the CAO should be able to prosecute offenders and employ and direct security services to maintain order in the district.

7.5.4 Background to the centralised appointment of CAOs

Before 2005, district councils used to appoint all district staff through their respective District Service Commissions. The powers of the DSC have been limited by an amendment to the Constitution,[128] to the effect that it no longer empowers the DSC to appoint the CAO. The CAO is now centrally appointed by the Public Service Commission.[129] Before the amendment to the Constitution, the procedure to remove a CAO was similar to that for removing the chairperson of a district council.[130] There is little evidence to suggest that a separate personnel system of district council staff in the past registered great success in Uganda's

125 See also section 174 of the LGA which renders local government political or administrative officers personally liable for financial losses incurred by local governments on account of malpractice or negligence.
126 Section 64(2)(i) of the LGA.
127 Tusasirwe 2007: 32. See also para. 2 of the Sixth Schedule to the Constitution, which lists 'Defence, security, maintenance of law and order' as competencies of the central government.
128 Article 188(2) of the Constitution provides: 'Notwithstanding articles 176(2) and (3) and 200 of this Constitution, the Public Service Commission shall appoint persons to hold or act in the office of chief administrative officer and deputy chief administrative officer, including the confirmation of their appointments and the exercise of disciplinary control over such persons and their removal from office'. Article 172 of the Constitution generally provides for the prerogative of the President to appoint persons in public service, other than members of the DSC. Articles 176(2) and (3) of the Constitution provide for the principles of devolution of powers to lower orders of government with emphasis on grassroot democratic control of the decision-making process.
129 Section 55(1A) of the LGA.
130 See *Gladys Aserua Orochi* 8. Two common features in the procedure for the removal of the district chairperson were the tribunal procedure and the medical board procedure. The only difference between the removal of the district council chairperson and the removal of the CAO was the role of the DSC that was mandated to effect the decision of either the tribunal or medical board. A further difference was that since the CAO was not a political officer, he or she could not be subject to recall by the electorate.

decentralisation.[131] It is conceded that the procedure to remove the CAO before the constitutional amendment presented numerous challenges. For instance, the procedure was prone to political manipulation, exhibition of nepotism, enormous costs and unprecedented delays.

The question as to who appoints district council staff under the Constitution therefore raises the following questions: first, why is it not the district council that appoints its own staff directly; and second, why is it the PSC, and not the DSC, that appoints all the senior district council employees? The CAO and other district staff should ordinarily be directly appointed by the district council.[132] Since the CAO is now directly appointed by the Public Service Commission (PSC), Article 176(2)(f) of the Constitution has been rendered redundant.

The rationale for the present unified personnel system for CAOs centres on two main grounds: the shortage of skilled human resources in many district councils and the need to uniformly promote efficiency in the service delivery sectors of all district councils.

According to Steiner, there is a shortage of qualified and skilled human resources in the district council civil service, with high deficiency levels in areas such as accounting, planning, engineering, teaching and health.[133] The latest *Annual Assessment of Minimum Conditions and Performance Measures for Local Governments* 2009 also paints a somewhat bleak picture for district councils. The report sought among other things to examine the ability of district council's staff to utilise the central government transfers. The report relied on the district council's staff capacity to comply with financial and accounting guidelines. Linking central government transfers to the quality of district council administrative performance, the report found evidence of a dysfunctional system administration.[134] These findings also find support in the views expressed by Lubanga, who ascribes the failure of district councils to develop a suitable career development path for district council administration staff to poor human resource management.[135]

Clearly, the above findings suggest a lack of skills. The central government may argue that the centralisation of the CAO sought to address deficiencies in skilled human resource in district councils by ensuring that highly skilled CAO can be transferred from one district council to another through the country.

There were problems with the appointment of CAOs by the DSC. The problems related to the supervision of CAOs and the cumbersome procedure for their

131 Reddy 1999: 44 cited in Isingoma & Red 2006: 102.

132 Section 67(1) of the LGA.

133 See Steiner 2006: 14. Although Steiner's study is contradicted by Ts'oele and Goldman, whose research findings reveal an abundance of qualified and skilled staff in many district councils.

134 See the Annual Assessment of Minimum Conditions and Performance Measures for Local Governments 2009. Synthesis Report March 2010: 8.

135 Lubanga 1998: 93.

removal.[136] In addition, a separate personnel system had no in-built mechanisms to ensure that district council staff moved from one administrative position to another. The effect was that the district staff became de-motivated, which led to under-performance.[137] Furthermore, there were constant allegations of nepotism in the recruitment process that resulted in the recruitment of inefficient and incompetent staff, two examples of which will be discussed below.[138] The most notorious example is the case of *Gladys Aserua Orochi v Kabale District Government*, where Kabale district council paid an enormous amount in damages and litigation costs as a result of flouting the rules of procedure in dismissing a CAO.[139] In this case, the purported allegation against the CAO by the Kabale district council was ironically that the CAO had followed the right procedures in awarding a tender for the supply of services, a fact that must have angered those members of the district council with vested interests in the tender process.[140] It is worth noting that even when the Kabale district council was ordered by the tribunal headed by a high court judge to reinstate the CAO, the order was ignored.[141] It is noted that Ms Aserua Orochi comes from the northern part of the country, far from the Kabale district, which is in the south-western part of the country. It is probable that the leaders of the Kabale district council looked at her as a 'foreigner', in spite of her experience and good managerial skills.

In *Tommy Obongo Ojok v Apac District Local Government*, the CAO sued the Apac district council for wrongful termination of his contract of employment.[142] The Apac district council had appointed the CAO even though the CAO was not eligible for the job, because of his previous bad record in another district where he had served in the same capacity. At the interview, the information regarding his retirement was brought to the attention of the interviewing panel. At the trial,

136 See Report of the Commission of Inquiry (Constitutional Review): Findings and Recommendations 2003: 9–110.

137 Kakumba 2008: 100.

138 Makara 2009: 140.

139 See *Gladys Aserua Orochi v Kabale District Government* CHC Civil Suit No. 0093 of 2003. See also the cases of *Tommy Obongo Ojok v Apac District Local Government* HCT-02-CV-CS-0015-2005 and *Onywello Ceaser V Pader District Local Government* HCT-02-CV-CS-009-2007, which had similar illegal conduct of members of the district council. In this case the court awarded a total of 127,440,952 Ugandan shillings or approximately 72,823 dollars at the then exchange rate of 1:1750. In addition, the entire sum carried a court interest rate p.a. from 12 August 1999, till payment in full, excluding 10,000,000 Ugandan shillings, which was awarded as general damages. This award excluded the costs. It is also noted that the CAO had been dismissed on 30 January 1999 and obtained judgment on 6 February 2009. In this case, the decision was based on section 69 of the LGA that catered for the tribunal. This procedure was abolished long before the 2005 constitutional amendment in that the CAO would be removed from office upon a two-third resolution of the members of a district.

140 *Gladys Aserua Orochi* 8.

141 *Gladys Aserua Orochi* 2.

142 *Tommy Obongo Ojok* 1.

the issue was whether Mr Ojok had been validly employed.[143] There was evidence that the central government threatened to withhold financial support from the Apac district council if Mr Ojok's appointment was not rescinded.[144]

The High Court held that since the circumstances of his retirement (Mr Ojok had been retired in the public interest) had been brought to the attention of the interviewing panel, his subsequent appointment was valid. The termination of the contract was, therefore, unlawful.[145] The High Court noted that the decision to dismiss the CAO based on a fear that central government funding would be withheld, was invalid. The High Court noted that under the provisions of section 58 of the LGA, 'the Apac District Service Commission ought to have carried out its work independently without being subjected to the direction or control of any person or authority'.[146] The court was wrong insofar as it validated the appointment of a CAO whose personal integrity, competency and experience was legally questionable.

The point here is that, given that people with a proven history of misconduct could be appointed even when the evidence of misconduct had been brought to the attention of the district appointing authority, the introduction of a unified personnel system may be justified. The previous separate personnel system of the CAO was prone to elite capture.[147] The CAO's job approval or job security was dependent upon his or her willingness to succumb to local politicians' corrupt behaviour.

This case points to the inadequacies of the DSC in appointing qualified staff and the central government's manipulation of the appointment process of senior district managers.

7.5.4.1 Current law on disciplining the CAO

In Chapter Three the point made was that local government administrative autonomy includes not only the power to appoint local government employees, but also the power to exercise discretion in determining the terms and conditions of local government staff.[148] Arguably, such a power includes the discretion to confirm appointments, to exercise disciplinary control and to remove them from office.[149] In terms of Article 188(1) of the Constitution, the CAO is now subject to disciplinary control by the PSC under Article 166(1)(b) of the Constitution.[150] This is despite the provision of Articles 176(2) and (3) and 200

143 *Tommy Obongo Ojok* 6.
144 *Tommy Obongo Ojok* 6.
145 *Tommy Obongo Ojok* 7.
146 *Tommy Obongo Ojok* 6
147 Chapter Two 2.3.2.3. See also Makara 2009: 143.
148 Chapter Three § 3.7.4.1.
149 Stanton 2009: 47.
150 Article 166(1)(b) of the Constitution provides: 'Except as otherwise provided in this Constitution, the functions of the Public Service Commission include: to appoint, promote and exercise disciplinary control over persons holding office in the public service of Uganda as provided in article 172 of this Constitution'.

of the Constitution which envisage the exercise of discretion over all persons employed in the district by the district council, through the DSC as the appointing authority. In the section below, the legal framework of the Public Service Commission (PSC) is discussed.

7.5.4.2 Public Service Commission and its role

The PSC is an independent constitutional body[151] composed of a chairperson, a deputy chairperson and seven other members appointed by the President with the approval of Parliament.[152] Members of the PSC serve for a term of four years but are eligible for reappointment.[153] The function of the PSC is to advise the President before appointing any public officers; to appoint, promote and exercise disciplinary control over persons holding public offices; and to review the terms and conditions of service, standing orders, training and qualifications of public officers. The PSC is mandated to deal with all matters connected with personnel management and development of the public service and to guide and coordinate district service commissions (DSCs), including hearing and determining grievances from persons appointed by DSCs.[154] Parliament is obliged to ensure that the PSC makes regulations in order to execute its mandate.[155] The Uganda Public Service Standing Orders, F – r 13 provides that 'It is the Appointing Authority who has the power to remove a public officer from office'.[156] What this ultimately means is that a CAO can only be removed from office by the President on the recommendation of the PSC.[157]

7.5.4.3 Assessment

The fact that the CAOs are now centrally appointed and controlled infringes on the constitutional autonomy of the district councils. The role of the PSC in the appointment of the CAO points to the resurgence of the recentralisation phenomenon, and is thus a threat to the constitutional value of decentralisation.[158] In the past, the power of the DSC to remove administrative staff, including the CAO, on the recommendation of a district council, was testimony to the real powers the district councils wielded. The appointment of the CAOs by the PSC and not by a DSC presents additional challenges to district councils' administrative autonomy.

151 Article 165(2) of the Constitution.
152 Article 165(2) of the Constitution.
153 Article 1657(7) of the Constitution.
154 Article 166(1)(c) of the Constitution.
155 Article 168(4) of the Constitution.
156 Cited as the Uganda Public Service Standing Orders 2010.
157 Article 167(1)(a) of the Constitution.
158 See 'Mukwaya, Lukooya clash over removal of CAO' *New Vision*, available at http://www.newvision.co.ug/D/8/19/713884 (accessed 23 March 2010).

As a result of the amendment to the Constitution, the district councils no longer have control over the heads of administration in a district. The CAOs now pay allegiance to the central government, as had been the case prior to the 1995 Constitution. In fact, the CAOs are practically employees of the central government (and not of the district councils). The CAOs may choose to ignore the district councils' development priorities.

The unified personnel system in which CAOs are no longer subject to the disciplinary control of the DSC and the district councils is a disguised form of recentralisation.[159] The constitutional value of decentralisation lies in the district councils' ability to determine their own development needs through a democratic process. The unified personnel system for CAOs contradicts the principles on which decentralisation is based under Article 176 of the Constitution. In the words of one of the CA delegates: '[i]f you give people political power and you do not give them administrative capacity to put their decisions into effect, you are in a way giving them *byoya bya nswa*'.[160]

While commenting on the proposed amendment that resulted in the promulgation of Article 188(2) of the Constitution, the Commission on Constitutional Review had in fact reasoned that there was no need to have centrally appointed CAOs because adequate provision for checks on the appointment of the CAOs already existed.[161] In the section below, the legal framework of the DSC, a body that the Commission on Constitutional Review had referred to, is examined.

7.6 Appointment and dismissal of other district council staff

Article 176(2)(f) of the Constitution states that persons employed by district councils must be employees of the district council.[162] This means that any person employed in the district council must be appointed by the district council itself. The Constitution calls on every district council to establish a DSC as the appointing authority.[163] The power of the district councils to control staff promotes efficiency and accountability by ensuring that local communities through their elected representatives can exert pressure on local managers, hence improving service delivery. Other than waiting for central government action in cases of non-performance and indiscipline, the DSC can take disciplinary measures such as reprimands, issuing a warning to or even a dismissing a district council staff

159 Tusasiwe 2007: 37.

160 See *Proceeding of the Constituent Assembly Official Report* 1994: 3825 para. 2 per Hon Amanya Mushega. The expression *byoya bya nswa* in Uganda's political talk literally means 'empty power'.

161 See the Report of the Commission of Inquiry (Constitutional Review): Findings and Recommendations 2003: 9–113 para. 9.6.5.

162 As one of the principles applied to district council system Article 176(2)(f), 'persons in the service of local government shall be employed by the local governments'.

163 Article 198(1) of the Constitution; section 54(1) of the LGA.

member. The problem is that although all the district council staff are subject to the direction of council, they are responsible to the CAO.[164] In the discussion below, the composition and role of the DSC is examined.

7.6.1 The District Service Commission (DSC)

The Constitution provides for the DSC in every district,[165] whose membership is composed of 'a chairperson and such other members as the district council shall determine, at least one of whom shall represent urban authorities and all of whom shall be appointed by the district council'.[166] Members of the DSC are appointed by the district council on the recommendation of the district council's executive committee, and approved by the Public Service Commission (PSC).[167] The Constitution provides that members of the DSC should be of high moral character and proven integrity.[168] The Constitution further provides for the term of office of members of a DSC to be a period of four years, although the members of a DSC are eligible for re-appointment for one more term.[169] It is noted that under Article 166(1)(c) of the Constitution, all the appointment decisions of the DSC can be appealed to the PSC.

The LGA in part repeats the provisions of the Constitution regarding the composition of the DSC. The LGA also states that the number of members of the DSC must not exceed four, excluding the chairperson.[170] The LGA further provides that at least one-third of the members of the DSC should be women, and that at least one member of the DSC must be a person with a disability. [171]

The LGA provides additional criteria for membership of the DSC, such as ordinary residence in the district, an advanced qualification or its equivalent and extensive work experience.[172] The Constitution provides for the removal of a member of the DSC by the district council's executive committee in consultation with the PSC and with the approval of the district council.[173] The Constitution lists three grounds upon which a member of the DSC can be removed from office: inability to perform their functions, arising from physical or mental incapacity; misbehaviour or misconduct; and incompetence.[174]

164 Section 67(3) of the LGA.
165 Article 198(2) of the Constitution.
166 Article 198(2) of the Constitution.
167 See Article 198(2) of the Constitution. Section 54(2) of the LGA.
168 Article 198(3) of the Constitution.
169 Article 198(4) of the Constitution.
170 Section 54(2A)(a) of the LGA.
171 Section 54(2A)(b) of the LGA.
172 Section 56(1) of the LGA.
173 Article 198(6) of the Constitution.
174 Article 198(6) of the Constitution; section 54(4) of the LGA.

While the Constitution does not mention the independence of the DSC, section 58 of the LGA vouches for its independence[175] subject to the provisions of Article 166(2) of the Constitution.[176] The exclusion of MPs, district councillors or a member of an executive body of a political party or organisation from eligibility for appointment to the DSC, manifests its independence.[177]

7.6.2 The role of the PSC vis-à-vis the DSC

In Chapter Three the emphasis was that local government administrative autonomy ensures that local council staff as technical bureaucrats are able to make decisions free from central government influence.[178] The role of the DSC is discussed below in the context of its ability to appoint and discipline district council staff, free from the central government control. First, members of the DSC are appointed by the district council with the 'approval' of the PSC.[179] The key words under Article 198(2) of the Constitution are 'with the approval of'. The word 'approve' as used in Article 198(2) of the Constitution means to 'officially accept as satisfactory'.[180] However the word 'approval' should be contextualised. The word 'approval' is intended to ensure that there must be conformity with official standards established by the PSC in the appointment of civil servants, without the PSC necessarily controlling the actual appointment process, an interpretation that accords with subsidiarity.[181] The second issue relates to the obligation on the district council's executive committee to consult the PSC before removing any of the members of the DSC under Article 198(2) of the Constitution. The key phrase as used under Article 198(6) of the Constitution is 'after consulting with' the PSC. This phrase implies that unless the opinion of the PSC is sought, the removal of any of the members of the DSC from office by the district local council would be invalid.

The initial interpretation of Article 198(6) of the Constitution may suggest that the requirement to consult the PSC by the executive committee of the

175 Section 58(1) of the LGA provides: 'Subject to article 166(1)(d) of the Constitution, the district service commission shall be independent and shall not be subject to the direction or control of any person or authority'. Article 166(1)(d) of the Constitution provides for the guidance and monitoring role of the PSC over the DSC.

176 Article 166(1)(d) of the Constitution provides that '[i]n the exercise of its functions, the Public Service Commission shall be independent and shall not be subject to the direction or control of any person or authority; except that it shall take into account government policy relating to the public service'.

177 Section 56(2) of the LGA.

178 Chapter Three § 3.7.3.

179 Article 198(2) of the Constitution provides that '[t]he district service commission shall consist of a chairperson and such other members as the district council shall determine, at least one of whom shall represent urban authorities and all of whom shall be appointed by the district council on the recommendation of the district executive committee with the approval of the Public Service Commission'.

180 Kavanagh 2002: 52.

181 Article 198(5) of the Constitution.

district council is mandatory. In practice, the PSC seems to consider the word 'approval' as if it has the power to control the appointment process, a position that is clearly erroneous.[182] However, on a closer scrutiny of Article 198(6) of the Constitution, the use of the word 'may' reveals a discretionary power as the district council's executive committee is merely to consult with the PSC.[183] All that is required of the DSC is to seek advice from the PSC, whose advice can be taken or rejected. The other argument is that it would be foolhardy to simply ignore the advice of the PSC which in fact sets the standards of public employment. The intrusive role of the PSC allows for the phenomenon of 'recentralisation' to creep into every aspect of district council administration, given the narrow constitutional and legislative mandate of DSCs.[184]

However, the power that vests in the PSC to approve the terms and conditions of the DSC and the obligation on the district council to consult that PSC before a member of the DSC can be removed from office may guard against what is generally referred to as 'elite capture' of local staff. The need to consult the PSC before the district council's executive committee may remove a member of the DSC from office reduces the risk of possible victimisation of members of the DSC by the local politicians.[185]

Earlier in this chapter, the appeal function of the PSC against the appointment decisions of the DCS was highlighted.[186] In the discussion below, the appeals rate against the decisions of the DSCs is examined. The number of the appointment decisions that are either upheld or overturned by the PSC is indicative of the fact that the DSCs are conducting themselves reasonably and responsibly. It attenuates the argument that DSCs need to be protected from elite capture. If the large number of overturned appointment decisions is scrutinised, it reveals incompetence and abuse in a very small number of district councils.

Figures 7.2 and 7.3 show that from 1 July 2010 to 30 June 2011 the PSC received a total of 141 appeal cases from 26 DSCs. This number includes three cases from former Kampala City Council and one from Kamwenje Town Council. Of these cases, 53 appeals succeeded while 83 appeals were rejected. Five cases were under review. In fact, one DSC of Manafwa district council had 81 of its decisions appealed against at the PSC. Of the 81 from Manafwa district council's DSC, 21 cases succeeded while 60 cases were rejected, with only one pending

182 See the *Public Service Commission Annual Report* 2010–2011: 10. The numerous appeals from DSC decisions that the PSC handles concerning 'irregularities in appointment process and procedures' shows a paternalistic and domineering pattern towards the DSC.

183 Kavanagh 2002: 247 defines the word 'consult' to mean to seek information or advice from someone, especially an expert or professional. This implies that the obligation of a district local government council's executive committee to consult the PSC should only arise when in the view of the district local government council's executive committee; the DSC does not have the ability to guide itself.

184 Makara 2009: 142.

185 Makara 2009: 141.

186 See Chapter Seven § 7.5.4.2.

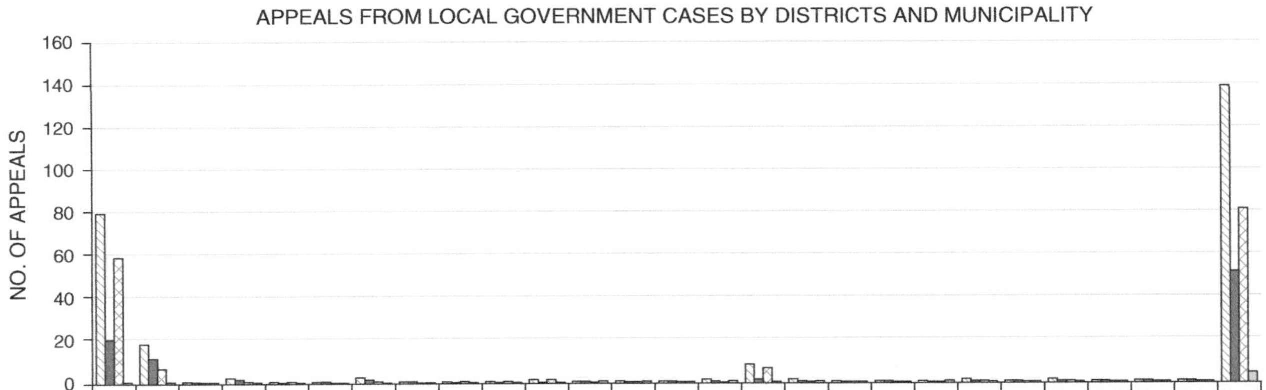

	Man afwa	Bud uda	Kam uli	KCC	Masi ndi	Amu ru	Kabe ram aido	Kaab ong	Buke dea	Buk wo	Jinja	Hoi ma	Ruku ngiri	Amu ru	Mpigi	Muk ono	May uge	Kiba ale	Kam wen ge TC	Ruku ngiri	Neb bi	Kaba role	Bun dibu gyo	Bulii sa	Kayu nga	Kaba role	Total
	1	2	3	4	5	6	7	8	9	10	11	12	13	14	15	16	17	18	19	20	21	22	23	24	25	26	
Received Appeals	81	19	1	3	1	1	3	1	1	1	2	1	1	1	2	9	2	1	1	1	2	1	2	1	1	1	141
Accepted Appeals	21	12	1	2	0	1	2	1	0	0	0	1	0	1	1	2	1	0	1	0	1	1	1	1	1	1	53
Not Accepted	60	7	0	1	1	0	1	0	1	1	2	0	0	0	0	7	0	0	0	0	1	0	1	0	0	0	83
Under Review	0	0	0	0	0	0	0	0	0	0	0	1	1	0	1	0	1	0	0	1	0	0	0	0	0	0	5

Figure 7.2 Performance of DSCs in 26 district councils in Uganda.

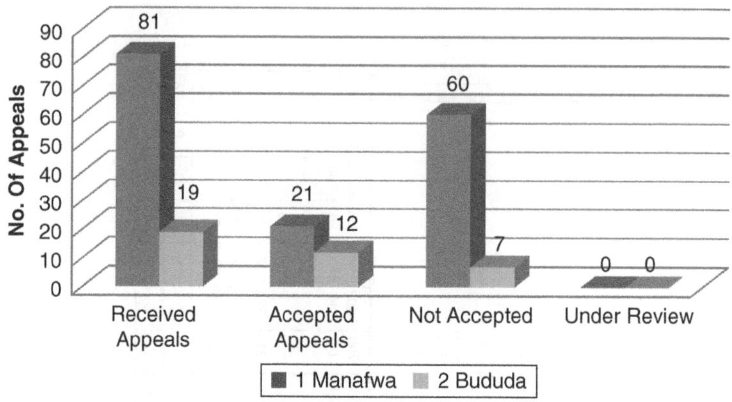

Figure 7.3 Appeals from Bududa and Manafwa Districts.

Source: Adopted from the Public Service Commission Annual Report 2010–2011: 10–11.

review.[187] Bududa district council's DSC presents another interesting case: it had 19 of its decisions appealed to the PSC. Of these, 12 succeeded, while only seven failed. It is noted that Manafwa and Bududa districts are new districts, whose capacity-building may be very limited.[188] In my view, the figures do not show evidence of incompetency and abuse of the recruitment process by the DSCs. On the contrary, Figure 7.2 demonstrates the ability of the DSC to appoint district staff independently, given the low appeal rate against DSC decisions. Instead Figure 7.3 illustrates the intrusive nature of the PSC in the decisions of the DSC. The apparent success rate of appeals of DSC decisions is noted in newly created districts that may not have acquired the requisite capacity. The large number of overturned appointment decisions in a very small number of district councils point towards the need for specific interventions in those localities, rather than a blanket instrument of intrusion across all districts.

7.6.3 Assessment

As already mentioned, the central government appointment of the CAO, on the one hand, and its subtle control of the DSC through the intrusive role of the PSC, on the other, undermines decentralisation. This subtle control is revealed in five ways:

- first the PSC guides and coordinates all the activities of the DSCs;
- second, appeals from appointment decisions of the DSCs are heard and determined by the PSC;

187 See the Public Service Commission Annual Report 2010–2011: 10–11.

188 See the detailed discussion on the creation of new districts in Uganda in Chapter Five § 5.3.2.4. Manafwa and Bududa districts were created in 1999 and 2006 respectively.

- third, the PSC is vested with the disciplinary control of all members of the DSCs as any public officers;
- fourth, the PSC must approve all the appointments of members to the DSC; and
- last, the district council executive committees must consult the PSC before removing from office any of the members of the DSC.

The district council's discretion to appoint and discipline staff under Article 176(2)(f) of the Constitution flows from the district council executive power under Article 180(1). Articles 188(2) and 198(2) which centralised the appointment and discipline of the CAO therefore contradict the intended purpose of decentralisation. To the extent that these two constitutional provisions have the effect of undermining the district council's discretion to appoint, discipline and dismiss its senior managers, they create an ambiguity that can only be remedied by a constitutional amendment.

7.7 Conclusion

The discussion in this chapter has highlighted the importance attached to the sharing of powers between the central government and local government. After highlighting the limited mandate that vested in the district administrations in the past, the chapter points out that the 1995 Constitution vaguely defines district powers and functions. The vagueness with which the Constitution defines district councils' power and functions ultimately causes an overlap. The overlap may easily confuse the local electorate in that they may not easily know which order of government is responsible for poor service delivery. The chapter therefore purposely interprets the powers and functions of district councils. The chapter finds:

- first, that there is an urgent need to clearly define the district councils' competencies in order to avoid the possibility of overlap of their functions with the central government's roles;
- second, that the centralisation of senior district senior managers that ultimately limits the district councils' discretion to fire and hire them is unjustified and should be reconsidered;
- third, that the central government subtle control of the DSC through the intrusive role of the PSC limits the developmental role of district councils; and
- last, that the limited legislative space accorded to the district councils undermines their developmental and democratic role and that their legislative role should be complementary of, and not subservient to, the central government.

In the next chapter, the district councils' fiscal powers are examined against the backdrop of their narrow functional, legislative and administrative powers.

8 District council finances

8.1 Introduction

In this chapter more evidence of limited, intrusive, 'hard edged' top-down centralism is presented using the limited district council financial autonomy as an example. In Chapter Three the call for the local governments to exercise their discretion to determine and manage their 'own revenue' in order to match their functional mandates with finances was made. The phrase 'own revenue' was defined with reference to the discretionary power to raise revenue through different sources and the discretion to spend it.[1] What follows is an assessment of Uganda's district councils' revenue raising autonomy.

8.1.1 Constitutional legal framework

Article 176(2)(d) of the Constitution provides that 'there shall be established for each local government unit a sound financial base with reliable sources of revenue'. The Constitution therefore suggests that the existence of strong district councils is dependent on a 'sound financial base with reliable sources of revenue'.[2] The Constitution seems to suggest that district councils should have a strong financial base in order to fulfil their roles.[3] Under the Sixth Schedule of the Constitution, taxation is a central government competency. In fact, the Constitution prohibits the imposition of any tax unless authorised by an Act of Parliament.[4] The question then is: do district councils have original power to raise revenue? In very clear terms, Article 192 provides: 'Parliament shall by law provide (a) for the taxes that may be collected by a local government for or on

1 See Chapter Three § 3.7.1.

2 Article 176(2)(d) of the Constitution.

3 Article 152(2) of the Constitution provides: 'Where a law enacted under clause (1) of this article confers powers on any person or authority to waive or vary a tax imposed by that law, that person or authority shall report to Parliament periodically on the exercise of those powers, as shall be determined by law'.

4 Article 152(1) of the Constitution provides: 'No tax shall be imposed except under the authority of an Act of Parliament'.

behalf of the Government for payment into the Consolidated Fund' and that '(b) for a local government to retain for the purposes of its functions and services, a specified proportion of the revenues collected for or on behalf of the Government from the district'.

Article 192 seems to suggest that Parliament is merely under an obligation to allow district councils to collect taxes on behalf of the central government and to retain a portion thereof. At this point it may appear that no original taxing powers vest in district councils. However, Article 191(1) of the Constitution grants original taxing authority to the district councils. It provides: 'Local governments shall have power to levy, charge, collect and appropriate fees and taxes in accordance with any law enacted by Parliament by virtue of article 152 of this Constitution'.

The words 'by virtue of article 152 of this Constitution', used in Article 191(1) of the Constitution, suggest that even if taxation is a competency of the central government, Parliament is implored to delegate the authority to impose a tax. The Constitution lists specific taxes which district councils may levy and spend, with a discretion by Parliament to expand the list.[5] The district councils have the authority as per the Constitution to exercise their original taxing authority, but they must exercise it in accordance with the statute.[6] District councils have original constitutional taxing powers under Article 191(1) of the Constitution. The district council taxing power is neither diminished by Article 151(1) of the Constitution, nor limited by Article 152(2) of the Constitution. The two articles are merely ancillary to the need for a strong financial base that is established under Article 176(2)(d) of the Constitution. The Constitution instructs Parliament to strengthen the district council taxing power, and not to weaken it.

8.1.2 Statutory framework

The LGA operationalises Articles 191(1) and (2) of the Constitution. It vests the district council with the discretion to exercise its taxing authority as provided under the Constitution. It provides: 'Local governments may levy, charge and collect fees and taxes, including rates, rents, royalties, stamp duties and registration and licensing fees and fees and taxes that are specified in the Fifth Schedule to this Act'.[7]

The Fifth Schedule of the LGA includes categories of taxes for district councils. These taxes are in addition to what is specified under Article 191(2) of the Constitution and section 80(1) of the LGA. In fact, the Schedule is open-ended in that any other taxes not included in the Schedule may be included by Parliament.[8]

5 Article 191(2) of the Constitution provides: 'The fees and taxes to be levied, charged, collected and appropriated under clause (1) of this article shall consist of rents, rates, royalties, stamp duties, cess, fees on registration and licensing and any other fees and taxes that Parliament may prescribe'.

6 Article 191(1) of the Constitution.

7 Section 80(1) of the LGA.

8 Section 2 of the Local Government Amendment Act (LGAA).

Thus, in addition to what is added to the already constitutionally specified taxes and those under the Fifth Schedule of the LGA, Parliament enacted other district council taxes.

8.2 Four types of district council taxes

Several types of local government taxes under the LGA are discussed below, namely property rates,[9] hotel and service taxes[10] and the now suspended graduated tax. These four types are discussed because they account for the vast majority of district council revenue. Further, the discussion explains how the central government is not responding adequately to the Constitution's instruction to ensure that the fiscal autonomy of the district council is protected.

8.2.1 Property taxation

8.2.1.1 Introduction

Local government property taxes are a common source of local government revenue.[11] According to Bird and Slack,

> the extent to which local governments have control over property taxes is often an important determinant of the extent to which they are able to make autonomous expenditure decisions. The level, design and control of property taxation are thus critical elements in effective decentralization policy in many countries.[12]

A key debate on property taxes in many countries is the extent to which central governments should interfere with the determination of property tax rates by local governments.[13] In Chapter Two, the common narrative that central governments distribute wealth better than local governments was challenged.[14] In Chapter Three, it was shown that the success of decentralisation depends on local governments' discretion to raise and spend revenue.[15] It is against this background that the district council property tax in Uganda is assessed.

The Constitution does not provide specifically for property rates as a form of district council tax. It only provides for '…rents, rates, royalties as part of the taxes to be levied by the district government'.[16] Arguably, rents, rates and royalties may

9 See the Local Government Rating Act (LGRA) of 2005.
10 Section 1 of the LGAA. These two taxes were introduced by the Local Governments (Amendment) Act No 2/2008 (LGAA).
11 Article 191(3) of the Constitution.
12 Bird & Slack 2003: 1.
13 Bird & Slack 2003: 33.
14 See Chapter Two § 2.3.1.3.
15 See Chapter Three § 3.7.1.
16 Article 191(2) of the Constitution.

be linked to the interest in the property but are not necessarily a form of a tax. The description of rents, rates and royalties as district council taxes is therefore problematic. This is because rents, rates and royalties relate to user rights from land which are quite distinct from property, service and hotel taxes. The above distinction ultimately limits the potential tax yield from property service and hotel taxes. In addition, as already mentioned, the district council's authority to levy taxes is regulated by an Act of Parliament.[17]

8.2.1.2 Rateable property

The LGRA provides for district council property rates.[18] The LGRA defines the term 'property' as 'immovable property and includes a building (industrial or non-industrial) or structure of any kind, but does not include a vacant site'. The term 'rate' is defined as 'a rate on property levied by a local government'.[19]

The LGRA identifies three kinds of property that are subject to a local government tax rate: 'commercial building', 'industrial building' and 'non-industrial building'. A commercial building under the LGRA is defined with reference to a business purpose, while an industrial building is defined with reference to an industrial purpose, for example, factory mills 'and other premises of similar character'. On the other hand, a non-industrial building is defined with reference to its non-industrial use.[20] As long as the building is no longer used for industrial purposes then it cannot be subject to property tax.

Only properties in urban areas are subject to the property rate unless such a property, even if located in a rural area, is for commercial use.[21] This means that a commercial building which is located outside an urban area is subject to property taxation. However, a residential building that is located outside an urban area is not subject to property tax.[22] The above provision limits the ability of rural district councils to generate revenue from property tax. It narrows the scope for property taxation in rural areas.

The LGRA provides for exempted properties specified in the Second Schedule.[23] These are: any of the official residences of the President;[24] any official residence of a traditional or cultural leader as defined by Article 246 of the Constitution;[25] an exclusive place of public worship; and a residence of a religious

17 Articles 152 and 191(1) of the Constitution.
18 The long title to the LGRA states the object of the law: 'An Act to provide for the levy [sic] of rates on property by local governments within their areas of jurisdiction; to provide for the valuation of property for the purpose of rating; to provide for the collection of the rates; to repeal the Local Government Rating Act and to provide related matters'.
19 Section 1 of the LGRA.
20 Section 1 of the LGRA.
21 Sections 3(3) and (4) of the LGRA.
22 Section 3(5) of the LGRA.
23 Section 5 of the LGRA.
24 Paragraph 1 of Part I the Second Schedule of the LGRA.
25 Paragraph 2 of Part I the Second Schedule of the LGRA.

leader.[26] The LGRA also exempt any property exclusively used as a cemetery or for cremation.[27] In addition, property used exclusively for charitable or education institutions (of a public character and supported by endowments or voluntary contributions) is exempted.[28] A detailed critique on these exemptions is offered later in this chapter.[29]

A property owner is personally liable for the payment of a property rate. Given the diverse forms of land ownership in Uganda, most of which is unregistered, and given the fact that most of the land interests are not easy to register, it is difficult to ascertain who the real owner is.[30] In cases where the name of the property owner is not known to a district council, the obligation to pay falls on the person in occupation.[31]

8.2.1.3 Determination of rates

It is mandatory for every district council to levy property rates at a rate determined by it on the rateable value of any property within its area of jurisdiction.[32] As explained above, the words 'any property within its area of jurisdiction' exclude residential buildings in rural areas.[33] The expression 'rateable value' means the 'net annual rental value of a property ascertained in accordance with the Act'.[34] However, the central government determines a threshold value (two thousand shillings, approximately US80 cents) below which no property taxation may apply. It also determines a ceiling: property taxation may not exceed 12% of the rateable value of the property. These thresholds are very rigid and therefore not legally unjustifiable, but certainly inappropriate for a decentralised system. A district council may levy a property rate below the minimum of two thousand shillings (approximately US80 cents) or beyond 12% of the rateable value of the property.[35]

A district council may reduce the payment of rates on any given property, say for specific groups of property owners such as the elderly. However, reduction of the payment of the rate of any property has to be determined by the Minister of Local Government.[36] The question then becomes: if the Minister determines when to reduce the property rate, can it be argued that district councils have autonomy over property rates? Because the law has determined who is to determine the rate, the question of who reduces or remits that property tax should fall

26 Paragraph 3 of Part I the Second Schedule of the LGRA.
27 See paragraph 4 of Part I the Second Schedule of the LGRA.
28 See paragraph 5 of Part I the Second Schedule of the LGRA.
29 See Chapter Eight § 8.2.3.2.
30 See section 3 of the Land Act 16 of 1998, which provides for customary land, freehold, *mailo* land and leasehold as forms of interest in land.
31 Sections 7(1) and (2) of the LGRA.
32 Section 3(1) of the LGRA.
33 Section 3(5) of the LGRA.
34 Section 1 of the LGRA.
35 Section 3(1) of the LGRA
36 Section 6 of the LGRA.

within the ambit of the district council.[37] The power to reduce or remit property taxes would enhance the district council's ability to effect redistribution within the district area. The Minister's powers are arbitrary and therefore unconstitutional.

8.2.2 Hotel taxation

The discussion below examines the contribution of hotel tax to the district council revenue. A district government hotel tax is a tax levied on all hotels and lodging room occupants, and is collected and paid by hotel owners.[38] The obligation of the hotel is to collect the tax from the occupant and remit it to the district council on a monthly basis.[39] Different hotel categories attract different sets of hotel rates.[40]

Income from hotel tax has to be spent in specific areas. These areas are described in general terms as 'basic local services', such as sanitation, education, health and construction and maintenance of roads in the area of jurisdiction.[41] That local governments should be empowered to manage local resources given that they can better match goods to local preferences than the central government is by now clear.[42] The strictures placed by section 80(1a)(c1) of the LGA on expenditure decisions making by the district councils limits the district council's budgeting freedom and therefore limits the district council's discretion to prioritise its expenditure decisions.

8.2.3 Service taxation

8.2.3.1 Overview

In 2008, Parliament introduced a new form of income tax known as district government service tax. The LGA in its amended form introduces taxation of the following categories of persons: (a) all persons in gainful employment; (b) professionals; (c) business persons; and (d) commercial farmers producing on a large scale.[43]

37 For instance, in a South African case, *CDA Boerdery (Edms) Bpk en Andere v Nelson Mandela Metropolitan Municipality* (526/05) [2007] SCA 1, [2007] SCA 1 (RSA) (6 February 2007), the Supreme Court held that given the new status of local government, it was no longer necessary to seek the consent of the provincial premier to increase the property rates.

38 Section 80(1a)(a) of the LGA as amended by the LGAA.

39 Section 80(1a)(b1) of the LGA as amended by the LGAA. See also the Fifth Schedule Part II Regulation 7 of the LGA as amended by the LGAA. See the Fifth Schedule Part II Regulation 8 of the LGA as amended by the LGAA. Any district government hotel tax that is collected and unremitted to the district council at the end of the financial year attracts a surcharge of 40%.

40 See Part II of the Fifth Schedule of the LGA as amended by the LGAA.

41 Section 80(1a)(c1) of the LGA as amended by the LGAA.

42 See Chapter Two § 2.3.1.1.

43 Section 80(1a)(b) of the LGA as amended by the LGAA. See also Part III of the Fifth Schedule Regulation 9(11) of the LGAA. If a person is taxed under any one of the categories, he or she cannot be taxed under any other.

The LGAA provides a long list of persons considered to be practising professional businessmen and women. The list even includes petty traders and self-employed persons.[44] Further, the LGAA exempts from service tax persons serving in the armed forces, diplomatic missions accredited to Uganda,[45] unemployed persons, peasants, persons engaged in subsistence or occasional economic activity, petty food vendors, *boda boda* cyclists,[46] petty artisans, the *jua kalis* and people living in abject poverty.[47]

The above list is a clear example of over-regulation of district council revenue sources by the central government. As already argued, local governments should be vested with the discretion to raise and spend their revenue.[48] The district council should have had the discretion to determine which categories of people are exempted.

8.2.3.2 Critique

In Chapter Three it was argued that local governments should be vested with the discretion to determine their sources of revenue and how to spend it in order to be able to fund their mandates.[49] The above mentioned constitutional and legal framework does not strike an adequate balance between the need for fiscal autonomy and moderate supervision of taxation. The LGRA vests district councils with the discretion to determine tax rates. However, the central government determines the parameters within which taxation may occur.[50] The above provision, commonly referred to as 'capping',[51] may in fact limit the ultimate tax yield achieved from the district council tax. Bird and Slack, however, argue that the capping of property rates ensures that local authorities do not impose unduly high property rates that might result in economic distortions. According to the authors, unfair tax competition as a result of low property rates may unfairly influence business decision-making in a given area, and thus negatively affect the level of investment in others.[52] Thus, '[o]ne way to minimize such undesirable

44 Sections 80(2b)(1)(b), (c) and (d) of the LGA as amended by the LGAA.

45 See the Fifth Schedule Part II Regulation 1(2) of the LGA as amended by the LGAA.

46 The term *boda boda* refers to the motorcycle 'taxis' that are used in many towns in Uganda as a means of transport. It derives its name from cross-border illicit trade between Kenya and Uganda where the smugglers use workers known as 'Border Porters' as their secret conduits. The Luhyas, one of Kenya's ethnic groups, mispronounced the word 'porter' as *boda* instead.

47 See the Fifth Schedule Part II Regulation 1(3) of the LGA as amended by the LGAA. The term '*jua kari*', although not defined by the Act generally, refers to people who do odd jobs such as loading farm produce and other merchandise onto lorries.

48 See Chapter Two § 2.3.1.1 and Chapter Three § 3.7.1

49 See Chapter Three § 3.7.1.

50 See Chapter Two § 2.3.1.

51 Bird & Slack 2003: 33.

52 Bird & Slack 2003: 36.

tax competition is for the central government to set minimum tax limits'.[53] Local governments may only exercise their discretion to reduce or increase their tax rates within a clearly defined threshold.

Arguably, the determination of the rateable properties by the central government narrows the district council tax base, hence reducing the tax yield from property tax. The common assumption is that district councils know best which properties and services should be taxed and which should be exempted. For example, a specific district council's policy may relate to the promotion of local tourism. In such cases, they should be able to decide whether hotels or casinos should enjoy tax exemption.[54]

However, it is equally arguable that vesting district councils with the discretion to determine which properties and services to subject to tax and which ones to exempt might lead to income inequities amongst local governments.[55]

Further, the central government policy may seek to promote national development goals through universal education or charity. In such cases it should be able to exempt education-related properties or charitable organisations. Whereas the central government may justifiably determine and/or exempt categories of properties to be taxed, it must be done in terms of national development goals. An examination of the current determination of and the exemption from property rates shows that the central government minimally considers the developmental role of district councils.

The trend towards undermining fiscal autonomy is further explained by the unilateral suspension of a major revenue source for district councils, the graduated tax.[56] This is discussed in the next paragraphs.

8.2.4 Graduated taxation

8.2.4.1 Overview

This section will explain that, although graduated tax is legally one of the district council's sources of revenue, it was suspended in 2005 by the President.[57]

Graduated tax in Uganda started as a form of poll tax in the colonial period, and was levied on every able-bodied working male adult and formally employed female adult.[58] Graduated tax was assessed on a scale determined by the district council, as advised by the Local Government Financial Commission (LGFC).[59] Graduated tax as a source of district council revenue has always been controversial. It was a form of forced revenue extraction, which was highly repressive

53 Bird & Slack 2003: 39.
54 Bird & Slack 2003: 10. This argument is valid on the assumption that the district councils are better suited to determine development priorities than the central government
55 Bird & Slack 2003: 39.
56 Ssewanyana & Okidi 2008: 4.
57 See the 2005/2006 Budget Speech by the Minister of Finance p 47.
58 Ssewanyana & Okidi 2008: 4.
59 Regulation 3 of the LGRR. The detailed discussion of LGFC is made in Chapter Nine.

and exploitative.[60] Graduated tax had a high level of evasion, especially by high income tax payers.[61] Ironically, studies showed that at the height of 2005, graduated tax contributed about 70% of the districts' own revenues.[62] Graduated tax contributed an estimated 10% of district councils' budget, marking a 0.9% share of GDP.[63] Graduated tax had no clear criteria upon which the assessment of a taxpayers' scale was based. Besides, the determination of an individual's income (and sometimes his or her age) in Uganda is usually based on estimates that are prone to statistical errors.[64] It did not matter whether a male or female resident was in fact 18 years old or not, given the use of the word 'apparent' in Regulation 2 of LGRR. This means that if a tax collector formed an opinion that someone looked like an 18-year-old, then they would have to pay tax irrespective of whether they were in fact younger.

There is also evidence to show that graduated tax was highly inequitable, with a higher tax burden on people with low incomes than people with high incomes.[65] Graduated tax also relied mainly on penal sanctions for enforcement. For instance, the liability for the offence of non-payment of graduated tax was strict, in that the onus of proving that payment had been made was on the tax defaulter.[66] Graduated tax had a higher incident of tax avoidance, and as a result many graduated defaulters were imprisoned.[67]

While there may thus have been good reasons to revisit the graduated tax, the actual decision was informed by political opportunism and was thus poorly executed. The decision to suspend graduated tax was prompted by the desire of the ruling party to forestall a private opposition member's bill that sought to abolish it.[68] In the 2001 election the opposition made the abolition of graduated tax an electoral issue on the grounds that it was an archaic and despotic way of raising district council revenue.[69] The President wrote to the Vice-President, asking him to suspend graduated tax within five months from the date of the letter.[70] Notwithstanding the suspension of graduated tax by the President, it is still legally part of the district councils' sources of revenue.

60 *Uganda Government, Report of the Commission of Inquiry into the Local Government System* 1987: 93 para. 242.

61 Ssewanyana & Okidi 2008: 21.

62 Kjær 2005: 1.

63 Ssewanyana & Okidi 2008: 21. Regulation 2 of the LGRR.

64 Emwanu 2008: 1.

65 Ssewanyana & Okidi 2008: 15; Chen, Matovu & Reinikka-Soininen 2001.

66 Regulation 10(3) of the LGRR. For example, non-payment of the tax attracted a term of imprisonment or a fine not exceeding double the amount of the tax due.

67 Makara 2009: 289.

68 The private member's Bill advanced three main reasons: (1) it is a form of poll tax that was associated with exploitative colonial rule; (2) it targeted poor people; and (3) it was highly prone to corruption. See also Makara 2009: 289.

69 Makara 2009: 289.

70 See 'Re-centralisation weakens the decentralisation process', available at http://www.ms.dk/sw94813.asp (accessed 14 November 2011).

8.2.4.2 An assessment of the suspension of graduated tax

Chapter Two linked fiscal decentralisation to accountability. Because local governments directly generate their revenue from local citizens, they may spend money with a higher degree of discipline that minimises waste, which in turn advances development. Thus, whenever locally elected leaders fail to honour their electoral pledges to the local citizens, at the next election they are likely to face the wrath of voters or even a recall.

Had Parliament properly exercised its role in regulating graduated tax, the tax could have been reformed instead of being suspended. Politics rather than good economics seemed to have played a significant role in suspending graduated tax, with no prudent financial considerations.[71] Reforming graduated tax policy was preferable to outright suspension.[72]

Furthermore, it would have been for the district council and not the central government to determine whether graduated tax was oppressive or not. The political fallout arising from the unpopularity of graduated tax would have been felt by the district councils and not the central government. The manner in which the central government suspended graduated tax constituted a violation of Articles 152 and 191(2) and was a direct infringement of Article 176(2) of the Constitution.

For instance, Table 8.1 shows that in the 2003/4 financial year, the total amount of property tax income generated by all district councils in the country was 6,788, shillings compared to 36,526,446 shillings that was generated from graduated tax during the same financial year. In the 2004/5 financial year, property tax generated 3,525,779 shillings compared to 60,038,704 shillings generated from graduated tax over the same period. In the 2005/6 financial year, property tax generated 26,716,387 shillings compared to 10,865,871 shillings from graduated tax over the same period. In the 2006/7 financial year, property tax generated 37,817,156 shillings while graduated tax collection declined to a paltry Shs. 4,429,273. In 2011, property tax generated 31,557,087,952 shillings. Between the 2007/8 and 2010/11 financial years, no revenue was generated from graduated tax.[73]

Figure 8.1 shows how much graduated tax contributed to district councils' revenue before it was suspended. It also shows how the contributions from business licences (or service taxes), which should have been compensated for the revenue loss occasions by the suspension of graduated tax, did not in fact replace the revenue lost. In essence, the table illustrates that district councils depend mainly on revenue sources categorised as 'others'. What is categorised as 'others' mainly refers to revenue from the central government in the form of transfers.

Table 8.2 shows the dependency on intergovernmental transfers and it also shows that district councils consistently raise less revenue than planned.

71 Makara 2009: 312.
72 Ssewanyana & Okidi 2008: 23.
73 The Local Government Finance Commission (LGFC) Fiscal Databank.

Table 8.1 Aggregate revenue

Financial year	*Property tax (Shs.)*	*Graduated tax (Shs.)*
2003/4	6,788,407	36,526,446
2004/5	3,525,779	60,038,704
2005/6	26,716,387	10,865,871
2006/7	37,817,156	4,429,273
2011	31,557,087,952	

Source: Adopted from the Local Government Finance Commission (LGFC) Fiscal databank.

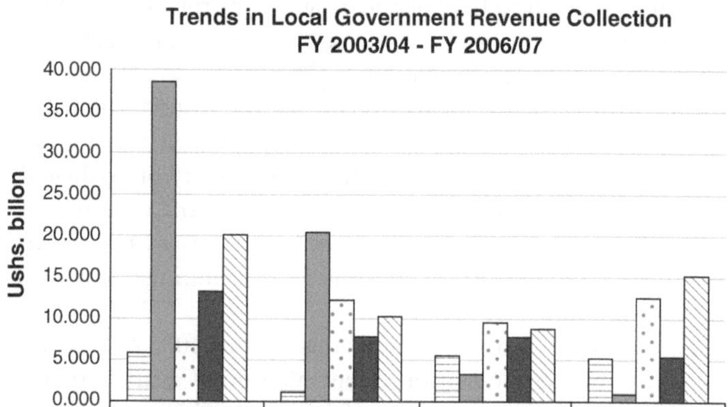

	2003/04	2004/05	2005/06	2006/07
Businesslicences	5.805	1.177	5.582	5.258
Graduated Tax	38.670	20.442	3.325	0.834
Property related duties/fees	6.789	12.255	9.671	12.605
User fees/charges	13.224	7.943	7.930	5.516
Other revenues	20.269	10.201	8.886	15.258

Figure 8.1 Trends in district council revenue generation before and after abolition of graduated tax.

Source: Fiscal decentralisation budget release performance – FY 2008/09 volume I, issue 3.

In Chapter Two, the argument was that local government should have the discretion to determine who pays the tax and the power to spend the revenue derived therefrom. This would likely make communities ensure that local leaders justify their actions to the electorate.[74] The central government's intrusive role in district councils' fiscal autonomy and the overdependence of the district councils on intergovernmental fiscal transfers undermines the ability of decentralisation to enforce accountability, a crucial element necessary for local development. The result is that the local electorate may not easily vote out district councils' elected leaders in cases of poor service delivery. The over-regulation of district councils' taxing authority discourages district councils from pursuing more methods of

74 See Chapter Two § 2.3.1.2. See also generally Oates 1972.

Table 8.2 District councils' revenue and expenditure for 2012/13 financial year

District council	*District councils' total revenue*			*District councils' own revenue*			*% share of district councils' own revenue against total evenue*	
	Budgeted	*Actual*	*(%)*	*Budgeted*	*Actual*	*(%)*	*Budgeted*	*Actual*
	377,998,133	276,927,776	73.3%	25,380,246	22,854,457	90.0%	6.7%	6.0%

Source: Adopted from the Local Government Finance Commission (LGFC) Fiscal databank. These figures are in Uganda shillings and include central government transfers, donations and district councils' 'own' revenues.

raising local revenue. The effect of low district council revenue-generating capacity is the overdependence on central government transfers,[75] which is further discussed below.

8.3 Intergovernmental fiscal transfers

As noted in Chapter Two, most revenues accrue to central governments, resulting in local governments' dependence on intergovernmental fiscal transfers.[76] Intergovernmental fiscal transfers are important because of their ability to redistribute, something that is crucial for local development. It was also argued in Chapter Three that intergovernmental fiscal transfers may limit the exercise of local government discretion and potentially discourage local government revenue mobilisation and investment.[77] Thus, in order to harness the benefits of fiscal transfers while at the same time mitigating its dangers, the process of transfers should be inclusive and aim at redistribution of resources.[78] As noted in Chapter Five, the Odoki Commission made strong recommendations for financially independent local governments.[79] The discussion below demonstrates that this recommendation was never seriously considered by the CA.

8.3.1 Three types of central government transfers

Every year, the President has to address Parliament, proposing the amount of money to be paid out of the Consolidated Fund as unconditional grants, conditional grants and equalisation grants.[80] It is noted that the President is advised by the LGFC.[81]

The Constitution spells out three types of central government fiscal transfer: (a) unconditional grants, (b) conditional grants and (c) equalisation grants.[82]

8.3.1.1 Unconditional grants

An unconditional grant is the minimum grant that the central government pays to the district council to deliver decentralised services.[83] According to the Constitution, unconditional grants serve to deliver decentralised services and,

75 Chapter Three § 3.7.7.
76 Chapter Two § 2.3.1.3.
77 Chapter Three § 3.7.7.
78 Chapter Three § 3.7.8.
79 See Chapter Five § 5.1.2.7.
80 See Article 193 of the Constitution and section 83(1) of the LGA. Article 153(1) of the Constitution defines the term Consolidated Fund' with reference to 'all revenues or other monies raised or received for the purpose of, or on behalf of, or in trust for the Government'.
81 See Chapter Nine § 9.6.2.
82 See Article 193(1) of the Constitution.
83 See Article 193(2) read together with the Seventh Schedule of the Constitution.

unlike other grants, are distributed according to a specific formula.[84] The formula considers the previous financial year's transfer, inflationary trends and the cost of running services.[85] Unconditional grants account for a smaller percentage of the central government transfers. Conditional and equalisation grants account for a larger percentage.[86]

8.3.1.2 Conditional grants

Conditional grants are payments which are made by central government and can only be spent subject to conditions specified in the agreement between the central government and district councils.[87] Strictly speaking, they are not considered part of district council revenue.[88] In fact, conditional grant funds must be separated from other sources of district council revenue in a district council's budget.[89] In addition, conditional grants are accounted for on conditions agreed to between the central government and district council.[90]

8.3.1.3 Equalisation grants

Equalisation grants are payments made to district councils by the central government as a form of subsidy for least developed districts. The purpose of equalisation payments from central government is to ensure uniform delivery of specific services.[91] For example, the central government must ensure that education or health services are uniformly delivered in every district in the country. Hence dis-

84 See Article 193(2) of the Constitution. The Seventh Schedule of the Constitution offers a further explanation for unconditional grants: 'an unconditional grant is equal to the sum of wage and non-wage components. Therefore, the wage components should be adjusted for the wage increase, if any, while the non-wage component is adjusted to the changes in the general price levels'.

85 See Regulation 55(1) of the LGFR.

86 Wash & Ottenoeller 2004: 196. According to Wash & Ottenoeller 2004: 196, in 1997/8 financial year, unconditional grants to district councils accounted for 24% of the district fiscal transfers while conditional grants accounted for 76% of district fiscal transfers. There were no equalisation grants to districts. In the financial year 1998/9 unconditional grants to district councils accounted for 23% of all fiscal transfers, while conditional grants accounted for 78% of all fiscal transfers to district councils. There were also no equalisation grants. In the financial year 1999/2000, unconditional grants accounted for 17% of all fiscal transfers to district councils while conditional grants accounted for 83% of all fiscal transfers to the district councils. Equalisation grants accounted for a mere 0.5% of all the fiscal transfers to district councils. In 2000/1 financial year, unconditional grants accounted for 15% of all fiscal transfers to district councils while conditional grants accounted for 78% of all fiscal transfers to district councils. Equalisation grants accounted for a paltry 0.8% of all fiscal transfers to the district councils.

87 See Article 193(3) of the Constitution.

88 See Regulation 55(1) of the LGFR.

89 See Regulation 55(2) of the LGFR.

90 See Regulation 55(3) of the LGFR.

91 See Regulation 55(4) of the LGFR.

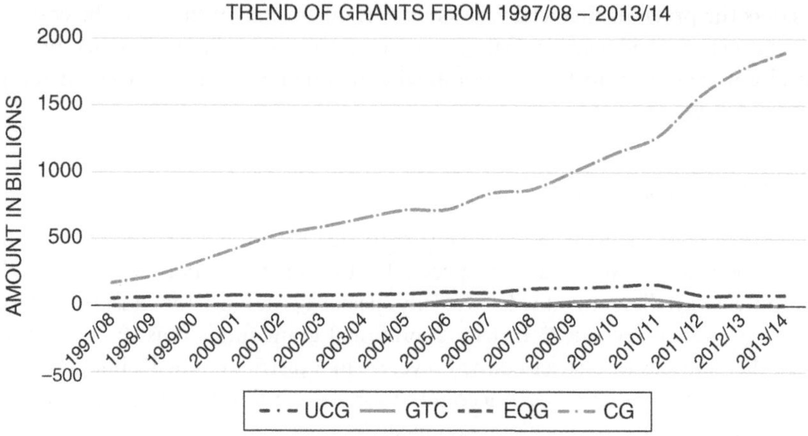

Figure 8.2 Impact of abolition of graduated tax on district council revenue autonomy.

Source: Local Government Financial Commission (LGFC) Fiscal databank 2014. UCG refers to the unconditional central grants, GTC refers to the graduated tax, EQG refers to the equalisation grants, while CG refers to the conditional grants.

trict councils with low incomes must be supplemented with equalisation grants in order to deliver those services. Equalisation grant transfers depend on the degree of economic disparity between the district and the national average standard of a particular service.[92]

8.3.2 Critique

Ugandan analysts argue that district councils are too dependent on conditional grants. They argue that the conditional grant is a form of subtle re-centralisation aimed at reversing the gains of devolution of powers to district councils.[93] Figure 8.2 shows the trend of central government transfers from 1997 to 2014. The trend reveals a stagnation in equalisation grants, a fluctuation in unconditional grants and a steady increase in conditional grants. Implicitly, the figure demonstrates that district councils depend, to a large extent, on central government transfers, rather than their 'own revenue'. The trend also shows a dramatic decline in graduated tax, a source of tax, as explained above, that in the past accounted for about 70% of district councils' revenues.[94]

For instance, the Rukungiri district budget in the 2010/11 financial year indicates that the central government funded about 98% of the budget, while

92 See Article 193(4) of the Constitution.
93 Tusasirwe 2007: 31.
94 Kjær 2005.

the district council's own revenue contribution was 1.6% of the budget.[95] The Rukungiri district council's dependence on the central government transfers compares well in general to central government transfers to district councils throughout the country.[96] The consequence of the suspension of graduated tax has been over-dependence by the district councils on central government grants. This trend undermines the district councils' political autonomy. It is also a direct infringement of Article 176(2)(d) of the Constitution that recommends a sound financial base for district councils.

Shah argues that Uganda's system of intergovernmental transfers offers a significant potential to reduce the trade-offs between district council autonomy and accountability while furthering access to locally preferred goods. The above view is based on three assumptions: the existence of district council planning and budgeting autonomy; the maintenance of proper accounting rules; and the ability to supervise engineering works.[97] The district council capacity to monitor the general provision of services is highly limited given the low educational qualifications of most councillors.[98] Besides, central government's own assessment of the performance of district councils shows serious weakness in adhering to basic accounting and financial management rules.[99] The contribution of the transfers system in deepening a developmental and accountable decentralised system is therefore very much limited by the district councils' institutional weaknesses.

In principle, Articles 176(2)(d) and 194(4)(b) of the Constitution envisage a flawless engagement process between the central government and the LGFC in the fiscal transfer system. However, in practice, there is little evidence to suggest any meaningful engagement with district councils in the determination of the formulae used in the central government transfers.[100] The failure by the LGFC to lobby for greater autonomy in the determination of district council tax rates or the identification of stable district council tax bases, such as electricity, water tariffs and trading licences, has led to its inability to meaningfully engage the central government on serious financial matters.[101]

95 *The New Vision*, 24 June 2010, available at http://www.newvision.co.ug/D/8/18/723830.

96 In her 2011–12 Uganda budget speech, para. 36, the Minister of Finance states:Transfers to Local Governments for purposes of meeting the local government wage bill and recurrent and development expenditures have continued to increase over the years. During the year, total local government transfers are projected to amount to 1,525 billion shillings compared to 1,461 billion shillings in the previous year. Of the total district local government transfers this year, 360 billion shillings is for development expenditure, 248 billion shillings for non-wage recurrent expenditures and 960 billion shillings for salaries and wages.For instance, in the 2012/13 financial year, the central government contribution of the district councils' revenue was 94% compared to the district councils' own revenue contribution of 6%.

97 Shah 2010: 13.

98 Singiza & De Visser 2011: 12.

99 The AAMC&PMLG Synthesis Report 2010: 9–52.

100 Article 194(4)(b) of the Constitution. See also Makara 2009: 183.

101 Lambright 2011: 119–20.

In spite of the advisory role of the LGFC, the central government retains the discretion to determine the amount of money that is allocated to the district councils.[102] Thus, Shah's examination of Uganda's intergovernmental transfer system is very much presumptive. For instance, the author's assessment is built on the assumption that first, district councils are able to adhere to proper accounting rules and second, that district councils have the requisite competency to execute their proper oversight functions in the utilisations of the intergovernmental transfers. This view is, however, disputed by the Uganda government's own assessment report on the performance of the district councils.[103]

8.4 Concluding remarks

This Chapter has outlined the difficulties that district councils face to raise own revenue. The district councils' financial difficulties are linked to the misunderstanding on the part of the central government as to what the Constitution provides regarding the true financial powers of district councils, and what is enacted under the LGA. Thus, the district councils' taxing powers become intertwined with and finally dependent on the central government. The narrowed district councils' financial space ultimately detracts from the overall point of decentralisation in Uganda.

It is submitted that the following are critical for Uganda's district councils' revenue:

- first, the district council's narrow discretion in determining the tax thresholds and exemptions ultimately lowers the overall district council tax yields;
- second, the policy behind the suspension of graduated tax was wrong and calls for its immediate reconsideration and possibly its reinstatement;
- third, the fact that conditional grants account for the majority of the central government transfers limits the district councils' discretion to initiate their own development agenda; and
- fourth, the existing fiscal transfer systems have the ability to improve service delivery and ensure accountability. However, many district councils have so far failed to adhere to the basic rules of accounting and financial management. This limits the ability of these grants to mitigate the dangers that may be associated with the district councils' autonomy.

The chapter therefore calls for immediate reform of the LGA to bring it in conformity with the Constitution that calls for a sound financial base for district councils. The next chapter assesses whether the disadvantages associated with devolution are adequately mitigated by sound intergovernmental relations between central government and district councils.

102 Article 194(4)(c) of the Constitution.
103 The AAMC&PMLG Synthesis Report 2010: 9–52.

9 Intergovernmental relations in Uganda

9.1 Intergovernmental relations in Uganda

As noted in Chapter Three, intergovernmental relations (IGR) can be categorised as both 'soft edge' and 'hard edge'. The 'hard edge' IGR refers mainly to supervision, while 'soft edge' IGR refers to co-operation. The approach to IGR depends on the nature of the decentralisation of powers and functions to the local governments. Where decentralisation takes the form of delegation, 'hard edge' IGR will be pronounced. On the other hand, where decentralisation takes the form of devolution, the 'soft edge' IGR becomes more important.[1]

By and large, IGR in Uganda is grounded in supervision, i.e. the 'hard edge' of IGR, because of the deliberate misunderstanding by the central government of the exact nature of district council powers and functions.

This chapter examines the regulation of district councils' institutions, elections, powers and functions. The chapter also describes the central government monitoring instruments of district councils and questions whether the regulation and monitoring thereof serves the overall objective of decentralisation. Lastly the chapter assesses the role of co-operation as a means of mitigating some of the weaknesses associated with regulation and monitoring in a decentralised system of government.

9.2 Supervision through regulation

9.2.1 Regulation of district council institutions, elections, powers and functions

In Chapter Three, three criteria for the supervision of local governments were noted. These were: predictability; respect for local government autonomy; and proportionality.[2] The discussion below questions whether the supervision of district council institutions, elections, powers and functions through regulation fulfils these criteria.

1 See Chapter Three § 3.8.3.
2 Chapter Three § 3.8.4.

The central government's regulation of district councils' powers is unpredictable. First, district council powers and functions are vaguely defined in that the Constitution provides for district councils' residual functions from the long list of central government powers. Furthermore, the Constitution introduces the doctrine of incidental powers, which creates a legal dilemma because what the LGA provides as the delegated functions of district councils overlaps with the exclusive list of central government competencies. Although Chapter Seven offered a strict interpretation of the doctrine of incidental powers,[3] it remains the case that the regulation of district councils' functions is not predictable.

There is not one single court judgement that deals with the regulation of a district council's institutions, elections, governance or powers by the central government. The attitude appears to be that central government can create as many districts as it deems fit. In addition, the central government regulation of district council elections has tended to favour the central government's political interests rather than the need to promote grassroots democracy. Further, in the absence of the courts' guidance, district council powers have been considerably limited, leaving little room for innovation.

In Chapter Five, it was noted that district councils are unilaterally created or altered.[4] The constitutional and LGA criteria are more often than not circumvented to serve central government's political purposes. The manipulation of district council institutions through the proliferation of many districts is facilitated by the absence of an independent body to rationally consider either splitting an old district or merging more than one. Further, there is no specific injunction on Parliament to seek all the stakeholders' views before a new district is created. Unfeasible districts that have been created with no tangible benefits to local communities and the political stalemate arising from the central government control of former KCC are clear examples of an unpredictable regulation of district council institutions.[5]

In any case, the creation of many districts and the centralisation of Kampala City have not been in line with the overall objective of decentralisation. Whereas the common narrative has been that creating many districts is linked to the desire to bring democracy and development closer to local communities, there is evidence that creating many districts increases the burden on tax-payers.[6] In any case, the political stalemate in Kampala City seems to have undermined the development and democratic prospects of the majority of the people in Kampala. The regulation of district council institutions is not achieving its intended purpose.

In Chapter Six, it was pointed out that district councils are exclusionary to certain social groups such as ethnic minorities.[7] Part of the reason why district council elections are exclusionary and less competitive is that the determination

3 Chapter Seven § 7.4.2.
4 Chapter Five § 5.3.3.
5 Chapter Five § 5.3.11.
6 Chapter Five § 5.3.11.
7 Chapter Six § 6.8.3.

of district council constituencies is not predictable. For instance, whereas Parliament determines district council boundaries, it is the Electoral Commission which determines district council constituencies. Moreover, the adoption of the first-past-the-post electoral system is not only confusing but unpredictable. The result has been that district council electoral outcomes are not legitimate, which undermines the goal of decentralisation.[8] The regulation of district council elections is employed to achieve dominance of the ruling party, and results in intolerance of the expression of different points of view and disrespect of district councils' autonomy. The regulation of district council elections that exclude ethnic minorities therefore works against the democratic and developmental objectives of district councils.

The central government plays an intrusive role in relation to the legislative and administrative powers of district councils. The central government has the discretion to legislate on all the delegated functions of the district councils and in this way may intrude into the district councils' legislative space. The fact that central government appoints the district council's CAO and controls the decision-making process of the DSC reveals the extent of its disregard for district council autonomy.

9.3 Monitoring of district councils

As argued in Chapter Three, monitoring is a form of supervision aimed at promoting and not controlling local governments.[9] In the discussion below, the monitoring roles of Parliament, the Minister of Local Government/Line Ministries, the Office of the Auditor General (OAG), the Inspector General of Government (IGG) and the Resident District Commissioner (RDC) are examined to determine whether the monitoring role of these institutions is predictable and respects the autonomy of district councils and whether their supportive role is proportional to the purpose of decentralisation as discussed in Chapter Three.[10]

9.3.1 Role of Parliament

Parliament plays a critical role in monitoring local governments' accounts. In order to effectively perform its oversight functions, the Constitution calls upon Parliament to establish different committees. The Constitution mandates Parliament to determine the powers, composition and functions of the Parliamentary committees that may be established.[11]

8 Chapter Six § 6.8.
9 Chapter Three § 3.9.2.
10 Chapter Three § 3.8.4.
11 Article 90 of the Constitution.

9.3.1.1 Committee on Local Governments Accounts

On the instruction of Article 90 of Constitution, 12 different committees of Parliament are established, including a 20-member Committee on Local Government Accounts.[12] The 20 members of this committee are appointed on the basis of a party's proportional membership in the House. Subject to Rule 134(6) of the Parliamentary Rules of Procedure, the chairperson and deputy chairperson of the Committee on Local Government Accounts have to be members of the official opposition party in Parliament.[13] This is to ensure that their reports are free from the ruling party's political control. In my view, the above provision is highly commendable as it safeguards the oversight role of Parliament from political manipulation. Article 90(2) of the Constitution provides for Parliament to make the rules of procedure and specify its own powers and functions.

The Parliamentary Committee on Local Government Accounts has the power to summon any person holding public office to submit memoranda or appear before it to give evidence. In addition, the Committee has the powers of the High Court insofar as it may summon witnesses and order the production of documents.[14]

The Committee has the power to examine the audited accounts showing the appropriation of sums granted by Parliament to district councils. Most public accounts committees of Parliament have vigorously scrutinised different public accounts and, in some cases, ensured that monies lost are recovered. On a number of occasions the Committee detected the misappropriation of district council finances by district council administrators and responded by making recommendations, threatening to arrest officials or withhold district council funds to ensure compliance with central government guidelines on public accountability.[15] However, given the fact that those parliamentary committees are dominated by the ruling party members, credible recommendations involving high profile politicians often do not result in recovery of lost government monies.[16] The central government may be tempted to 'over-monitor' district councils by using the Committee, for example, to withhold central government transfers to district councils.[17] However, the fact that the Committee's chair and deputy chair are members of the opposition minimises the possibility political manipulation on the

12 See Rule 131(1) of the Parliamentary Rules of Procedure 2006.

13 Article 90 of the Constitution provides for the appointment of the different committees of Parliament necessary for the discharge of its functions. Pursuant to Article 90, Rule 155 of the Rules of Procedure of the Parliament of Uganda, 2006.

14 Article 90(3)(c) of the Constitution.

15 Goodluck & Wasswa 'Katuntu clashes with Kabale district chief', *The New Vision*, 25 May 2010, available at http://www.newvision.co.ug/D/8/18/720751. Nalugo M 'MPs order arrest of ex-Kampala officials', *The Daily Monitor*, 7 July 2010, available at http: //www.monitor.co.ug/News/National/-/688334/953510/-/x20py7/-/index.html.

16 'Nine corruption scandals to look back' *The New Vision*, available at http://www.newvision.co.ug/mobile/Detail.aspx?NewsID=637209&CatID=1 (accessed 13 June 2014).

17 See detailed discussion on the central government transfers in Chapter 8 § 8.3.12.

part of the central government. In any case, it is Parliament and not the central government that may order the withholding of central government transfers.[18]

9.3.2 Monitoring by the Minister of Local Government/ Line Ministries

9.3.2.1 Legal basis

Article 176(2)(a) of the Constitution calls upon the central government to mutually interact with district councils in their developmental and democratic roles.[19] Arguably, the Constitution envisages that the central government may put in place appropriate operating guidelines in order to determine which particular powers and functions may be efficiently performed by district councils and which ones may not. In that respect, an obligation on the central government to co-ordinate district council powers and functions through central government agencies such as the Minister of Local Government (and Line Ministries) is inferred. Section 1(1)(k) of the LGA defines the term 'Minister' as the 'minister responsible for local government'.[20]

9.3.2.2 Mandate

The role of the Ministry of Local Government/Line Ministries is to inspect, to provide technical assistance and to establish operating standards for the delivery of services by district councils.[21]

There are numerous instances where the Minister of Local Governments/ Line Ministries will monitor district councils. For example, in respect of the process for removal of senior political leaders, the Minister of Local Government 'must be satisfied' that the procedures for removing district council elected leaders have been complied with.[22] In addition, the Minister of Local Government 'must ensure' that district council by-laws are certified by the Attorney-General, and adopted by following the prescribed procedure within the district council's legislative residual authority.[23] Further, the Minister of Local Government/Line

18 See Chapter Five § 5.2.2.1.

19 Article 176(2)(a) of the Constitution provides: '...the system shall be such as to ensure that functions, powers and responsibilities are devolved and transferred from the Government to local government units in a coordinated manner'. See also § 9.5.1 of this chapter.

20 However, section 2 of the Interpretation Act Cap 3 expands on the definition of the term 'Minister' to mean any minister of the central government. Arguably, then, the term 'Minister' includes Line Ministries.

21 See sections 95 and 97 of the LGA.

22 See section 11(6C), 14(2A)(4) and 68 of the LGA.

23 See section 38 of the LGA. Section 38 of the LGA requires the legislative powers of district council to be subject to 'any other laws made by Parliament'. Among other limitations, the LGA requires the Attorney-General through the Minister of Local Government to certify that any proposed district council by-law be consistent with the Constitution 'and any other law enacted by Parliament' before it can have any legislative force. Arguably, the LGA's limi-

Ministries 'must ensure' that the central government policies,[24] audit[25] and procurement rules[26] are complied with. For instance, under section 97 of the LGA, the central government is called upon to 'monitor and coordinate Government initiatives and policies as they apply to local governments', including the provision of advisory services, technical support and establishment of minimum standards of service delivery. Further, section 98 of the LGA empowers the central government ministries to inspect district councils' books of accounts so as to foster the rule of law, good governance and to eliminate corruption and abuse of office. Section 94F(1) of the LGA also mandates the Minister of Local Government to determine sanctions for contravening procurement rules under the LGA. These may include a penalty, forfeiture and/or compensation, severe reprimand, interdiction, dismissal and dissolution of contracts committee.[27]

The words 'must be satisfied' import notions of compulsion and control into the role of the Minister which is quite distinct from a supportive role. A type of 'monitoring' whose aim is to ensure that central government policies are complied with connotes intrusive supervision and little respect for district council autonomy. The ultimate result of the above ministerial monitoring is that the central government policies must always prevail.

There is an obligation on the Minister of Local Government/Line Ministries while exercising their monitoring mandate to promote and foster respect for the rule of law.[28] Thus, monitoring that involves the usurpation of the district councils' powers and functions would be unlawful. In addition, monitoring by the Minister of Local Government/Line Ministries must be geared towards the promotion of natural justice: in other words, it must be fair, just and promote good governance. Transparency and accountability ought to be respected in any act of monitoring by the Minister of Local Government/Line Ministries. Rather than enhance transparency and accountability, monitoring by ministries has in fact tended to undermine the good governance practices in district councils. For example, the education department guidelines for district councils on the use of the universal primary education (UPE) funds call for, among other things, timely provision of accountability and participatory formulation of UPE budgets[29] when those very guidelines were susceptible to local political manipulations and non-adherence to proper accounting rules.[30] In the discussion below, the roles of other state agencies are also examined.

---

tation of district councils' legislative powers is open to challenge as it automatically dilutes district councils' constitutional legislative powers. See also section 39 of the LGA.

24 See sections 96 and 97 of the LGA.

25 See section 98(2) of the LGA.

26 See section 94(F) of the LGA.

27 Sections 94F (2) and (3) of the LGA

28 See section 97 of the LGA.

29 See Ministry of Education and Sports *Guidelines; policy, planning and roles and responsibilities of stakeholders in the implementation of Universal Primary Education (UPE) for district and urban councils* Kampala: Ministry of Education and Sports 2008: 10.

30 Nambalirwa 2010: 34–7.

9.3.3 The role of the OAG, the IGG, etc. as monitoring tools

Section 98(1) of the LGA[31] highlights the role of 'other State organs' in inspecting and monitoring district councils. Investigative organs such as the Office of the Auditor General (OAG), the Inspector General of Government (IGG) and the police, on the one hand, and the Resident District Commissioner (RDC), on the other, come into the picture.

The legal basis and mandate of each of the organs are examined below.

9.3.4 Office of the Auditor General

The Constitution provides that the OAG is headed by the Auditor General, appointed by the President with the approval of Parliament.[32]

The mandate of the OAG is to audit and report on all public accounts, including district councils.[33] The role of the OAG is to conduct financial and value-for-money audits in respect of any project involving public funds by district councils, and report to Parliament annually.[34] In terms of regulation 171 of the Local Government Financial and Accounting Regulations (LGFAR), the OAG is required to submit a copy of report to Parliament, the Minister of Finance, the Minister of Local Government, the district council to which the audit relates, the district council Public Accounts Committee, the Local Government Finance Commission, the IGG and the RDC.

The OAG is obliged to ensure that the district council financial and accounting regulations are complied with.[35] As already mentioned, section 97 of the LGA places an obligation on the central government to provide technical support to district councils by establishing the minimum standards of service delivery. So within the context of section 97 of the LGA, the role of the OAG is to provide support to district councils in the areas of accountability and good governance.

9.3.4.1 Practice of OAG auditing district council accounts

In the year ending 30 June 2013, the Office of the Auditor General carried out financial audits in 111 district councils. The financial audits included the audit

31 Section 98(1) of the LGA provides: 'The inspection of local governments by line Ministries and other State organs authorised by the law shall promote adherence to the law and without limiting the generality of the foregoing shall – (a) promote and foster adherence to the rule of law and principles natural justice and good governance; (b) foster the elimination of corruption and abuse of office'.

32 Articles 163(1) and 163(2)(a) of the Constitution. The Auditor General must be a qualified accountant of not less than 15 years' standing and of high moral character and proven integrity.

33 Article 163(3)(a) of the Constitution.

34 Article 163(3)(b) of the Constitution; Annual Report of the Auditor General for the Year Ended 30 June 2009 Volume 3 Local Authorities p 7–47.

35 Regulation 5(1) of the LGFAR.

opinions of the previous 2010/11 and 2012/13 audit years.[36] According to the audit report, unqualified audit opinions on district councils increased from 36% from in 2009/10 to 45% in 2010/11, dropped to 32% in 2011/2013 and then increased slightly to 37.4% in 2012/2013. Qualified opinions decreased from 62% in 2009/10, to 50% in 2010/2011, increased again 62% in 2011/12 and decreased again to 60% in 2012/13. It is noted that the disclaimer to these audit opinions increased from 4% in 2010/11, increased to 5% in 2011/12 and reduced to 2.3% in 2012/13. At the same time, the adverse audit opinions remained unchanged between 2010/11 and 2011/12 at 1% but reduced to 0.3% in 2012/13.[37]

The audit report also documents district councils' procurement anomalies and poor accountability of funds. For example, the audit report shows that of all 18, 264,166,478 shillings worth of procured goods and services, 51.4% breached contract procedures, 35% showed contract management weaknesses, 10.7% lacked contract files, while 2.8% worth of procured good and services were altered without authorisation.[38] In addition the report shows that out of 17,040,364,920 shillings spent, 49% was categorised as 'outstanding administrative advances', 31.4% was categorised as 'incompletely vouched expenditure', 12.6% was categorised as 'doubtful expenditure', while 7% was categorised as 'un vouched expenditure'.[39]

Arguably the above audit report is a useful instrument for intergovernmental accountability in that evidence of culpability on the part of district administrators or district political leaders may trigger a criminal investigation resulting into prosecution in the courts of law. The more pertinent question becomes whether such an audit report may be used by local citizens and civil society to hold district councils' accounting officials and local political leaders accountable?

The above instruments may be a useful tool for enforcing local accountability in that local citizens can use evidence of financial abuse and impropriety as presented by the audit report in district councils to either recall their representatives, or cause the impeachment of district council chairpersons. The risk of backlash from the central government in the recall process of district councillors, and the onerous procedure of removing the district council chairpersons from office was discussed in detail in Chapter Six.[40] It is unlikely that the audit reports may be a reliable instrument to enforce local democratic accountability in a district council. Civil societies may rely on the audit reports on district councils to create

36 Office of the Auditor General 2013: 2.

37 Office of the Auditor General 2013: 3. According to Garner 2009: 1202, an unqualified audit report refers to an audit opinion made with minimal hindrances, stating that the financial statements of an entity fairly represent a true picture of its books of accounts and confirms that a business entity complied with generally accepted accounting principles and laws.

38 Office of the Auditor General 2013: 8.

39 Office of the Auditor General 2013: 9.

40 See detailed discussion on the vacation of district council political office bearers in Chapter Six § 6.8 and § 6.10.3.

public awareness of the extent of financial abuse and mismanagement in district councils. Arguably, public awareness on the district councils' financial abuse and mismanagement has the potential to translate into 'protest votes' against elected district council leaders in future elections. The limited number of civil society organisations in district councils through the country and their minimal interaction with local communities[41] limits their ability to use audit reports to enforce accountability in district councils.

9.3.5 The Inspector General of Government

9.3.5.1 Legal basis

The Constitution provides for the IGG and deputy IGG who are appointed by the President with the approval of Parliament.[42] The Inspectorate of Government Act (IGA) provides for the Inspectorate of Government (IG), consisting of the IGG and two Deputy Inspectors General.[43] The IGA provides for ten functions of the IGG.[44]

9.3.5.2 Mandate

The IGA establishes the office of the IGG with the mandate to inspect instances of corruption and misuse of power by government officials. The mandate of the IGG is to ensure adherence to the rule of law, combating corruption and abuse of office, and promoting fair and efficient governance in public offices.[45] The Constitution bestows on the IGG the powers to supervise and investigate malpractices by officers and leaders irrespective of whether they are employed in the public service.[46] In addition, the IGG has the mandate to educate members of the public 'about the values of constitutionalism'. The IGG reports to Parliament once every six months.[47]

41 See Lambright 2011: 246–54.
42 Article 223(5) of the Constitution. The IGA repeats the provisions of Article 233(5) of the Constitution in relation to the qualifications, appointment and term of office of the IGG. See sections 3(3), (4) and (5) and 4(3) of the IGA. The IGG must be qualified to be appointed as a High Court judge. The IGG must be a Ugandan, of high moral character, proven integrity, considerable experience, demonstrated competence and high calibre in the conduct of public affairs.
43 Section 3(1) of the Inspectorate of Government Act (IGA) cited as Act 5 of 2002.
44 Section 8(1) of the IGA.
45 Article 225(1) of the Constitution. Section 14(6) of the IGGA. section 29 of the LCA.
46 Articles 225(2) and 226 of the Constitution. Article 230(1) provides: 'The Inspectorate of Government shall have power to investigate, cause investigation, arrest, cause arrest, prosecute or cause prosecution in respect of cases involving corruption, abuse of authority or of public office'. Additionally, Article 233 of the Constitution provides for the Leadership Code of Conduct as the main instrument for enforcement of good behaviour by every public leader, and bestows the obligation to enforce the Code on the IGG.
47 Article 231 of the Constitution.

Under the Leadership Code Act (LCA), the IGG may receive complaints relating to a breach of the Leadership Code of Conduct,[48] and is mandated to 'inquire into, or cause the complaint to be inquired into'.[49] Specifically, the IGG has powers to investigate officers and leaders of district councils or committees in order to 'enforce the Leadership Code of Conduct'.[50] As mentioned earlier, the LCA generally provides for the minimum standard of behaviour or conduct of leaders and defines a 'leader' as 'a person holding any of the government offices specified in the First Schedule to this Code'.[51] The LCA also defines 'Government' to include district councils.[52] In enforcing the Leadership Code of Conduct, the IGG receives and examines complaints and instances of corrupt practice that breach the Leadership Code of Conduct. The IGG must also investigate and report on any alleged 'high handed, outrageous and infamous or disgraceful conduct' of a leader.[53] This implies that the IGG decision is a political rather than a quasi-judicial one.

9.3.5.3 The role of the IGG under the Leadership Code Act.

The LCA provides that once the inquiry is completed, the IGG is obliged to report the outcome of the inquiry to the 'authorised person' requiring such person to implement his or her decision.[54] The term 'authorised person' is defined by section 2 of the LCA to mean 'a person or body authorised by law to discipline the leader in relation to whom the expression is used'. The above provision suggests that the monitoring role of the IGG can amount to an intervention, given that, over and above his or her power of inquiry, he or she must also demand that the outcome of her inquiry is implemented by the disciplining officer. Yet existing jurisprudence, discussed below, suggests that the monitoring role of the IGG does not include a power to intervene in district councils.

9.3.5.4 The High Court's approach to the role of the IGG

Faced with numerous complaints against district councils by members of the public,[55] the IGG's initial response has tended to exceed the monitoring mandate of the Inspectorate of Government. In its most controversial recommendation, the IGG directed a Municipal Council to dismiss an elected political official.

48 Section 18(1) of the LCA.
49 Section 18(2) of the LCA.
50 Sections 9(k) and 8(1)(d) of the IGA.
51 Section 2(1) of the LCA.
52 Section 2(1) of the LCA.
53 Section 3 of the LCA. Section 2(1) of the LCA defines 'Minister' to mean 'the Minister responsible for ethics and integrity'.
54 Section 19(1) of the LCA.
55 The Inspectorate of Government, *Report to Parliament July–December 2007* (2007): 8.

This recommendation was challenged in the High Court in the case of *Hajji Mohammed Baswari Kezaala v The Inspector General of Government and Others.*[56]

In this case, the Jinja Municipal Council's resolution, which adopted the IGG's report and recommendations, and the interdiction/suspension of the Municipal Mayor was challenged. The main grounds of the application were that the Mayor was, by a resolution of Jinja Municipal Council, removed from office despite the existence of two court orders restraining them from implementing the recommendations of the IGG. There was evidence that the IGG in fact pressurised the Jinja Municipal Council to implement its recommendations.[57]

The High Court restated the oversight role of the powers of the IGG in its investigative and inquiry powers over public bodies such as district councils. The view of the High Court was that in a judicial review the court's role is to ensure that a lawful authority is not abused by unfair treatment.[58] The High Court was 'concerned with the process by which the decision was reached – whether the decision-making authority exceeded it powers, committed an error of law, committed a breach of natural justice etc'.[59]

The High Court concluded that it was inappropriate, illegal and oppressive of the IGG to pressurise the Jinja Municipal Council to implement her decision to remove the Mayor from office contrary to an existing court order.[60]

The High Court nullified the resolution of the Jinja Municipal Council to remove the Mayor and set aside the report of the IGG.[61]

9.3.5.5 *Comment*

The judgement generally reviewed and nullified the decision of the IGG to remove an elected official of a municipal council. The decision demonstrates that the monitoring of district councils must follow the law to the letter. It also shows that institutions that monitor district councils have to be checked by independent bodies to guard against abuse of their monitoring powers. In an earlier decision of the Constitutional Court on the powers of the IGG, a different approach was adopted to the effect that the IGG has no powers at all to remove an elected office bearer from office.[62] However, the correct position is that the IGG cannot recommend an elected district leader to vacate office.

56 *Hajji Mohammed Baswari Kezaala v The Inspector General of Government and others Miscellaneous application No.28 of 2009.*
57 *Hajji Mohammed Baswari Kezaala* p 10.
58 *Hajji Mohammed Baswari Kezaala* p 12.
59 *Hajji Mohammed Baswari Kezaala* p 17.
60 *Hajji Mohammed Baswari Kezaala* p 16.
61 *Hajji Mohammed Baswari Kezaala* p 27.
62 See *John Ken-Lukyamuzi vs. The Attorney General and Another Constitutional Court Petition No. 19 of 2006 – 3/26/2007.*

9.3.6 Case study of the monitoring role of the IGG in respect of district councils

The IGG has made numerous interventions in district councils. In fact, according to the IGG report of 2007, out of a total of 991 complaints received by the IGG in 2007, 16.9% related to local government leaders, i.e. district chairpersons, CAOs, RDCs, CFOs and district councillors. In the same report, 6.7% of the complaints related to Municipal Councils/Town Councils, 4.4% of the complaints related to other lower councils and 2.1% of the complaints related to subcounty chiefs. Thus, district councils generally had a combined share of 30.1% of the number of complaints.[63] The IGG report found widespread poor accountability of funds, shoddy construction work, poor maintenance of facilities and use of false accounting systems that had long been abolished.[64] The big number of complaints received by the IGG indicates two things: one the one hand, the big number of complaints reported to the IGG shows a considerable level of public trust in the institution of the IGG to address corruption related cases. On the other hand, the ever increasing number of complaints reported to the IGG demonstrates its institutional weakness to fight corruption and abuse of office, as it is mainly used by the central government as an instrument of intervention in district councils. The following discussion assesses the monitoring role of the RDC in the district councils.

9.3.7 The role of the of Resident District Commissioner (RDC)

The history and metamorphosis of the office of the RDC have already been examined.[65] During the CA debates, various reasons were advanced for and against the constitutional status of the office of the RDC. While it was clear that suspicion remained as to the true essence of the office of the RDC, the consensus was that there was need for a bridge to link the district councils with the central government.[66] In this part of the chapter, the role of the RDC is analysed not only as a 'link' between the central government and district councils, but also as a means to oversee district councils' service delivery.[67]

63 The Inspectorate of Government, *Report to Parliament July–December 2007* (2007): 9.

64 The Inspectorate of Government, *Report to Parliament July–December 2007* (2007): 10.

65 See Chapter Four § 4.9.3.

66 CA debates p 3962–84.

67 Azfar, Kahkonen & Meagher 2001: 49. See also Article 203(2) of the Constitution and Section 70(2) of the LGA. The LGA provides that the qualifications of an RDC, as a central government employee, must be similar to those of a Member of Parliament. An RDC must be a citizen of Uganda. He or she must be beyond reproach, with considerable experience and demonstrated competency. The RDC is appointed by the President.

9.3.7.1 Mandate

The primary function of the RDC is 'to monitor the implementation of central and local government services in the district'.[68] In addition, the Constitution vests the President with the discretion to assign to the RDC any other functions with the approval of Parliament.[69]

The RDC represents the President in a district[70] and co-ordinates the central government's services in a district.[71] Further, the RDC advises the chairperson of the district 'on matters of national importance', such as plans and programmes in the district.[72] In addition, the RDC monitors and inspects the activities of a district council[73] and educates local communities about the central government's programmes.[74] Furthermore, the RDC may advise the chairperson of a district council to initiate special audits and investigations by both the police and the OAG.[75] The RDC may also prompt the IGG to investigate instances of mismanagement or abuse of office.[76] The RDC checks whether a district council follows central government policies and therefore ensures that a district council's policies tow the central government line.[77]

9.3.7.2 Assessment of the RDC as an instrument of monitoring

The RDCs have kept most local governments' elected leaders under constant watch.[78] Whereas the existing legal framework appears to grant the RDC the requisite competency to perform their monitoring functions, a closer examination of the credentials and track records of many RDCs indicates a clear misunderstanding of the true essence of monitoring.

It is submitted that a number of RDCs do not have the appropriate qualifications to carry out their proper oversight functions, a concern voiced by the donor community (development partners), civil society and the media in Uganda.[79] Unfortunately, the reality is that in most cases the criteria for appointment of any person as a RDC is limited to their political 'credentials' and support for the

68 Article 203(3)(a) of the Constitution. Azfar *et al.* in Bardhan *et al.* 2006: 231.
69 Article 203(3)(c) of the Constitution.
70 Section 71(1)(a) of the LGA.
71 Section 71(1)(b) of the LGA.
72 Section 71(1)(c) of the LGA.
73 Section 71(1)(d) of the LGA.
74 Section 71(2)(a) of the LGA.
75 Section 71(2)(b) and (c) of the LGA.
76 Section 71(2)(d) of the LGA. It is noted that under the Constitution the OAG and the IGG are independent and are therefore not subject to directives from any person.
77 Section 71(2)(e) of the LGA.
78 Kiyaga & Olum 2009: 30.
79 Matsiko M & Mubatsi A 'New Districts and the Paradox of Taking Services to the People', *The Independent*, 17 May 2010, available at http://www.independent.co.ug/index.php/news/news-analysis/79-news-analysis/2916-new-districts-and-the-paradox-of-taking-services-to-the-people.

ruling party.[80] Hence, the focus of the RDC is on political support mobilisation for the ruling party, rather than carrying out oversight functions.[81] The result has been that increasingly the RDC is viewed as an instrument of central government hegemony in district councils, rather than as an instrument of monitoring as part of IGR.[82] For example the RDCs are now politically encouraged to 'vet guests on radio talk shows to take care of security in their jurisdiction ... if RDCs "sufficiently" suspect a guest is going to make statements with a negative bearing on security, they should block such a speaker from accessing a radio'.[83]

Thus, the RDCs are used as instruments for curtailing individual civil liberties in district councils, rather than for monitoring district council performance. In the past, a district council was vested with the power to recommend to the President the removal of an RDC from office.[84] The current Constitution, in its amended form,[85] no longer includes the power of the district council to recommend the removal of an RDC by the President, emphasising the central government's control of the RDC's actions in a district council. If the RDC is to monitor the implementation of the central government's and district council's service delivery, he or she must have the requisite skills and experience to do so. It is recommended that the academic qualifications of the RDC should be increased to that of a degree.

9.3.8 Reporting systems in local government

The legal basis for the provision of reporting on the district councils' performance is found in section 97(1)(d) of the LGA, which calls for the establishment of the minimum standards of service delivery by every sector ministry. In addition, section 98 of the LGA calls for the promotion of the rule of law, good governance and elimination of corruption through monitoring and inspection of district councils by line ministries.[86]

80 See *Amos Twinomujuni v The Attorney General & Another* (CIVIL Suit No. 0413 Of 2005) [2009] UGHC 145 (23 January 2009), where the RDC was sued by a Court of Appeal judge for alleging that the judge shared money from suits against the government with opposition politicians. See also 'Abaramuzi n'enkomba za DP-RDC Mwesigye' *Orumuri Newspaper* 5–7 July 2004. See also Azfar, Kahkonen & Meagher 2001: 55.

81 See Oloka-Onyango 2007: 39, who explains that the fact that RDCs are no longer civil servants but politicians implies that their functions are no longer technical in nature but rather of a political kind. See also *Rtd.Col.Dr.Kizza Besigye v Electoral commission, Yoweri Kaguta Museveni* (Election Petition No.1 Of 2006) [2007] UGSC 24 (31 January 2007) per Justice Odoki, CJ, where the Chief Justice condemned the partisan role of RDCs in Presidential elections.

82 Azfar in Bardhan 2006: 234.

83 Mulondo 'RDCs can vet radio talk show guests, says minister', *The Daily Monitor*, 24 September 2010, available at http://www.monitor.co.ug/News/National/-/688334/1017132/-/cnli3ez/-/index.html (accessed 25 September 2010).

84 Section 73 of the LGA.

85 Article 203 of the Constitution.

86 See also generally the LG (FA) R SI 243–15.

Three policy documents form the basis of reporting systems in local government in Uganda. These are:

- the Decentralisation Policy Strategic Framework;[87]
- the revised Framework for Monitoring and Evaluation[88] within the context of the Joint Annual Review of Decentralisation (JARD);[89] and
- the Annual Assessment of Minimum Conditions and Performance Measures for Local Governments (AAMC&PMLG) or the penalty/reward reporting scheme.[90]

These policy documents lay down parameters of reporting by district councils to the central government.

9.3.8.1 Reporting under the decentralisation policy framework

The legal basis for the DPSF is found in the eight directive principles of the state discussed in Chapter Seven.[91] The DPSF is a collection of different development policy interventions in decentralisation. It provides a mechanism for coordination through improved systems and effective reporting mechanisms on decentralisation in line with national development priorities. The DPSF is located in the Poverty Eradication Action Plan (PEAP),[92] which is Uganda's development strategy designed along the lines of United Nations Millennium Development Goals (UNMDGs).[93] The PEAP is founded on five principles: (a) micro-economic discipline; (b) improved productivity through competitiveness; (c) peace-building and disaster management; (d) human rights and democracy; and (e) human development through education.[94] Under the DPSF, these principles are reporting indices of compliance for every district council. The adoption of the PEAP

87 Ministry of local Government *Decentralisation Policy Strategic Framework* (2006).

88 The Revised Framework for Monitoring and Evaluation (M&E) of the Future of JARD (2008), Local Government International Consultancy Division.

89 See the Joint Annual Review of Decentralisation (JARD) 2009 under the theme: 'Meeting the Millennium Development Goals and Targets: The Critical Role of Local Governments' *New Vision*, available at http://www.newvision.co.ug/D/526/538/703831 (accessed 20 April 2010).

90 The Annual Assessment of Minimum Conditions and Performance Measures for Local Governments (AAMC&PMLG) Synthesis Report 2010.

91 Chapter Seven § 7.2.2.

92 The Ministry of Finance and Planning and Economic Development Poverty Eradication Action Plan (2004/5–2007/8).

93 The UNMDGs benchmarks are: to eradicate extreme poverty and hunger; to achieve universal primary education; to promote gender equality and empowerment of women; to reduce child mortality; to improve maternal health; to combat HIV/AIDS, malaria and other diseases; to promote sustainable development of the environment; and to develop a global partnership for development.

94 The Decentralisation Policy Strategic Framework (2006) Ministry of Local Government, Kampala p 4–5.

principles in the DPSF arose from the need for a simple, coherent mechanism for assessing district council performance.

The DPSF was published ten years after the promulgation of the 1995 Constitution.[95] The DPSF is the first comprehensive policy document for decentralisation in Uganda. Between 2006 and 2009, reporting under the DPSF was on a yearly interval. The fact that there is no specific interval under which reporting under the DPSF must take place renders its contribution to monitoring district councils rather unpredictable and difficult to assess.

9.3.9 Joint review of decentralisation

The DPSF calls on different district council stakeholders to jointly assess the performance of the district councils. On the basis of the DPSF, a joint review penal was established made up of key decentralisation stakeholders, comprising Ministries, Departments and Agencies (MDAs), Local Governments (LGs), Local Government Associations (LGAs), Civil Society Organisations (CSOs), Non-Governmental Organisations (NGOs), Development Partners and the Private Sector. It is noted that the JARD is not legally provided for. The legal status of the JARD may pose challenges for reporting on district councils given that the donor countries (development partners) and NGOs are not the authorised oversight institutions under the LGA.

Under JARD, it is the role of the Minister of Local Government/line ministries to assess whether the performance of a district council is in line with DPSF/PEAP benchmarks. JARD members must determine the common challenges that affect district councils' performance in the light of the five principles of PEAP.[96]

The tasks carried out by the JARD panel include the following: to assess the implementation of the decentralisation policy and review the performance of various stakeholders; to identify the challenges facing district councils and propose viable solutions; to identify strategies to monitor and refine the implementation of the decentralisation policy; and to review the impact of other government policies on the decentralisation programme.[97]

9.3.9.1 Penalty/reward scheme

> The joint review on the performance of district council is a corrective measure geared towards motivating district councils. The annual assessment of district councils is used by the central government to release funds meant for poverty reduction and simultaneously enhancing district councils' ability to

95 Chapter Seven § 7.1.3.

96 See JARD 2009.

97 See JARD 2009 under the theme: 'Meeting the Millennium Development Goals and Targets: The Critical Role of Local Governments'. See also *The Revised Framework for Monitoring and Evaluation (M&E) of the Future of JARD (2008)*, Local Government International Consultancy Division: 9.

> spend and raise revenue. The central government is then able to determine whether district councils are able to comply with the central government financial management and accounting rules. At the same time, district councils are vested with a discretion to spend central government grants according local development priorities.[98]

District councils' AAMC&PMLG is a penalty/reward scheme that is used to assess the performance of district councils annually.[99] Under this scheme, all district councils are annually examined in relation to common performance criteria adopted by an *ad hoc* National Assessment Team (NAT). Although the Ministry of Local Government is the leading agency of the assessment process, members of the NAT are drawn from district councils, line ministries, government institutions and civil society.[100]

The AAMC&PMLG measures the extent of compliance with the legal provisions relating to district councils; the district councils' capacity to manage development funds; the level of district capacity building; the ability of a district council to promote good administrative and service delivery practices; the ability of the district council to meet national sector specific targets and standards; and the level of downward accountability and closer co-ordination.[101]

As already stated, the penalty/reward scheme is the system of assessment where the NAT annually assesses the performance of district councils. The outcome of the performance assessment is then used to reward or penalise districts by either releasing more or withholding intergovernmental funding.

The NAT's performance measure may either be 'reward', 'static' or 'penalty'. District councils that efficiently utilise the funds under PEAP are rewarded with more funds in the next financial year while districts that fail to utilise the PEAP funds are penalised with a reduction in the amount of funds in the next financial year.[102] The Uganda's penalty/reward scheme is similar to what Shah describes as an output-based grant system (performance-oriented transfers). The output-based grant system is now common in what is generally referred to as the new public management (NPM) framework that places emphasis on performance.[103] According to Shah,

> [s]uch a managerial focus reinforces joint ownership and accountability of the principal and the agent in achieving shared goals by highlighting terms of mutual trust.[104]

98 The AAMC&PMLG Synthesis Report 2010: 16.
99 The AAMC&PMLG Synthesis Report 2010: 7. According to the executive summary of this report, the annual assessment of local governments is now in its ninth year. At its commencement, the main focus was on implementation of phase I of the LGDP.
100 The AAMC&PMLG Synthesis Report 2010: 6.
101 See the Objectives of the AAMC&PMLG Synthesis Report 2010: 8.
102 The AAMC&PMLG Synthesis Report 2010: 19.
103 Shah 2010: 5.
104 Shah 2010: 6.

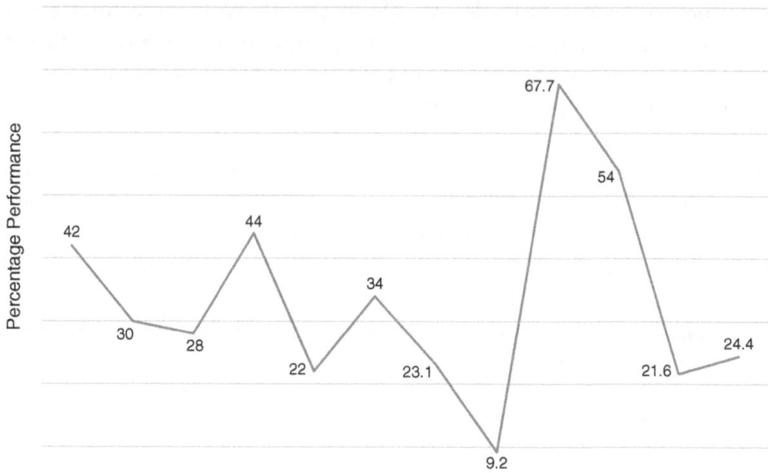

	Districts Councils			Municipal Councils			Sub County Councils			Municipal Divisions		
	Good Performance	Static Performance	Penalised	Good Performance	Static Performance	Penalised	Good Performance	Static Performance	Penalised	Good Performance	Static Performance	Penalised
—— Series1	42	30	28	44	22	34	23.1	9.2	67.7	54	21.6	24.4

Figure 9.1 Percentage performance of district, municipal, subcounty and divisions (2006–2009).

Source: MOLG *Annual Assessment of Minimum Conditions and Performance Measures for Local Governments 2009: Synthesis Report* pp 9–52.

The scheme provides incentives for good performance and sanctions for poor performance. There is evidence that highly performing districts have in the past been rewarded with more central government funds.[105]

9.3.9.2 Penalty/reward scheme findings

The discussion below illustrates annual compliance with the minimum conditions of performance by district councils in Uganda in 2009 on the one hand (Figure 9.1), and their cumulative trend of compliance with the minimum conditions of performance over a period of three years, on the other (Figure 9.2). The aim of presenting the above information is to show that whereas few district councils have complied with minimum conditions, a bigger number of district councils have totally failed to comply with the minimum conditions. Further, the information shows that between 2006 and 2008, district councils' compliance with the minimum conditions drastically declined, but stabilised between 2008

105 Lambright 2011: 39.

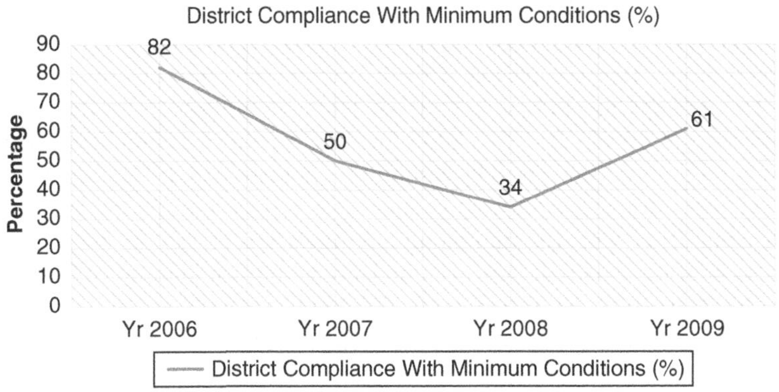

Figure 9.2 Performance trends in district councils.

Source: MOLG *Annual Assessment of Minimum Conditions and Performance Measures for Local Governments 2009: Synthesis Report* p 12.

and 2009. The stabilisation in performance demonstrates the positive contribution of the penalty/reward scheme.

For instance, the performance of 80 districts, 13 municipalities, five city divisions and 1006 subcounties and town councils from 2006 to 2009 shows a less than average level of performance.[106] Of the 80 district councils assessed, only 42% were rewarded with more funds for good performance, 30% were static, meaning there was no improvement and hence no funding was extended to them, while 28% were penalised meaning that they were subject to withholding of their funds. Of the 13 municipal councils assessed, 44% were rewarded, 22% were static and 34% were penalised. Of all the subcounty councils assessed, only 23.1% were rewarded, 9.2% were static and 67.7% were penalised. Of the 37 municipal divisions assessed, 54% were rewarded, 26.6% were static and 24.4% were penalised.

For political reasons, the central government rarely penalises district councils by withholding funds due to underperformance.[107] Thus, the practical relevancy of the penalty/reward scheme in ensuring that the existing financial management accounting and accounting rules are complied with is very much limited by the central government. Part of the reason the central government has not withheld the funds under the scheme is because the central government uses the scheme to promote co-operation rather than to penalise and thus destabilise the relationship. For instance, the decision to withhold funds on account of failure to comply with mutually agreed targets may damage the much-needed co-operation between the central government and the penalised district council(s).

106 See MOLG, *Annual Assessment of Minimum Conditions and Performance Measures for Local Governments 2009: Synthesis Report*, March 2010.

107 Azfar, Livingston & Meagher in Bardhan 2006: 232.

A comparison may be made between the district councils' compliance with the minimum conditions in 2009 and the trend of performance over a period of the previous three years. The overall performance of district councils over a period of three years indicates that compliance with the minimum conditions was at 82% in 2006. The findings also indicate a sharp decline in compliance with the minimum conditions to 50% in 2007. In 2008 the district council's compliance with minimum conditions declined to 34%, although it improved in 2009 to 61%.[108]

The overall performance of district councils over a period of three years indicates that compliance with the minimum conditions was at 82% in 2006. The findings also indicate a sharp decline in compliance with the minimum conditions to 50% in 2007. In 2008 the district council's compliance with minimum conditions declined to 34%, although it improved in 2009 to 61%.[109]

9.3.9.3 Assessment

Lambright argues that the performance of district councils in Uganda is directly related to the degree of central government supervision and finds no evidence that stringent central government supervision of a district council leads to an improvement in the district council's performance. On the contrary, district councils with few administrative links to the centre performed extremely well.[110] The intrusive monitoring role of the above institutions in part explains the poor performance of many district councils in Uganda.

Arguably, Uganda's penalty/reward scheme, as observed by Shah, is an honest example of results-based intergovernmental finance that is capable of minimising trade-offs between district councils' autonomy and accountability in service delivery.[111] The absence of any legal basis for the penalty/reward scheme may discredit it as a subtle means of control of district councils by the central government.

Kugonza and Namara in principle agree with the observations of Shah. However, the authors find that the information on district council performance is misleading for a few reasons. First, the penalty/reward scheme focuses on 'workload and cost measures (which are relatively easy to collect and apply) and not on the results of service delivery, such as quality of service and achievement of goals and standards'.[112] Second, the penalty/reward scheme lacks a commitment to the principal elements of openness. In other words, the indicators of good performance were not clearly and transparently stated to the district councils in advance. The authenticity and usefulness of the information relied on to reward

108 See MOLG *Annual Assessment of Minimum Conditions and Performance Measures for Local Governments 2009: Synthesis Report* March 2010 p 9.

109 See the *Annual Assessment of Minimum Conditions and Performance Measures for Local Governments 2009: Synthesis Report* March 2010 p 9.

110 Lambright 2011: 107–10.

111 Shah 2010: 13.

112 Kugonza & Namara 2012: 4. See also Lambright 2011: 39, who adopts a similar criticism of the scheme.

or penalise a district council is questionable. Moreover, according to the authors, the 'irregular releases and arbitrary budget cuts' for district councils that performed well in the earlier stages of the scheme seemed to have demotivated many other district councils.[113] Third, there are allegations that some of the figures on the district councils' performance were tampered with by the assessors. The alleged fraud in the scheme fundamentally undermined its credibility. The creation of many districts weakened the inbuilt district council capacity to comply with future benchmarks.[114]

Reiterating the criteria established in Chapter Three on supervision,[115] the reporting systems discussed above are unpredictable, do not respect the autonomy of district councils and go beyond the intended purpose of reporting. For instance, the DPSF was published in 2006. It is difficult and potentially confusing for district councils to link the DPSF to the current legal framework on decentralisation that came into existence in 1995. This confusion is not mitigated by the unclear role the various members of the JARD. In any case, because it is prone to manipulation, the penalty/reward scheme may undermine the autonomy of the district councils.

9.4 Interventions in district councils

In Chapter Three, the importance of interventions in district councils by the central government was highlighted. Despite the fact that an intervention in a district council may appear oppressive by its nature, it is an inevitable and temporary corrective measure.[116] As a rule, intervention in local governments should be predictable, must respect the autonomy of local government and must be proportional to the pursued objective.[117] In the discussion below, the legal framework governing the central government interventions in district councils is examined.

9.4.1 Intervention by presidential assumption of a local government's powers

Article 202(1) of the Constitution provides for the assumption of the executive and legislative powers of a district council by the President. Three main grounds for the assumption of executive and legislative powers are given.

9.4.2 Grounds for Intervention

The first grounds for intervention is under Article 202(2)(a) of the Constitution. The President may intervene on the request of a district council as long as it is

113 Kugonza & Namara 2012: 4.
114 Kugonza & Namara 2012: 15–16.
115 Chapter Three § 3.8.4.
116 See Chapter Three § 3.9.3.
117 See Chapter Three § 3.9.3.

in the public interest. Even when the President is requested to intervene, the autonomy of the district is not diminished. The word 'request' does not imply that a district council can, without strong reasons, abdicate its constitutional, political and developmental roles to the central government.

The second grounds for intervention by the President in a district council is upon the declaration of a state of emergency in a district or in Uganda. Article 202(2)(b) of the Constitution regulates the manner in which a state of emergency can be declared:

- the President must only declare a state of emergency in consultation with the Cabinet and with the approval of Parliament;
- there must be a threat of war or external aggression, a threat to the security or economic life of the country, or part thereof, an insurgency or a natural disaster;
- a state of emergency may be declared where conditions exist that warrant taking measures to secure 'public safety, the defence of Uganda and the maintenance of public order'. For instance, the outbreak of a civil war or a highly contagious disease may trigger a Presidential intervention in a district council; and
- where the developmental needs of the district council warrant an intervention, such as failure to deliver 'supplies and services essential to the life of the community'.[118] For example where a district council is unable to provide rural roads, or rural ambulance services so that local pregnant women are unable to attend access antenatal services, an intervention therein should be justified.

The third grounds for intervention by the President in a district council is where there is 'extreme difficulty or impossibility' for the district local government to function.[119] The phrase 'extreme difficulty or impossibility' is open to various interpretations. The word 'extreme' denotes exceptional circumstances, a severe situation.[120]

The word 'difficulty' implies an element of a serious situation.[121] In other words, the exceptional circumstances on which the President has to base his or her intervention in a district council have to be of such a nature that something serious may happen in the district council. The word 'impossibility' implies an element of restraint on the part of a district council to exercise its powers and perform its functions.[122] The use of 'or' between the words 'difficulty' and 'impossibility' suggests that the exceptional circumstances need not be of both a difficult and serious nature. Once it is proven that exceptional circumstances

118 Article 110(1)(c) of the Constitution.
119 Article 202(1)(a), (b) and (c) of the Constitution.
120 Kavanagh 2002: 409.
121 Kavanagh 2002: 325.
122 Kavanagh 2002: 580.

are of a 'difficult' nature, there is no need for determining that the exceptional circumstances are of an 'impossible' kind.

An intervention must be predictable, respect the autonomy of local governments and be proportional. Instances such as maladministration, incompetence, ethnically based violence, natural calamities such as famine and civil war, qualify to be described as 'extreme difficulty or impossible' so as to legally justify an intervention. Although Article 202 of the Constitution does not provide any helpful insights, the Odoki Report gives a hint of what the phrase 'extreme difficulty or impossibility' could mean: 'widespread corruption, abuse of office, gross financial mismanagement, breakdown of law and order, and activities which threaten national unity or sovereignty of the country'.[123] It is noted that a threat to 'sovereignty', as recommended by the Odoki Report, is not a sufficient and adequate definition because it is linked to an act of aggression against the state for which a district council may not be responsible.

9.4.3 Consequence of intervention

As will be explained below, an intervention in a district council places an onerous financial burden on the central government and radically limits a district council's political autonomy.

Section 100 of the LGA repeats verbatim the provisions of Article 202(1) of the Constitution. Two additional conditions are provided for under section 100A of the LGA. First, once the political authority of a district council has been assumed by the President, the central government must finance all decentralised services from the national budget that are allocated by a district council vote ran by the CAO.[124] Second, for the period that the President assumes the district council's political authority, the central government's conditional grant to it must be 'utilised under the supervision of the permanent secretary for local governments'.[125] This means that where the President intervenes in a district council, the central government's grants to a district council that is subject to intervention are in fact retained and re-channelled through a specific budget vote controlled by the central government accounting officer.

The above provision amounts to a 'bailout'. Conventional wisdom in the literature on intergovernmental financing is that bailouts provide the wrong incentive and suggest that district councils can expect to receive 'easy money' from the central government as long as they perform poorly.[126] Not only does the promise of a bail-out provide the wrong incentive, it also seems to go against the intentions of the penalty/reward scheme. Ordinarily, financial incentives should be

123 Odoki Commission p 515 para 18.170.
124 Section 100A(2) of the LGA.
125 Section 100A(2) of the LGA.
126 De Visser 2005: 25.

given to districts that perform exceptionally well and not those that have failed to perform their functions.

Where the unexpired term remaining for the district council leaders is more than 12 months, the President must order fresh elections.[127] This means that there is no need for conducting fresh elections where the remaining term of office is less than 12 months.

9.4.4 Checks and balances

The President's intervention in a district council is generally limited to 90 days. The President's period of intervention in a district council may be extended beyond 90 days with the approval of Parliament.[128] However, it is the role of Parliament to determine if circumstances have indeed changed to end the intervention.[129] It is noted that that even if conditions existed justifying the continuation of a presidential intervention in a district council, Parliament cannot extent a Presidential intervention in a district council beyond 12 months (one year). This is an essential safeguard that is aimed at protecting the integrity of the district council.

9.4.5 Assessment

Since 1995, the President has never invoked his powers to intervene in any district council. Clearly, the two-decades-old civil war in northern Uganda, which has been described as 'social torture',[130] would have been legitimate grounds for the President to take over most district councils' powers in that part of the country, on the basis of Article 202(1)(b) of the Constitution. The presidential interventions in district councils have been conducted outside the above legal framework. For instance, the central government generally allocates funds and human resources to the districts in the northern Uganda region, the districts in the Karamoja region and the districts in 'the Luweero Triangle' region, districts that lack the requisite financial ability and human resource capacity necessary to deliver essential services to their local communities as a result of civil wars and historical economic imbalances.[131] It is maintained that preferential treatment of

127 Article 202(4)(b)(i) of the Constitution.

128 Article 202(3) of the Constitution.

129 Article 202(4)(b) of the Constitution.

130 Dolan 2009: 39.

131 These districts have special development programmes under the Prime Minister's office with specific dockets of the Minister of State for Northern Uganda, the Minister of State for Luwero Triangle and a full cabinet Minister for Karamoja Affairs. See GoU (Office of the Prime Minister), *Second Northern Uganda social action fund (NUSAF2) operations manual*, 2010, covering 40 districts, and GOU, *Luwero Rwenzori Development Programme* (LRDP), 2012/2013, covering 40 districts from Central and Western Uganda. The main objective of these development programmes is to address the post-war socio-economic challenges in these districts.

districts in the above three regions is evidence that the legal framework on presidential intervention in district councils has not been complied with.

The nature of the intervention in district councils by the central government is assessed under the criteria of predictability, respect of district council autonomy and proportionality.[132] It is not clear to district councils when the central government is permitted to intervene in their affairs. For example, for two decades, the central government did not intervene in many northern Uganda districts, yet those districts had failed to deliver the essential services such as primary education, primary healthcare and the rural ambulance services. Moreover, the fact that intervention in a district council may result in a 'bailout' suggests that an intervention is not every time intended to support district councils, but rather to address underlying political questions like in the case of war torn districts in Uganda. The fact that fresh district council elections must be conducted where the remaining term after the intervention is more than 12 months is a feature that demonstrates respect for district councils' autonomy.

9.5 Co-operative government

In Chapter Three, the point was made that co-operation as a feature of IGR manifests a collective exercise of power for the common good. Co-operation operates on the assumption that decentralisation can only succeed if national policies are sensitive to local preferences and priorities. Co-operation is therefore built on the interconnectedness of both the central government and local governments.[133]

9.5.1 The constitutional framework

The Constitution imposes an obligation on the state to foster national unity, peace and stability.[134] In addition, there is an obligation on the state to promote a culture of co-operation, appreciation, tolerance and respect.[135] Although the 'culture' of co-operation is confined to 'customs, traditions and beliefs', the above obligation can be expansively interpreted.

In addition, there is a constitutional obligation to nurture institutions and procedures that aim to solve conflicts 'fairly and peacefully'.[136] Article 176(2)(a) of the Constitution calls for co-operation (commonly referred to as the co-ordinate principle in federal countries), between the central government and district councils in the pursuits of the country's development objectives.[137]

132 See Chapter Three § 3.8.4.
133 Chapter Three § 3.8.5.1.
134 See the NODPSP No.2 (i).
135 See the NODPSP No.2 (ii).
136 See the NODPSP No.2 (iii).
137 See Hills 1998: 815 and De Villiers 1994: 431, who discuss the co-ordinate theory in federalism.

9.6 Instruments of co-operative government in Uganda

There are many instruments of IGR that are linked to co-operation in Uganda. These are: the Uganda Local Governments Association (ULGA), the Local Government Financial Commission (LGFC), Intergovernmental Agreements and Integrated Development Plans (IDP). Each of these instruments shall be analysed below.

9.6.1 Uganda Local Governments Association

The Constitution does not provide for organised local governments. Hence, the legal status of the ULGA is not very clear. The only place in the Constitution where role of the ULGA is found is Article 194(2). Under this article, organised local governments must nominate four members to the LGFC.[138] The legislative status of the ULGA can be located in the Companies Act[139] and the Trustees (Incorporation) Act, as a registered trustee, just like any other incorporated trust.[140] This means that by and large the ULGA is governed by the Companies Act as a non-profitmaking incorporated trust. The ULGA derives its mandate from the voluntary adoption of its Constitution by the member local government councils.[141] The ULGA consists of all the local governments of Uganda and their affiliate organisations and professional bodies.[142] The mandate of the ULGA is to promote unity and efficiency in local government. In addition, the ULGA is mandated to create a forum for the discussion of matters of mutual interest. Further, the ULGA has the duty to prepare reports for members and stakeholders dealing with matters affecting local government.[143] Arguably, the duty to prepare

138 During the CA debates at p 3927, it was suggested that the nomination of members by the district councils (under Article 194(2) of the Constitution) to the LGFC would be made by 'some kind of trade union of local governments'. In South Africa, for instance, section 163 of the Constitution expressly provides for organised local governments as forums for consultation in the legislative process, and mandates Parliament to make provision for the procedure by which they may carry out their constitutional mandate. Further, section 3(3) of the Systems Act provides for the object of organised local government: For the purpose of effective co-operative government, organised local government must seek to—(a) develop common approaches for local government as a distinct sphere of government;(b) enhance co-operation, mutual assistance and sharing of resources among municipalities;(c) find solutions for problems relating to local government generally; and(d)facilitate compliance with the principles of co-operative government and intergovernmental relations.

139 See sections 1(g) and 3(2)(b) of the Companies Act Cap 110.

140 See section 1(3) of the Trustees Act Cap 164 and section 1(3) of the Trustees Incorporation Act Cap 165.

141 Article 3(1) of the ULGA Constitution.

142 Article 3(2), (3), (4) and (5) of the ULGA Constitution. Under Article 3(5) of the ULGA Constitution the Association of District Speakers (UDICOSA), the Association of Chief Administrative Officers (ALGAOU), and the Association of Chief Finance Officers (CFOs) are listed as affiliate members.

143 See generally Article 2 of the ULGA Constitution. Article 2(2)(a) of the ULGA Constitution.

reports is linked to the ULGA ability to conduct research for the benefits of members and stakeholders.

The ULGA's critical areas of focus have been district council financing, sectoral policies, capacity building and democracy.[144] For example, the ULGA raised concerns about the absence of guidelines for multiparty politics in district councils,[145] poor remuneration of district councillors, Value Added Tax (VAT) arrears and the increasing domestic debt of district councils.[146]

In its advocacy role, the ULGA has for example made a detailed submission to Parliament on the challenges created by the establishment of RGs and the fear of 'recentralisation'.[147]

The role and extent of the ULGA in ensuring effective participation is crucial to co-operative governance.[148] At a thematic level the ULGA seeks to limit centrally imposed targets for service delivery by complementing them with locally driven ones. The ULGA also seeks to develop a mechanism for oversight and scrutiny, such as the district council anti-competitiveness and anti-corruption strategies.[149]

The role of the ULGA in peace building can be seen from the special attention that it accords to the local governments in areas emerging from conflict. For example, the ULGA's strategic plan proposes to increase flexibility in grants to Northern Uganda and to promote peace efforts in areas emerging from conflicts.[150]

The ULGA seems to have made these significant contributions to co-operative governance despite the existence of serious legal impediments arising from its obscure legal status.

As long as the ULGA depends on voluntary membership and the goodwill of the central government for its existence, its contribution will remain limited. The views expressed by the ULGA may never be taken into account by both the central government and district councils. A legally recognised ULGA is helpful in that its opinions and recommendations may be considered by both the central government and district councils. It is recommended that the LGA should be amended to provide for a principle of consultation with organised local governments.

144 See the achievements of the ULGA, available at http://www.ulga.org/achievements.html. It could be implied that whenever the ULGA makes submissions on local government finances, it is against the backdrop of Articles 194(2) and (4) of the Constitution dealing with the LGFC. These Articles provide for four members of the Commission as nominees of the local governments, while carrying out its advisory role. Moreover, the OAG must give a copy of it reports under section 87(3)(f) of the LGA to the LGFC.

145 The ULGA Corporate Strategic Plan p 14.

146 See the achievements of the ULGA, available at http://www.ulga.org/achievements.html.

147 See the ULGA submission of issues on the Constitution (Amendment) No. 2 Bill of 2005 to the Parliamentary Sessional Committee on Public Services and Local Government May 2005 p 6–7; the ULGA Corporate Strategic Plan p 13.

148 The ULGA Corporate Strategic Plan p 16.

149 The ULGA Corporate Strategic Plan p 21.

150 The ULGA Corporate Strategic Plan p 13.

9.6.2 The Local Government Finance Commission (LGFC)

The Constitution calls for the establishment of a seven-member LGFC by the President. Under the Constitution, four of the seven members have to be nominated by district councils in the country.[151] Members of the LGFC are vested with the power to elect from amongst themselves a chairperson and a vice-chairperson. In theory, members nominated by the ULGA have control of the Commission.[152]

The LGFC is mandated to advise the President on the distribution of revenue between the different orders of government and the allocation of funds from the Consolidated Fund.[153] The LGFC also considers and recommends to the President potential district council revenue sources.[154] In addition, the LGFC advises district councils on appropriate 'tax levels to be levied by local governments'.[155] It is not clear what the phrase 'tax levels' means. It may refer to district council tax rates and taxable income. It probably refers to the question of what is an appropriate tax burden on district council residents. Thus, the LGFC may advise the central government on the rate of district council property tax or on the determination of the district council residents' incomes that should be subject to taxation or exempted.

In the CA debates the LGFC was considered an 'arbiter' between the central government and district councils and a 'lobbying' and 'negotiating body' for district councils.[156] What came out of the CA debates was that the LGFC had to be independent and act as a link between the central government and the district councils, while avoiding the fray of politics.[157] Given that the majority of the members of the LGFC are the ULGA's nominees, the assumption here is that the LGFC represents the district councils' interests. The LGFC therefore provides a mechanism through which district councils can engage the central government on matters of district council revenue generation and sharing.

An assessment of the LGFC should be viewed in relation to its two critical roles: as a platform on which the central government and district councils can discuss matters of mutual interest, on the one hand, and as a lobbying group for district councils, on the other. There is no tangible evidence that the LGFC is taken seriously by the central government. Other than carrying out a study to expand district councils' revenue sources, the LGFC has been unsuccessful in lobbying for more autonomy in the determination of district council tax rates or the identification of stable district council tax bases, such as electricity, water tariffs and trading licences, to mention but a few. The approach adopted by the LGFC in making a case for reinstatement of the graduated tax as a source of

151 Article 194(1) of the Constitution.
152 Article 194(2) and (3) of the Constitution.
153 Article 194(4)(b) of the Constitution.
154 Article 194(4)(c) of the Constitution.
155 Article 194(4)(d) of the Constitution.
156 CA debates p 3920.
157 CA debates p 3920–1.

district council revenue has so far borne no fruit.[158] Its ability to build consensus and mutual respect between the two orders of government is therefore limited.

9.6.3 Integrated Development Plans (IDPs)

In Chapter Three the point was that decentralisation is crucial for prioritising the developmental needs of local communities. Development needs, the argument went, are better identified by the local communities, rather than dictated by local governments or imposed on them by central government. The Chapter called for joint plans between the central government and district councils.[159] In the discussion below, the legal framework for district councils' joint plans is examined.

9.6.3.1 Constitutional framework

Planning is a central government competency.[160] According to the National Objectives and Directive Principles of State Policy (NODPSP), the Constitution directs the state 'to adopt an integrated and co-ordinated planning approach'.[161] The words 'integrated and co-ordinated' as used by the Constitution direct the central government to consider district council plans before the central government plans are adopted. In turn, district councils are obliged to ensure that before any district council's plans are forwarded to the National Planning Authority, the lower council's plans are incorporated therein.[162]

9.6.3.2 Legislative framework

On the basis of the principles that follow from Articles 176(2)(b)[163] and 190 of the Constitution, section 36 of the LGA was enacted. Section 36(1) of the

158 For example, in 2007 district council leaders, through the LGFC, boycotted a National Budget Consultative meeting organised by the Ministry of Finance, protesting against non-remittance of Graduated Tax Compensation Funds. The district council leaders were not happy that the then Minister of Finance, Dr Ezra Suruma, had deliberately ignored 'their concerns and [the LGFC] refused to meet with the ministry again until the issue was resolved'. See Andrew Bagala, 'District Bosses Storm out of the Government Meeting', *The Daily Monitor*, 7 December 2007, cited in Lambright 2011: 119–20.

159 See Chapter Three § 3.10.2.

160 Article 125 of the Constitution. See also the Sixth Schedule which makes reference to Article 189 of the Constitution: Item 13 of the Sixth Schedule states that functions and services for which Government is responsible include '[m]aking national plans for the provision of services and coordinating plans made by local governments'. Not all the powers under the Sixth Schedule are exclusive to the central government, which clearly makes planning a local government competency that is shared with the central government.

161 NODPSP para 12(1).

162 Article 190 of the Constitution.

163 Articles 176(2)(b) provides: 'decentralisation shall be a principle applying to all levels of local government and, in particular, from higher to lower local government units to ensure peoples' participation and democratic control in decision making'.

LGA provides that the exercise of the district local government planning powers is vested in the district planning committee and planning units. A district local government planning committee is chaired by the COA and consists of the heads of department of the district and any members co-opted by the COA. Section 36(2) of the LGA provides that the role of the district planning committee is to co-ordinate and integrate all the sectoral plans of the lower local governments before any such plans can be presented to the district local government council.

9.6.4 District councils' planning cycles

District council plans in Uganda take the form of Public Investment Plans (PIP). District council plans must sufficiently consider the interest of both private and public sector demands. All district council plans essentially follow six phases, namely (1) identification, (2) screening and selection, (3) preparation, (4) appraisal, (5) implementation and monitoring and (6) project evaluation and ex-post evaluation of a project.[164] All the district plans follow the same cycle (see Figure 9.3).

First, the identification of projects involves defining its objectives and the means to achieve those objectives. In theory, local communities should be involved in the process of identifying particular projects. The reasoning here is that identification of projects should match local preferences. Second, a district council project must be screened. The process of screening a project helps to ensure that the priorities are agreed upon. At this stage the merits and demerits of the project are considered by the Technical Planning Committee and the respective district council standing committee. Third, the district council project must be prepared. The preparation of the project entails designing the project and considering the alternatives in the light of technical, socio-economic and financial implications by the TPCs, standing committees and lower councils. It is important at this stage to ascertain the source of funding.

Fourth, the district council project must be implemented and monitored. It is the role of district councils, the TPCs and the Executive Committees to implement and monitor district council projects.[165] At this stage, workplans are presented and resources mobilised for the project. No project can be implemented unless the district council has approved the budget.[166]

Fifth, district council projects must be appraised. At this stage, the performance reports are prepared and analysed with the aim of altering the project design, if necessary. Finally, the district council project must be evaluated by district councils, the TPCs, the district council standing committees, the external support agencies (ESAs), donors (commonly referred to as development

164 Henry K *Decentralised District Development Planning: A Guide to Development Planning* p 1–4.

165 Section 17(a) of the LGA.

166 Article 191(1) of the Constitution and Section 82(1) of the LGA.

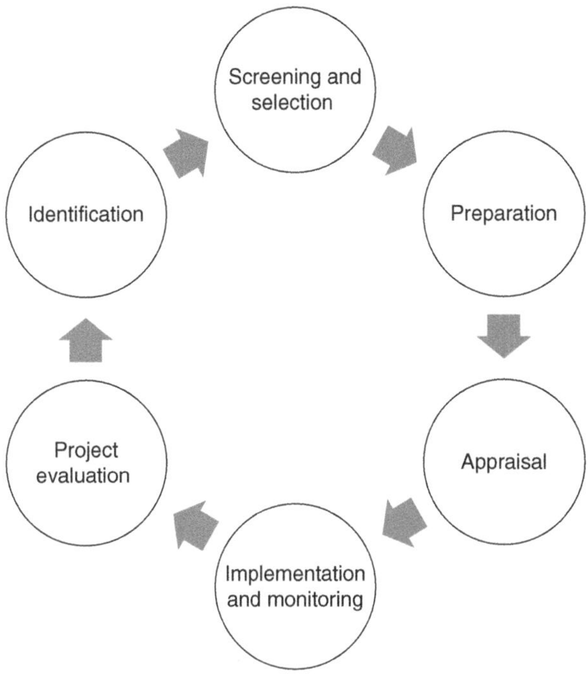

Figure 9.3 Planning cycle of district councils.

partners), NGOs, interest groups and central government. At this stage, performance reports are examined, possible changes in project design may be mooted and ideas can be generated for new projects.[167]

Within the broader framework of IGR, the above planning cycle must be linked to the central government oversight role in ensuring that future district council plans result in improved service delivery.

9.6.4.1 Assessment

The office of the COA has been described in Chapter Seven.[168] An important aspect of the COA is that he or she is a technical civil servant in the district and the accounting officer that chairs the technical planning team in every district council. So the question here is: to what extent do district councils exercise their discretion to initiate their development plans through the CAO since the central government directly appoints the CAO? A centrally appointed CAO may, in

167 Henry K *Decentralised District Development Planning: A Guide to Development Planning* p 5.
168 Chapter Seven § 7.5.6.2.

certain instances, ignore local priorities in the design of district plans. In practice, the design of district council plans through the office of the CAO reveals central government hegemony in the IDP. In any case district council discretion to prioritise their plans is limited by budget ceilings imposed by the central government.[169] For example, as discussed in Chapter Eight, district councils depend on central government conditional grants to fund their functions.[170] These grants have detailed guidelines for their use and the amount thereof is determined by the respective ministries, with little input from the district councils. The district councils are, in theory, prohibited from adopting budgets for education, primary health care or rural roads that exceed the conditional grants.[171] Lambright, however, finds little evidence that district councils that violated the budget ceilings were penalised by the central government.[172]

The intergovernmental utility of planning system is undermined by two major factors. First, district councils depend primarily on conditional grants which leave little room for local discretion to be deployed in these local plans. Secondly, district councils' ability to raise their own revenue is very much limited by the over-regulation of their taxing power by the central government. In effect, the district planning system is actually centrally directed.

9.6.5 Dispute resolution mechanisms in IGR

Given the central government regulation of local governments, conflicts are bound to emerge. If these conflicts are not well managed they may undermine the intended objective of decentralisation. The practice in other countries has been that courts will not entertain an intergovernmental dispute unless efforts have been made by the state organs involved to resolve it amicably outside the mainstream adjudication systems.[173]

There is no specific provision for an intergovernmental dispute resolution mechanism in Uganda. Yet there is evidence that there are numerous instances of intergovernmental disputes in Uganda's decentralised system. For instance, conflicts have arisen in areas such as district councils' law-making processes,[174] district council budget processes, the allocation of central government fiscal transfers and the district councils' taxing discretion. A case in point is the unilateral suspension of graduated tax by the President.[175] Conflicts have arisen in the creation of districts, especially in the determination of district boundaries, in cases where

169 Azfar *et al.* in Bardhan *et al.* 2006: 226. For example, according to the Local Government Financial and Accounting Regulations (LGAFR), a district council cannot spend more than 15% of its annual local revenue on the allowances and salaries of the district council officials.
170 See Chapter Eight § 8.3.2.
171 Lambright 2011: 126–7.
172 Lambright 2011: 127.
173 Chapter Three § 3.10.5.
174 Chapter Seven § 7.5.2.
175 Chapter Eight § 8.2.3.2.

ethnic tensions are rife in particular areas,[176] and in cases of unilateral central government intervention in conflicts between the district speakers and district council chairpersons.[177] Further, intergovernmental disputes have arisen from the correct procedure for removing elected leaders from district councils[178] and in the appointment and disciplining of the CAO.[179]

The absence of intergovernmental dispute resolution mechanisms is in part explained by the overregulation of district council institutions, powers and functions that provides little incentive for finding alternative ways to resolve disputes. The majority of intergovernmental conflicts are referred to courts with all the attendant financial inconveniences and disruptions to the delivery of services.[180] Where recourse to court is not considered viable, these intergovernmental disputes are either managed by the Ministry of Local Government or personally resolved by the President. Intergovernmental disputes appear to be resolved through the centralised party structure. The central government is therefore the final arbiter on any intergovernmental conflict.

9.7 Conclusion

This chapter has examined IGR in Uganda from two main angles: supervision and co-operation. As argued at the outset of the chapter, supervision is considered the 'hard edge' of IGR, while co-operation is considered the 'soft edge'. In answering the question of whether the framework and practice of supervision in Uganda comply with the criteria of predictability, respect for autonomy and proportionality, as provided in Chapter Three, it is reiterated that they do not. For instance, there is clear evidence of overregulation of the district council institutions, powers and functions. Besides, the monitoring of district councils, which is open to abuse, seems to clog the political space of district councils. As noted, whereas the OAG is an important instrument to enforce accountability in district councils, the ability of many district councils to use its reports in order to demand more accountability is limited by lack of skills on the part of the majority of district councillors. In addition, as was discussed, the monitoring role of the IGG in district councils is inclined to intervention, a weakness that undermines the role of monitoring in IGR. Last, the use of RDCs to monitor district councils is limited by their skills deficiencies as well as their inclination towards enforcing central government policies and limiting local civil liberties rather than monitoring service delivery. Some writers argue that institutions such as the OAG, the IGG and RDC are 'external control and accountability mechanisms' in district

176 Chapter Five § 5.3.3.
177 Chapter Six § 6.12.2.
178 Chapter Six § 6.7.4.4.
179 Chapter Seven § 7.5.6.4.
180 See the *Hajji Mohammed Baswari Kezaala* cases discussed in Chapter Six § 6.9.4.6.

councils.[181] This is misleading as they are in fact part of IGR.[182] The central government uses the above organs to 'force' district councils to be more accountable to the electorate.[183]

Further, in answering the question of whether the practice of co-operation in Uganda's decentralisation system complies with the criteria given in Chapter Three, it is clear that it does not. The muted roles of the LGFC and the ULGA (essential institutions of co-operation in IGR) do not support a finding of co-operation in Uganda's decentralised system of government. Instead the chapter presents evidence of the central government's subtle control of the district council plans, as merely a loose form of co-operation in Uganda's IGR. It is maintained that the absence of formal mechanisms for intergovernmental dispute resolution has also resulted in the clogging of the mainstream courts with district council cases that that are political in nature, which ordinarily would have been resolved through IGR. The absence of a formal mechanism of intergovernmental dispute resolution has therefore added more strain to an already struggling system of decentralisation in Uganda that requires immediate legal reform.

181 Kakumba & Fourie 2008: 122. Shah 1997: 15–16.
182 Azfar, Kahkonen & Meagher 2001: 49.
183 Kakumba & Fourie 2008: 123.

10 General conclusions and recommendations

10.1 Introduction

Building on the emerging international soft law on decentralisation, the book has argued that decentralisation has become a focal point for reforming developing states, especially those emerging from conflict. A crucial element in the argument of this book is that ethnicity is an important sociological and constitutional question in the devolution of power in multi-ethnic countries such as Uganda and that the exclusion of ethnicity in the devolution process typically has dire consequences.

The book's central argument is that for decentralisation to be successful as a state reform strategy, developing countries should consider protecting the integrity of decentralising measures by constitutionally recognising local governments, establishing an independent boundary demarcation system, designing an adequate local government electoral model and recognising the role of traditional leaders. Second, developing countries should vest local governments with a clear functional authority and with the discretion to exercise an adequate degree of fiscal and administrative autonomy. Last, developing countries must provide for an equitable system of intergovernmental transfers and a sound system of intergovernmental relations.

The book has argued that in theory decentralisation is good for development, democracy and the accommodation of diversity, and therefore the institutions, powers and functions of local government must be designed to achieve these goals.

10.2 Has decentralisation failed in Uganda?

The book finds that decentralisation, as a state reform measure in Uganda, has neither failed nor succeeded. The Ugandan government's own assessment of the decentralisation seems to come to a similar conclusion. On the scale of one to ten, Uganda's decentralisation scores an average of 5.7 points.[1] The description

1 See the *Annual Assessment of Minimum Conditions and Performance Measures for Local Governments 2009: Synthesis Report*, March 2010: 9.

of Uganda's legal and institutional architecture on decentralisation began with an overview of the historical development of local government. The decentralisation program in Uganda was initiated by the military government formed after a five-year guerrilla war that formally ended in 1986, but in reality continued in the northern part of the country until 2010. Thus, decentralisation in Uganda may be considered a political and military strategy of the victorious against the vanquished. It is likely that some of the district council institutions were adopted with a military culture that places emphasis on 'order and discipline', rather than on consultation and dialogue.[2]

The brief findings were that post-independence political instability and economic underdevelopment are explained by over-centralisation of state power that limited the right of local communities to participate in the decision-making process. Thus, the new constitutional order that recognises district councils desired to reform the nature of the state in Uganda and to establish a democratic state geared at improving the material well-being of local communities.

The book argued that decentralisation is predicated on the idea of social freedom and democratic governance. However, there is little evidence that the devolution of power to district councils has significantly changed the nature and character of post-independence Uganda. For instance, the available research shows that the quality of political freedoms in Uganda is below average and is not different from many other developing countries that are described as 'partly free', 'undemocratic' or 'not fully democratic'.[3] Decentralisation is also associated with improvement in the material well-being of local communities as a result of improvement in the delivery of local services. However, the mapping of poverty in Uganda by Emwanu in 2008, covering 52 districts over the period 2002 to 2005, shows mixed results. On one hand, the study shows a marked decline in the incidence of poverty nationally from 39% to 31%,[4] but at the same time, rural districts in the northern parts of the country have higher poverty levels of 64.9% when compared with levels in rural districts in western Uganda of 21.4%. In addition, the districts in the northern parts of the country have a higher poverty gap of 23.5% compared to the poverty gap of 4.52% in districts in the western parts of the country.[5]

2 Makara 2009: 64.

3 See Oloka-Onyango 2007: 24. See also Freedom House Report 2011, available at http://www.freedomhouse.org/report/freedom-press/2011/uganda (accessed 13 June 2012). In the 2012 Freedom House report, Uganda is conspicuously excluded from the 115 countries in the world that are described as 'Electoral Democracies'.

4 Emwanu 2008: 6. It is noted that as of 2011, Uganda had 112 districts, implying that the above poverty mapping percentage figures have considerably changed. See also Singiza & De Visser 2011: 4–5, who discuss the effect of creating many districts in Uganda.

5 Emwanu 2008: 7. Emwanu *et al.* 2008: 4 explain that the '[p]overty gap (IP), provides information on the depth of poverty. It captures the average expenditure shortfall, or gap, for the poor in a given area to reach the poverty line. It measures the poverty deficit of the population or the resources that would be needed to lift all the poor in that area out of poverty if one were able to perfectly target cash transfers towards closing the gap'.

These figures are in accord with the latest 2010 report on the performance of local governments throughout the country.[6] The poverty mapping figures in 52 districts, and the continued evidence of administrative malady, underpin the fact that the economic efficiency and fiscal discipline that are associated with decentralisation have not translated into the improved material well-being of the majority of the people at grassroots level. This book, on account of the above figures, in no way finds that decentralisation as a system of government has failed. Rather, the book maintains that serious flaws in the legal and policy framework have contributed to the low rating levels of decentralisation as a system of government in Uganda. The irony is that a quick glance at Uganda's legal and policy framework on decentralisation reflects a genuine desire to transform the country's democratic and economic path by engaging local communities. However, a detailed, critical study of Uganda's decentralisation system reveals institutional failure that demands immediate reform in order to harness the real benefits of decentralisation.[7] As Aung San Suu Kyi warns, 'The most difficult time in any transition is when we think that success is in sight ... Then we have to be very careful that we're not lured by the mirage of success'.[8]

10.3 Essential findings

Even though the 1995 Constitution bestowed a new status on district councils at the inception of decentralisation, there was not a concomitant, comprehensive policy providing a rationale for devolving power to lower orders of government. The policy void in the new constitutional status of local governments partly explains why there has been exponential growth in numerous district councils with little tangible rise in the material well-being of the local communities that district councils were intended to serve.

10.3.1 Local government Institutions

As was argued in Chapter Three, an independent boundary demarcation body in the demarcation process is vital to ensure that the process is free from political manipulation. It was further argued that a boundary demarcation process must be more transparent and participatory for the communities concerned.[9] It is recommended that Article 179(4) of the Constitution of Uganda should be amended to provide for an independent body to demarcate district boundaries. This body should be able to operate free from political influence. Any proven

6 See the *Annual Assessment of Minimum Conditions and Performance Measures for Local Governments 2009: Synthesis Report*, March 2010: 8.

7 The *Annual Assessment of Minimum Conditions and Performance Measures for Local Governments 2009: Synthesis Report*, March 2010: 8.

8 Kuhnhenn, 'Obama to people of Myanmar: America "is with you"', *Associated Press*, 19 November 2012.

9 Singiza & De Visser 2011: 33.

attempt at political influence should be subject to criminal prosecution and possible legal sanction. Second, the amendment should include a provision for public hearings and objections from stakeholders and members of the public so that the wishes of the people are heard before a new district is created.

One of the major critiques of Uganda's decentralisation is what is generally considered the 'recentralisation phenomenon', particularly that of the former Kampala City Council. The recentralisation phenomenon is also apparent in the centralisation of all district councils' senior managers. Further, the suspension of the district council graduated tax is also cited as evidence of the recentralisation phenomenon.

The book finds an urgent need to strengthen the autonomy of district councils in order to limit the excesses of state power. For instance, if district councils are to serve as instruments of peace, they should be strengthened enough to compete with the central government in order to mitigate the dangers associated with a highly centralised state. Further, district councils, as local institutions of democracy, should seek to build consensus with the central government under a broader umbrella of the nation state and not to antagonise it. Testing whether Uganda's district councils' institutional design promotes democratic governance, the book finds that there is a fair environment in which democratic governance can take root. However, the wall-to-wall institutional design of district councils, together with the proliferation of district councils, creates weak lower orders of government that are dependent on central government, with little ability to check the excesses of state power.

The institutional design of Uganda's district councils reveals the following: the Buganda Kingdom's demand for special federal status was rejected on account of it threatening the nation state of Uganda, yet many district councils have been created mainly on the basis of ethnicity. This suggests that the promotion of ethnicity at lower orders of government does not necessarily threaten the integrity of the nation state, as was argued with respect to the Buganda Kingdom. The Buganda Kingdom should be awarded a special federal status, a status that poses no risk to Uganda's sovereignty. The book therefore rearticulates the Buganda Kingdom's quest for special federal status through strong district councils. The Buganda Kingdom's special federal status within Uganda presents no incentive for secession, as long as there are strong district councils within it.

10.3.2 Local democracy

The general argument has been that the success of decentralisation lies in the acknowledgement of district councils as deliberative democratic assemblies for local communities. The book finds that all district council political office-bearers are elected by local citizens with the provision for revoking their mandate. This is an essential feature that protects their constitutional democratic autonomy and integrity. When local democracy is viewed through the prism of periodic elections only, then, in this narrow sense, it seems that local government is genuinely democratic as an expression of local communities' preference.[10]

10 Oloka-Onyango 2007: 17.

Essentially, district councils as deliberative assemblies are grounded in the idea of free and fair elections that are inclusive and transparent. This view is based on the assumption that the existence of elected community representatives ensures that district council political leaders must constantly justify their actions to local communities through their elected representatives. The finding of the book is that the quality of district council elections presents outcomes that are antithetical to grassroots democracy given the allegations (proven and unproven) of election malpractice. Besides, the legal framework seems to have resulted in people with no skills being elected to district councils. Inevitably, district councils are dominated by councillors with almost no skills and are therefore incapable of demanding critical explanation on behalf of communities from the national and district political leaders.

It is noted that district councils are the supreme political authority within the jurisdiction of every district council. On the other hand, the directly elected district council chairperson is the political head of every district council. The apparent absence of clear political authority in a district council may be potentially dangerous for a local democracy. It is reiterated that the absence of a clear and dominant political authority in a district council is a recipe for political conflicts.

In addition, whereas provision is made for the political participation of different social groups, such as women, the youth and the elderly, traditional leaders are constitutionally excluded from participation in politics, specifically district councils. Furthermore, ethnic minorities are not recognised as a special interest group in district councils. District councils are supposedly founded on inclusive democratic principles. An electoral system that does not make any special effort to afford ethnic minority representation amounts to political discrimination and violates these principles. It is also noted that the exclusion of traditional rulers from district councils is based on a misconception that traditional leaders are inherently undemocratic and divisive.

District councils were originally grounded in the ideology of 'non-party democracy', which is in practice undemocratic. In fact, in 1993, when the decentralisation legislation was enacted, multiparty political activities had been banned for seven years. The promulgation of the 1995 Constitution further sealed the fate of political pluralism, in that from 1995 to 2005 political parties were constitutionally excluded from competing for any political office. Notwithstanding the 2005 constitutional amendment that provided for political pluralism, the book finds that ideologically Uganda's decentralisation is still infused with the single-party political doctrine that is intolerant towards alternative political opinions.[11]

10.3.3 Local government powers

One of the critical findings of the book is that district council administrative technocrats are protected from district council elected leaders' direct control. On the one hand, the separation of senior district council managers from district

11 Oloka-Onyango 2007: 10–11, 24–5. See also Francis & James 2003: 327

council political control ensures that district council technocrats are free from district council political manipulation. On the other hand, the book questions the decision to re-centralise the appointment of senior district council managers. The book finds that the re-centralisation of the district council senior administrators makes it politically impossible for district councillors to seriously demand explanations from district council technocrats. Ultimately, the book finds that the absence of district council political control over its senior managers means that district councils can no longer determine their own developmental priorities.

The book also highlights the importance of sharing powers and functions between orders of government. Placing emphasis on the emerging international soft law on decentralisation, the book makes a case for clearly defined powers to devolve to district councils on the principle of subsidiarity. The book notes that the powers and functions that devolve to Uganda's district councils are not only vague, but contradict the emerging soft law and existing literature on decentralisation.

The book finds that the Constitution provides for a detailed list of central government exclusive competencies under the Sixth Schedule of the Constitution. In addition, item 29 of the Sixth Schedule of the Constitution has an open-ended effect in that any of the residual district councils' competencies that are incidental to the execution of the central government competencies automatically reverts to the central government. Last, the Sixth Schedule of the Constitution then seems to suggest that Parliament will prescribe and detail the residual functions of district councils from a very narrow list.

It is noted that the manner in which Parliament prescribes the district councils' powers and functions ultimately causes an overlap of central government and district council functions. This has rendered parts of the legislative scheme for district powers unconstitutional and subject to constitutional challenge in court. Arguably, the 1995 Constitution offers room for constitutional litigation to purposefully add meaning to the real powers and functions of district councils in order to protect the integrity of district councils in Uganda.

Testing the nature of powers and functions that devolve to district councils, the book finds that vaguely defined district council powers narrow the political space of district council legislative and executive powers. The book also finds that vaguely defined district council functions make it difficult for local communities to demand explanations from specific orders of government.

10.3.4 Intergovernmental relations

The book's examination of the nature of intergovernmental relations (IGR) in Uganda's decentralisation shows that district councils are institutionally over-regulated. A clearest example is the suspension of district graduated tax by the President by a mere letter without considering the views of district councils. The relationship between central government and district councils is characterised by too much supervision and monitoring, with little emphasis on co-operation and mutual respect. The book argues that the success of decentralisation hinges on the adoption of both supervision and co-operation as important tools for IGR. Preferably, the book maintains, emphasis should be placed on co-operation as a means of promoting a culture of dialogue necessary for grassroots democracy.

In summary, the findings of this book concern a political environment that in many ways is nostalgic of a highly centralised state.[12]

10.4 Recommendations

The findings of this book are important for further institutional reform of district councils in Uganda. The book offers lessons to other multi-ethnic countries (especially those emerging from conflict) that desire to adopt devolution through decentralisation as means of consensus building. The book has highlighted opportunities as well as serious shortcomings in the legal framework for decentralisation, with an emphasis on practical suggestions for reform. There are as follows:

- That decentralisation is an appropriate state reform measure for less-developed countries, especially those emerging from conflict.
- That a wall-to-wall institutional design of district councils is inappropriate for multi-ethnic countries, especially for ethnic groups with a unique history; hence a specially crafted form of asymmetrical decentralisation is highly recommended.
- That there is no international legal obligation to adopt decentralisation as a state reform measure, but there is a trend, evident in many international declarations and ministerial statements, which suggests that decentralisation as a system of government could in the near future become an international norm.
- That democracy, development and accommodation of diversity are the main principles on which a good decentralised system should be predicated.
- The success of decentralisation, however, hinges on six critical features. These are: (a) integrity of local government institutions; (b) functional local government authority; (c) adequate fiscal autonomy; (d) administrative autonomy; (e) equitable intergovernmental transfers; and (f) sound intergovernmental relations.
- Parliament should revisit the important role of traditional leaders in district councils. For example, the Constitution and the LGA should be amended so as to ensure that traditional leaders are included in district council structures by lifting a ban on traditional leaders from participating in elections.

12 Tusasirwe 2007: 31–2.

- That in order to establish 'functional district councils', the institutions, functions and powers of district councils must serve the purpose of grassroots democracy, development and accommodation of diversity by ensuring the promotion of democratic citizenship, improvement of efficiency in public service delivery systems and protecting territories of communities.
- That the failure of decentralisation to promote democratic governance and improve the material well-being of many communities in Uganda points to the need for further reform.

Bibliography

Books

Apter D *The Political Kingdom in Uganda: A Study of Bureaucratic Nationalism* (1967) Portland: Frank Cass Publishers.

Apter D *Rethinking Development: Modernization, Dependency, and Postmodern Politics* (1987) London: SAGE Publications.

Aristotle *Politics* (1932) (translated by H Rackham) Cambridge: Cambridge University Press.

Ayele Z *Local Government in Ethiopia: Advancing Development and Accommodating Ethnic Minorities* (2014) Baden-Baden: Nomos Verlagsgesellschaft.

Azfar O, Kahkonen S & Meagher P *Conditions for Effective Decentralized Governance: A Synthesis of Research Findings* (2001) Maryland: IRIS, University of Maryland.

Azfar O & Livingston J *Federalist Discipline or Local Capture: An Empirical Analysis of Decentralization in Uganda* (2001) Maryland: IRIS, University of Maryland.

Bird R & Slac, E (eds) *International Handbook of Land and Property Taxation* (2003) Northampton, Massachusetts: Edward Elgar.

Breton A & Scott A *The Economic Constitution of Federal States* (1978) Toronto: Toronto University Press.

Brownlie I *Principles of Public International Law* (1998) Cambridge: Cambridge University Press.

Callahan K *Elections of the Elective Governance: Measurement, Accountability and Participation* (2007) New York: CRC Press.

CLGF *Time for Local Democracy, the Aberdeen Agenda: Commonwealth Principles on Good Practice for Local Democracy and Good Governance* (2005) London: Commonwealth Local Government Forum.

De Villers B (ed) *The Review of Provinces and Local Governments in South Africa: Constitutional Foundations and Practices* (2008) Johannesburg: Konrad Adenauer Stiftung.

De Villiers B *Local Provincial Intergovernmental Relations: A Comparative Analysis* (1997) Johannesburg: Konrad Adenauer Stiftung.

De Visser J *Developmental Local Government: A Case Study of South Africa* (2005) Antwerp: Intersentia.

De Visser J, Steytler N & May A *The Quality of Local Democracies: A Study into the Functionality of Municipal Governance Arrangements* (2009) Cape Town: Community Law Centre, University of the Western Cape.

Dolan C *Social Torture: The Case of Northern Uganda, 1986-2006* (2009) New York: Berghahn Books.

Duchacek I *Comparative Federalism: The Territorial Dimensions of Politics* (2nd ed) (1987) Lanham: University Press of America.

Dugard J *International Law: A South African Perspective* (2007) Cape Town: Juta.

Ebel R & Yilmaz S *Concept of Fiscal Decentralisation and Worldwide* (2001) Washington: World Bank.

Emwanu T *et al.* (eds) *Spatial Trends of Poverty and Inequality in Uganda: 2002–2005* (2008) Kampala: Bureau of Statistics.

Erk J & Anderso LM (eds) *The Paradox of Federalism: Does Self-Rule Accommodate or Exacerbate Ethnic Divisions?* (2010) New York: Routledge.

Garner B (ed) *Black's Law Dictionary* (abridged) (2005) Eagan, Minnesota: West Publishing.

Garner B (ed) *Black's Law Dictionary* (9th ed) (2009) New York: Thomson Reuters.

Gluckman M *The Judicial Process Among the Barotse of Northern Rhodesia* (1967) Manchester: Manchester University Press.

Hubert A & Andersen B *Draft Decentralization of Government in Uganda: Reports on Uganda* (1993) Greve: Nordic Consulting Group.

Ibingira G *The Forging of an African Nation: The Political and Constitutional Evolution of Uganda from Colonial Rule to Independence, 1894–1962* (1973) Nyack: Viking Press.

Kabwegyere T *People's Choice, People's Power: Challenges and Prospects of Democracy in Uganda* (2000) Kampala: Fountain Publishers.

Kanyeihamba G *Constitutional and Political History of Uganda: From 1994 to the Present* (2002) Kampala: Centenary Publishing House.

Kaplan S *Fixing Fragile States: A New Paradigm for Development* (2008) London: Praeger Security International.

Karugire S *Roots of Instability in Uganda* (1988) Kampala: New Vision.

Kavanagh K (ed) *The South African Concise Oxford Dictionary* (10th ed) (2002) Oxford: Oxford University Press.

Kavanagh K (ed) *Oxford Dictionary Advanced Learner's Dictionary* (10th ed) (2002) Oxford: Oxford University Press.

Kelsen H *The General Theory of Law and the State* (1945) (translated by A Wedberg) Cambridge, Massachusetts: Harvard University Press.

Kymlicka W *Multicultural Citizenship: Liberal Theory of Minority Rights* (1995) Oxford: Clarendon Press.

Ladd H & Yinger J (eds) *America's Ailing Cities: Fiscal Health and the Design of Urban Policy* (1989) Maryland: Johns Hopkins University Press.

Lambright G *Decentralization in Uganda: Explaining Successes and Failures in Local Governance* (2011) Boulder, Colorado: Lynne Rienner Publishers.

Loughlin M *Local Government in the Modern State* (1986) London: Sweet & Maxwell.

Lugard F *The Dual Mandate in the British Tropical Africa* (1922) London: Frank Cass Publishers.

Lugard F *The Rise of Our East African Empire vol. II* (1893) Edinburgh: William Blackwood & Sons.

Mamdani M *Politics and Class Formation in Uganda* (1979) Princeton: Princeton University Press.

Mamdani M *Imperialism and Fascism in Uganda* (1983) London: Heinemann.

Mamdani M *Citizen and Subject: Contemporary Africa and the Legacy of Colonialism* (1996) Princeton: Princeton University Press.

Margery P Lugard *The Years of Authority 1898–1945* (1960) London: Collins.

Markakis J *Ethiopia: Anatomy of a Traditional Polity* (2006) London: Clarendon Press.

Morris H & Read J *Uganda: The Development of its Laws and the Constitution* (1966) London: Stevens & Sons.

Murry C & Nijzing L *Building Representative Democracy: South Africa's Legislatures and the Constitution* (2002) Cape Town: Parliamentary Support Programme.

Museveni Y *Sowing the Mustard Seed: The Struggle for Freedom and Democracy in Uganda* (1997) London: Macmillan.

Museveni Y *What is Africa's Problem?* (2000) Minneapolis: University of Minnesota Press.

Nabudere W *Imperialism and Revolution in Uganda* (1980) Dar es Salaam: Onyx Press.

Nkrumah K *Africa Must Unite* (1963) London: Heinemann.

Nyerere J *Ujamaa: Essays on Socialism* (1968) Oxford: Oxford University Press.

Oates W *Fiscal Federalism* (1972) New York: Harcourt Brace Jovanovich.

Oomen B *Chiefs in South Africa: Law, Power & Culture in the Post-Apartheid Era* (2005) Oxford: James Curry.

Peirce N *Citistates: How Urban America Can Prosper in a Competitive World* (1993) Washington: Seven Locks Press.

Reynolds A *Electoral Systems and Democratization in Southern Africa* (1999) Oxford: Oxford University Press.

Reynolds F *Bowstead and Reynolds on Agency* (1996) London: Sweet & Maxwell.

Rodden, J., Gunnar S E & Litvack J (eds) *Fiscal Decentralization and the Challenge of Hard Budget Constraints* (2003) London: Cambridge University Press.

Shah A *Balance, Accountability and Responsiveness: Lessons about Decentralisation* (1998) Washington: World Bank.

Shah A *Sponsoring a Race to the Top: The Case for Results-Based Intergovernmental Finance for Merit Goods* (2010) Washington: World Bank.

Shah A *Fiscal Federalism and Macroeconomic Governance: For Better or For Worse?* (1998) Washington: World Bank.

Smith B *Good Governance and Development* (2007) New York: Palgrave Macmillan.

Soanes C & Stevenson A. (eds) *Concise Oxford English Dictionary* (2004) New York: Oxford University Press.

Sorensen V & Lubanga F (eds) *Democratic Decentralisation in Uganda: A New Approach to Local Governance* (1996) Kampala: Fountain Publishers.

Steytler N & De Visser Y *Local Government Law of South Africa* (2007) Durban: LexisNexis.

Tamale S *When Hens Begin to Crow: Gender and Parliamentary Politics in Uganda* (1999) Boulder, Colorado: Westview Press.

Twaddle M & Kakungulu S *The Creation of Uganda 1868–1928* (1993) London: James Curry.

Walubiri P *Uganda: Constitutionalism at Cross Roads* (1988) Kampala: Uganda Law Watch Centre.

Watts R *Comparing Federal Systems* (2008) Montreal & Kingston: McGill-Queen's University Press.

Wheare K *Federal Government* (4th ed) (1963) Oxford: Oxford University Press.

World Bank *The Uganda District Management Study* (1992) Washington: World Bank.

World Bank *Sub-Saharan Africa: From Crisis to Sustainable Growth* (1989) Washington: World Bank.

World Bank *World Development Report: The State in a Changing World* (1997) Washington: World Bank.

World Bank *World Development Report (1997)* (1998) Washington: World Bank.

Chapters in books

Asbjørn E 'Good governance, human rights and the rights of minorities and indigenous peoples' in Hans-Otto S Alfredsson G (eds) *Human Rights and Good Governance: Building Bridges* (2002) The Hague: Martinus Nijhoff Publishers.

Azfar O & Livingston J 'Decentralization in Uganda' in Bardhan P, Mookherjee D, Baiocchi G, Hofman B, Kaiser K *et al.* (eds) *Decentralization and Local Governance in Developing Countries: A Comparative Perspective* (2006) Cambridge, Massachusetts: MIT Press.

Banks J 'Multicultural education' in Asante M & Mazama A (eds) *Encyclopedia of Black Studies* (2005) Thousand Oaks, California: SAGE Publications.

Bird R 'A comparative perspective on federal finance' in Banting K, Brown DM & Courchene TJ (eds) *The Future of Fiscal Federalism* (1994) Kingston: School of Policy Studies, Queen's University.

Cameron R 'Local government reorganisation in South Africa' in Meligrana J (ed) *Redrawing Local Government Boundaries: An International Study of Politics, Procedures and Decisions* (2004) Vancouver: University of British Columbia Press.

De Torrente N 'Pragmatism as principle? The donors and "no-party democracy" in Uganda' in Nakanyike B *et al.* (eds) *Transformations in Uganda* (2002) Kampala: Makerere Institute of Social Research.

Devas N 'Local revenue administration' in Alam M, Devas N, Venkatachalam P, Koranteng RO & Delay S (eds) *Financing Local Government* (2008) London: Commonwealth Secretariat and Local Government Reform Series.

Devas N 'Revenue sources for local government' in Alam M, Devas N, Venkatachalam P, Koranteng RO & Delay S (eds) *Financing Local Government* (2008) London: Commonwealth Secretariat and Local Government Reform Series.

Devas N 'Intergovernmental fiscal transfers' in Alam M, Devas N, Venkatachalam P, Koranteng RO & Delay S (eds) *Financing Local Government* (2008) London: Commonwealth Secretariat and Local Government Reform Series.

De Visser J 'South Africa: local government development in an uncertain partnership' in Blindenbacher R & Pasma C (eds) *A Global Dialogue on Federalism: Dialogue on Local Government and Metropolitan Regions in Federal Countries* (2006) Montreal: Booklet Series Vol. 2 Forum of Federations/International Association of Centre for Federations.

Golooba-Mutebi F 'Local councils as political and service delivery organs: limits to transformations' in Nakanyike B & Cole P (eds) *Transformations in Uganda* (2002) Kampala: Makerere Institute of Social Research.

Golooba-Mutebi F 'Chiefs, politicians and the community in Uganda: a historico-analytical narrative' in Reddy PS & Naidu RA (eds) *Traditional Leadership and*

Local Governance in a Democratic South Africa: Quo Vadis? (2007) Durban: Southern Sun-Elangeni.

Haysom N 'The Origins of Co-operative Debates in the Constitutional Making Process' in Levy N & Tapscott C (eds.) *Intergovernmental Relations In South Africa: The Challenges of Co-operative Government* (2001) Cape Town: IDSA, School of Government UWC (2001).

Hoffschulte H 'The UN guidelines on decentralization and the strengthening of local authorities' in De Villiers B (ed) *Review of Provinces and Local Governments in South Africa: Constitutional Foundations and Practice* (2008) Johannesburg: Konrad Adenauer Stiftung.

Hooja R & Mathew G 'Partners in development: local governments in India' in Blindenbacher R & Pasma C (eds) *A Global Dialogue on Federalism: Dialogue on Local Government and Metropolitan Regions in Federal Countries* (2006) Booklet Series Vol. 2 Forum of Federations/International Association of Centre for Federations.

Kabumba I 'Conflicts between elected and appointed officials in districts' in Asiimwe D & Musisi NB (eds) *Decentralisaion and Transformation of Governance in Uganda* (2007) Kampala: Fountain Publishers.

Katono W 'Planning and budgeting for decentralisation' in Asiimwe D & Musisi NB (eds) *Decentralisation and Transformation of Governance in Uganda* (2007) Kampala: Fountain Publishers.

Levy N & Tapscott C 'Intergovernmental relations in South Africa: the challenges of co-operative government' in Levy N & Tapscott C (eds) *Intergovernmental Relations in South Africa: The Challenges of Co-operative Government* (2001) IDASA and School of Government, University of the Western Cape.

Lubanga F 'Human resources management under decentralization' in Nsibambi A (ed) *Decentralisation and the Civil Society in Uganda: The Quest for Good Governance* (1998) Kampala: Fountain Publishers.

Magi L & De Villiers B 'Principles underlying demarcation: implications for provincial boundaries' in De Villiers B (ed) *Review of Provinces and Local Governments in South Africa: Constitutional Foundations and Practice* (2008) Johannesburg: Konrad-Adenauer-Stiftung.

Makumbe J 'Local government and traditional leadership' in De Visser J, Steytler N & Machingauta N (eds) *Local Government Reform in Zimbabwe: A Policy Dialogue* (2010) Cape Town: Community Law Centre, University of the Western Cape.

Markku S 'Good governance in the electoral process' in Hans-Otto S & Alfredsson G (eds) *Human Rights and Good Governance: Building Bridges* (2002) The Hague: Martinus Nijhoff Publishers.

Murray C 'The constitutional context of intergovernmental relations in South Africa' in Levy N & Tapscott C (eds) *Intergovernmental Relations in South Africa: The Challenges of Co-operative Government* (2001) Cape Town: IDASA and School of Government, University of the Western Cape.

Miller D 'Secession and the principle of nationality' in Moore M (ed) *National Self-Determination and Secession* (1998) Oxford: Oxford University Press.

Netzer D 'Property taxes: their past, present, and future place in government finance' in Swartz T & Bonello FJ (eds) *Urban Finance Under Siege* (1993) New York: ME Sharpe.

Nohlen D, Krennerch M & Bernhard T 'Elections and electoral systems in Africa' in Nohlen D, Krennerich M & Thibaut B (eds) *Elections in Africa: A Data Handbook* (1999) New York: Oxford University Press.

Paddison R 'Redrawing local government boundaries: delivering the principles for politically just procedures' in Meligrana J (ed) *Redrawing Local Government Boundaries: An International Study of Politics, Procedures and Decisions* (2004) Vancouver: University of British Columbia Press.

Quieroz De Ribeiro L & Garson S 'Brazilian municipalities and metropolitan regions: economic and institutional obstacles to cooperation' in Blindenbacher R & Pasma C (eds) *A Global Dialogue on Federalism: Dialogue on Local Government and Metropolitan Regions in Federal Countries* (2006) Booklet Series Vol. 2 Forum of Federations/International Association of Centre for Federations.

Scheinin M 'State responsibility, good governance and indivisible human rights' in Hans-Otto S & Alfredsson (eds) *Human Rights and Good Governance: Building Bridges* (2002) The Hague: Martinus Nijhoff Publishers.

Seidman R 'Law and stagnation in Africa' in Ndulo M (ed) *Law in Zambia* (1984) Nairobi: East African Publishing House.

Seidman A, Seidman R & Wälde T 'Building sound national legal frameworks for development and social change' in Seidman A, Seidman RB, & Walde T (eds) *Making Development Work: Legislative Reform for Institutional Transformation and Good Governance* (1999) London: Kluwer Law International.

Stauffer T & Töpperwien N 'Balancing self-rule and shared rule' in Basta Fleiner LR & Fleiner T (eds) *Federalism and Multiethnic States: The Case of Switzerland'* (2nd ed) (2000) Geneva: Helbing and Lichtenhahn.

Steiner H 'Political participation as a human right' in Panner M *et al.* (eds) *Harvard Human Rights Year Book 1* (1988) Harvard: Harvard Law School.

Tapscott C 'Intergovernmental relations in South Africa: a comparative analysis' in *Intergovernmental Relations: An International Comparative Study* (1998) Pretoria: Department of Constitutional Development and Provincial Affairs.

Taylor J 'Urban autonomy in Canada: its evolution and decline' in Steler G *et al.* (eds) *Power and Place: Canadian Urban Development in the North American Context* (1986) Vancouver: University of British Columbia Press.

Trubek D & Santos A 'Introduction: the third moment in law and development theory and the emergence of a new critical practice' in Trubek D & Santos A (eds) *The New Law and Economic Development: A Critical Appraisal* (2006) New York: Cambridge University Press.

Wash J & Ottenoeller D 'Uganda: multiple levels of local government' in Olowu D & Wunsch JS. (eds) *Local Government in Africa: The Challenges of Democratic Decentralization* (2004) Boulder, Colorado: Lynne Rienner Publishers.

Watts R 'Intergovernmental relations: conceptual issues' in Levy N & Tapscott C (eds) *Intergovernmental Relations in South Africa: The Challenges of Co-operative Government* (2001) Cape Town: IDASA.

Watts R 'The dynamics of decentralisation' in Bird R & Stauffer T (eds) *Intergovernmental Fiscal Relations in Fragmented Societies* (2001) Geneva: Helbing & Lichtenhahn.

Young R 'Canada: a creaking system' in Blindenbacher R & Pasma C (eds) *A Global Dialogue on Federalism: Dialogue on Local Government and Metropolitan Regions in Federal Countries* (2006) Ottawa: Booklet Series Vol. 2 Forum of Federations/International Association of Centre for Federations.

Dissertations

Jjemba M *Local Council Courts and Local Conflict Resolution: A Case of Lubaga Division, Kampala District, Uganda* (unpublished MA thesis, University of KwaZulu-Natal, Durban, 2009).

Kakumba U *The Challenges of Personnel Decentralization and Local Government Performance in Uganda: The Case of Luwero District* (unpublished MA thesis, Makerere University, Kampala, 2003).

Kakumba U *External Control Systems in Enhancing Accountability in Local Government: The Case of Uganda* (unpublished PhD thesis, University of Pretoria, 2008).

Kjær A *Exploring Local Government Extractive Capacity: Illustrations from Graduated Tax Collection in Uganda* (unpublished thesis, University of Aarhus, 2005).

Makara S *Decentralisation and Urban Governance in Uganda* (unpublished PhD thesis, University of the Witwatersrand, Johannesburg, 2009).

Nambalirwa S *The Implementation of Universal Primary Education in Uganda* (unpublished MA thesis, University of Pretoria, 2010).

Singiza D *Exorcising the Antiquity spirit of Intolerance: Possibilities and Dilemmas of Decriminalising Sodomy Laws in Uganda* (unpublished LLM thesis, University of Pretoria, 2007).

Stanton A *Decentralisation and Municipalities in South Africa: An Analysis of the Mandate to Deliver Basic Services* (unpublished PhD thesis, University of KwaZulu-Natal, Pietermaritzburg, 2009).

Journal articles

Aleinikoff T 'Constitutional law in the age of balancing' (1987) 96(5) *Yale Law Journal* 943.

Andrews J 'European charter of local self-government' (1986) *European Law Review* 180.

Barron D 'The promise of Cooley's city: traces of local constitutionalism' (1999) 147 (3) *University of Pennsylvania Law Review* 487.

Bermann G 'Taking subsidiarity seriously: federalism in the European community and the United States' (1994) 94 *Columbia Law Review* 332.

Bernstein M 'Identity politics' (2005) 31 *Annual Review of Sociology* 47.

Blanco S & Carrasco E 'The functions of the IMF and World Bank' (1999) 9 *Transnational International Law & Contemporary Problems* 67.

Blank Y 'Localism in the new global legal order' (2006) 47 *Harvard International Law Journal* 921.

Bosire C 'Local government and human rights: building institutional links for the effective protection and realisation of human rights in Africa' (2011) 11 *African Human Rights Law Journal* 147.

Botchway N 'Good governance: the old, the new, the principle, and the elements' (2001) 2 *Florida Journal of International Law* 159.

Briffault R 'Who rules at home?: one person/one vote and local governments' (1993) 60 *University of Chicago Law Review* 339.

Briffault R 'The local government boundary problem in metropolitan areas' (1996) 48 *Stanford Law Review* 1115.

Carozza P 'Subsidiarity as a principle of international human rights law' (2003) 97 *American Journal of International Law* 38.

Carrasco E 'The 1980s: the debt crisis and the lost decade of development' (1999) 9 *Transnational International Law & Contemporary Problems* 119.

Carrasco E & Ayhan K 'Income distribution and the Bretton Woods institutions: promoting an enabling environment for social development' (1996) 6 *Transnational International Law & Contemporary Problems* 1.

Carreau D 'Why not merge the International Monetary Fund (IMF) with the International Bank for Reconstruction and Development (World Bank)?' (1994) 62 *Ford Law Review* 1989.

Craik A 'Recalcitrant reality and chosen ideals: the public function of dispute settlement in international environmental law' (1998) 10 *Georgian International Environmental Law Review* 551.

Flood R & Velick M 'Questions and answers about intergovernmental agreements' (1997) *Illinois Bar Journal* 112.

Føllesdal A 'Survey article: subsidiarity' (1998) 6(2) *Journal of Political Philosophy* 190.

Fossum E & Menéndez A. 'The Constitution's gift? A deliberative democratic analysis of constitution making in the European Union' (2005) 11(4) *European Law Journal* 380.

Francis P & Robert J 'Citizen participation: the contradictions of Uganda's decentralisation program' (2003) 31(2) *World Development* 325.

Ginsburg T, Elkins Z & Blount J 'Does the process of constitution-making matter?' (2009) 5 *Annual Review of Law and Social Science* 201.

Hilliard J 'To accomplish fairness and justice: substantive due process' (1996) 30 *John Marshall Law Review* 95.

Howard R 'The full-belly thesis: should economic rights take priority over civil and political rights? evidence from Sub-Saharan Africa' (1983) 5 *Human Rights Quarterly* 467.

Isingoma P & Red P 'Local government in Uganda: trends, constraints and prospects' (2006) 36(1) *Africanus* 88–104.

Kakumba U & Fourie D 'Enhancing local government systems and processes towards accountability: the case for external control agencies in Uganda' (2008) 43(3.1) *Journal of Public Administration* 121.

Kane I 'The implementation of the African Charter on democracy, elections and governance' (2008) 17(4) *African Security Review* 43.

Kiyaga J & Olum Y 'Local governance and local democracy in Uganda' (2009) 1(2) *Commonwealth Journal of Local Governance* 26.

Kjær A 'Sources of local government extractive capacity: the role of trust and pre-colonial legacy in the case of Uganda' (2009)29 (3) *Public Administration and Development* 228.

Kleymeyer C 'What is "grassroots development"?' (1991) *15 Grassroots Development* 38.

Knouse J 'From identity politics to ideology politics' (2009) (3) *Utah Law Review Society* 749.

Kumar R 'Personnel administration in urban local bodies in India: a study' 2011 *International Referred Research Journal.*

Kunal P 'The history of experience: on the historical imagination of Oliver Wendell Holmes, Jr' (2003)26(2) *Political and Legal Anthropology Review* 60.

Meehan E, Chiarelli R & Major M 'The constitutional legal status of municipalities 1849–2004: success is a journey, but also a destination' (2007) 22 *National Journal of Constitutional Law* 1.

Milner G 'Early treaties in Uganda 1888–1891' (1948) *Uganda Journal* XII.

Mohnach M 'Intermunicipal agreements: the metamorphosis of home rule' (1999) 17 *Pace Environmental Law Review* 161.

Mugambwa J 'The legal aspects of the 1900 Buganda Agreement revisited' (1987) (2/3) *Journal of Legal Pluralism* 244.

Murray C 'Municipal integrity and effective government: the Butterworth intervention' (1999) 14(2) *South Africa Public Law* 332.

Murray C 'Recognition without empowerment: minorities in a democratic South Africa' (2007) 5 *International Journal of Constitutional Law* 699.

Ndulo M 'The democratization process and structural adjustment in Africa' (2003) 10 *Indiana Journal of Global Legal Studies* 315.

Ndulo M 'The democratic state in Africa: The Challenges for Institution Building' (1998/9) 16 *National Black Law Journal* 70.

Nsibambi A 'Political integration in Uganda: problems and prospects' (1968) 2 *Eastern African Journal* 13.

Oliver D 'Adopting the UK "accounting officer" model in Canada' (2009) 2 *Journal of Parliamentary and Political Law* 233.

Oloka-Onyango J 'Expunging the ghost of Ex. Parte Matovu: challenges facing the Ugandan judiciary in the 1995 Constitution' (1996) (1) *Makerere Law Journal* 141.

Pieterse M 'Beyond the welfare state: globalisation of neo-liberal culture and the constitutional protection of social economic rights in South Africa' (2003) 14 *Stellenbosch Law Review* 3.

Prempeh H 'Africa's "constitutionalism revival": false start or new dawn?' (2007) 5 *International Journal of Constitutional Law* 469.

Prempeh H 'Presidential power in comparative perspective: the puzzling persistence of imperial presidency in post-authoritarian Africa' (2008) 35 *Hastings Constitutional Law Quarterly* 761.

Prud'homme R 'The dangers of decentralization from the viewpoints of redistribution, stabilization, and allocation' (1995) 10(2) *World Bank Research Observer* 201.

Reynolds L 'Intergovernmental cooperation, metropolitan equity, and the new regionalism' (2003) 78 *Washington Law Review* 93.

Romero F 'Legal challenges of globalization' (2005) 15 *Indiana International and Comparative Law Review* 501.

Rosen M 'From exclusivity to concurrence' (2010) 94 *Minnesota Law Review* 1051.

Rugege S 'Traditional leadership and its future role in local governance' (2003) 2 *Law Democracy and Development* 171.

Sewell D '"The dangers of decentralization" according to Prud'homme: some further aspects' (1996) 11(1) *The World Bank Research Observer* 143.

Simon W 'The market for bad legal advice: academic professional responsibility consulting as an example' (2008) 60 *Stanford Law Review* 1555.

Singiza D & De Visser J 'Chewing more than one can swallow: the creation of new districts in Uganda' (2011) 15 *Law Democracy and Development* 1.

Singiza D & De Visser J 'The unresolved ethnic question in Uganda's district councils' (2015) 19 *Law Democracy and Development* 107.

Ssekandi F & Gitta C 'Protection of fundamental rights in the Uganda constitution' (1994) 26 *Columbia Human Rights Law Review* 191.

Steytler N 'The strangulation of local government' (2008) 3 *Journal of South African Law* 528.

Steytler N & Fessha Y 'Defining provincial and local government powers and functions' (2007) 124 *South African Law Journal* 320.

Stiles D 'Classical versus grassroots development' (1987) 11 *Cultural Survival Quarterly* 3.

Tiebout C 'A pure theory of local expenditure' (1956) 64(5) *Journal of Political Economy* 416.

Trubek D 'The owl and the pussy-cat: is there a future for "law and development"?' (2007) 25 *Wisconsin International Law Journal* 235.

Working papers

Akin J, Hutchinson P & Strumpf K 'Decentralization and provision of public goods: the public health sector in Uganda' (2001) Draft Paper, MEASURE Evaluation Project/USAID, Carolina Population Center, University of North Carolina, Chapel Hill.

Bainomugisha A & Mushemeza E 'Deepening democracy and enhancing sustainable livelihoods in Uganda: an independent review of the performance of special interest groups in Parliament' (2006) Kampala: ACODE Policy Research Series No. 13.

Boucher F 'Deep diversity and multinational federalism in Canada' (2008) Students' Best Papers, Summer University, Institute of Federalism, Fribourg.

Chen D, Matovu J & Reinikka-Soininen R 'A quest for revenue and tax incidence in Uganda' (2001) Washington: IMF Working Paper 01/24.

De Visser J 'Cities in federal and decentralized systems in Africa' (2010) 5th International Conference on Federalism, Addis Ababa.

Fossum, J & Menéndez AJ (eds) 'The Constitution's gift: a constitutional theory for a democratic European Union' (2010) Recon. Working Paper No. 25.

Golooba-Mutebi F 'Collapse, war and reconstruction in Uganda: an analytical narrative on state-making' (2008) Working Paper No. 27 Makerere Institute of Social Research, Makerere University.

Kugonza S & Namara R 'Dynamics of public sector performance measurement: national annual assessment of local governments in Uganda public policy and government' (2012) Uganda Management Institute, Kampala and National Institute of Development Administration (NIDA), Bangkok.

Kymlicka W 'The global diffusion of multiculturalism: trends, causes and consequences' (2004) Conference paper at International Conference on Leadership, Education and Multiculturalism in Armed Forces, La Paz, Bolivia.

Nyerere J 'Stability and change in Africa' (1969) Address to the University of Toronto, printed in *Africa Contemporary Record* 2 (1969–70) C30–1.

Okidi J & Guloba M 'Decentralisation and development: emerging issues from Uganda's experiences' (2006) Kampala: Economic Policy Research Centre.

Oloka-Onyango J '"Decentralisation without human rights?" Local governance and access to justice in post-movement Uganda' (2007) HURIPEC Working Paper 12.

Sennoga E 'Local government revenues and expenditures in Uganda: a VAR approach' (2008) 13th Annual Conference on Econometric Modelling in Africa, University of Pretoria.

Sewanyana S & Okidi J 'A microsimulation of the Uganda tax system and the poor from 1999 to 2003' (2008) UGATAX Kampala: Economic Policy Research Centre.

Shah A & Thompson T 'Implementing decentralized local governance: a treacherous road with potholes, detours and road closures' (2004) World Bank Policy Research Working Paper 3353 Washington: World Bank.

Siegle J & O'Mahony P 'Assessing the merits of decentralization as a conflict mitigation strategy' (2006) USAID Office of Democracy and Governance Paper.

Singiza D 'Unity in diversity through federalism: a case for the Buganda Kingdom's demand for a special federal status in Uganda' (2010) 5th International Conference on Federalism, Addis Ababa.

Steiner S 'Decentralisation in Uganda: exploring the constraints for poverty reduction' (2006) GIGA Research Programme: Transformation in the Process of Globalisation No. 31.

Trubek D 'Developmental states and the legal order: towards a new political economy of development and law' (2008) University of Wisconsin Legal Studies Research Paper No. 1075 16, available at http:// ssrn.com/abstract=1349163 (accessed 14 September 2009).

Ts'oele M & Goldman I 'Case study 1: decentralization in Uganda' (2006) *Sustaining Livelihoods in Sub-Saharan Africa* No. 19.

Tumushabe G 'Trends in public administration expenditure in Uganda: the cost of the executive and its implications on poverty eradication and governance' (2009) ACODE Policy Research Series 27.

Tusasirwe B 'Enforcing civil and political rights in a decentralized system of governance' (2007) HURIPEC Working Paper 14.

Work R 'Overview of decentralisation worldwide: a stepping stone to improved governance and human development' (2002) Conference Paper at the 2nd International Conference on Decentralisation and Federalism: The Future of Decentralizing States? Manila, Philippines, available at http://www.undp.org/governance/docs/DLGUDPuboverview-decentralisationworldwidepaper.pdf.

Newspaper articles

'Abaramuzi n'enkomba za DP-RDC Mwesigye' *Orumuri Newspaper* 15 (54) 5–7 July 2004.

Abimanyi K 'Uganda's districts grow beyond size' *Daily Monitor* 12 November 2009.

Butagira T 'Ugandans want smaller districts' *The Daily Monitor* 6 June 2010.

Byaruhanga M 'Local leadership should monitor service delivery' *The Daily Monitor* 3 May 2010 available at http://www.monitor.co.ug/OpEd/Commentary/-/689364/910914/-/a2bue7z/-/index (accessed 3 May 2010).

'Deaths in riot after Uganda fire' *Al Jazeera* available at http://english.aljazeera.net/news/africa/2010/03/20103183262649981 (accessed 17 March 2010).

Goodluck & Wasswa A 'Katuntu clashes with Kabale district chief' *The New Vision* 25 May 2010 available at http://www.newvision.co.ug/D/8/18/720751 (accessed 10 June 2010).

'Govt to create more municipalities' *The Daily Monitor* 1 December 2009 available at http://www.monitor.co.ug/artman/publish/regionalspecial/Govt_to_create_more_municipalities_95357 (accessed 3 December 2009).

Kadiresan K & Onyach-Olaa M 'Are we serious on improving service delivery in local govts' *The Daily Monitor* available at http://www.monitor.co.ugn/ artman/publish/opinions/Areweseriousonimprovingservicedeliveryinlocalgovts83936 (accessed 28 April 2009).

Katende J 'Bishop Lwanga's federo remarks are a tip on unresolved national issues' *The Independent* 26 April 2010.

'Lazy chiefs irk Kabarole councillors' *The Sunday Vision* 30 May 2010 available at http://www.newvision.co.ug/D/8/18/721223 (accessed 30 May 2010).

'Masaka mayor must quit-LC5 chief' *The New Vision* 30 October 2009 available at http://www.newvision.co.ug/D/8/13/699613 (accessed 3 November 2009).

Matsiko M & Mubatsi A 'New districts and the paradox of taking services to the people' *The Independent* 17 May 2010 available at http://www.independent.co.ug/in dex.php/news/news-analysis/79-news-analysis/2916-new-districts-and-the-paradox-of-taking-services-to-the-people (accessed June 2010).

'Mayuge district council fires LC5 chairman' *The New Vision* 7 April 2010 available at http://www.newvision.co.ug/D/8/17/715491 (accessed 10 April 2010). 'Mengo in Bulange Takeover Scare' *The Red Pepper* available at http://www.redpepper.ug/details.php?item=3130 (accessed 4 February 2010).

'MPs oppose autonomy for minority tribes' *The New Vision* 30 October 2009 available at http://www.newvision.co.ug/D/8/13/699607 (accessed 4 November 2009).

Mubatsi A 'Court nullified LCs: who will govt pay the Shs10bn?' *The Independent* 28 June 2010 available at http://www.independent.co.ug/index.php/news/news-analysis/79-news-analysis/3094-court-nullified-lcs-who-will-govt-pay-the-shs10bn- (accessed 29 August 2009).

Mugerwa Y 'Government tables bill to take over Kampala' *The Daily Monitor* available at http://www.monitor.co.ug/artman/publish/news/GovttablesBilltotakeoverKampala87025 (accessed 16 July 2009).

Mugumya A 'Drop those insults in making the case for Obugabe' *The Daily Monitor* 22 April 2010 available at http://www.monitor.co.ug/OpEd/Commentary/-/689 364/904172/-/a2us58z/-/index (accessed 22 April 2010).

Mukisa L & Mulndo E 'Court to rule on Bushenyi division' *The Daily Monitor* 27 April 2010 available at http://www.monitor.co.ug/News/National/-/688334/907282/-/wy0ql7/-/index (accessed 27 April 2010).

Mulondo E 'RDCs can vet radio talk show guests, says minister' *The Daily Monitor* 24 September 2010 available at *http://www.monitor.co.ug/News/National/-/688334/101 7132/-/cnli3ez/-/index* (accessed 25 September 2010).

Musoke C 'Museveni bans farm pruduce [sic] tax' *The New Vision* 5 March 2010.

Nalugo M 'MPs order arrest of ex-Kampala officials' *The Daily Monitor* 7 July 2010 available at *http://www.monitor.co.ug/News/National/-/688334 /953510/-/x20py7/-/index.html* (accessed 16 July 2010).

Namutebi J & Kiwanuka F 'LC bosses to get bonus cash' *The New Vision* 31 May 2010 available at *http://www.newvision.co.ug/D/8/19/721330* (accessed 31 May 2010).

Naturinda S 'Dr Otaala Runs Amok Over Tororo' *The Daily Monitor* available at http://www.monitor.co.ug/artman/publish/news/DrOtaalarunsamokoverTororo88080.shtml (accessed 30 August 2009).

Nganda S *MS Uganda Newsletter* April 2008 available at http://www.ms.dk/sw94813.asp (accessed 28 February 2010).

Osinde M 'Not all Jopadhola reject splitting of Tororo district' *The Sunday Monitor* available at http://www.monitor.co.ug/artman/publish/insights/notalljopadholarejectsplittingoftororodistrict86387 (accessed 27 May 2009).

'President orders fresh demarcation of Sironko' *The Daily Monitor* 16 November 2009 available at http://www.monitor.co.ug/artman/publish/regionalspecial/President_orders_fresh_demarcation_of_Sironko_Kapchorwa_boundary_94651 (accessed 17 November 2009).

Segawa M 'No doctor for 200,000 people in new district' *The Daily Monitor* 7 April 2011 available at http://www.monitor.co.ug/News/National/-/688334/1140316/-/c2sydnz/-/index.html (accessed 23 May 2011).

Other sources

A Constituent General Assembly the Africities 3 Summit, Yaoundé on 02-06-012-2003, available at http://www.uclgafrica.org/AboutUC LGA.htm (accessed 9 September 2008).

CESCR General comment 1, Reporting by States parties UN doc. document E/1989/22, 24/02/1989 para 1, available at http://www.unhchr.ch/tbs/doc.nsf/%28Symbol%29/3 8e23a6ddd6c0f4dc12563ed0051cde7?Opendocument (accessed 20 September 2010).

Core Program: Report of the Panel of Experts on Technology Missions Advisory Committee on Science and Technology for Development, 11th Sess., Prov. Agenda Item 3(c), at 4, 7, UN.Doc A/CN.11/AC.1/XI/2 (1990).

ECOSOC, Sub-Committee on Prevention of Discrimination & Protection of Minorities, Study of the Problem of Discrimination against Indigenous Populations, 20, U.N. Doc. E/CN/4/Sub.2/1986/7/Add.4 (1987).

Good Governance: The IMF's Role. Washington D.C.: IMF, available at http://www.imf.org/external/pubs/ft/exrp/govern/govindex.htm (accessed 20 January 2007).

Millennium Development Goals and Targets: The Critical Role of Local Governments, available at http://www.newvision.co.ug/D/526/538/703831 (accessed 20 April 2010).

President Barack Obama's address to Gay Rights Group, Washington, 10 October 2009, available at http://www.whitehouse.gov/the_press_office/Remarks-by-the-President-at-Human-Rights-Campaign-Dinner/ (accessed 20 November 2009).

Resolution 7/6: Mandate of the Independent Expert on Minority Issues, available at http://ap.ohchr.org/documents/E/HRC/resolutions/A_HRC_RES_7_6.pdf (accessed 17 July 2009).

Shireletso T 'Participatory research: a development world research paradigm for change' in Saugestad S (ed) *Indigenous Peoples in Modern Nation-States* Occasional Papers Series A No. 90, 141.

The Advisory Group of Experts on Decentralisation (AGRED), available at http://www.unhabitat.org/downloads/docs/1701_45838_journal_04_E.pdf (accessed 20 April 2009).

The African Charter on Human and People's Rights, available at http://www.achpr.org/english/info/charteren.html (accessed 18 March 2009).

The Commonwealth Principles on Good Practice for Local Government (the Aberdeen Principles) available at http://www.lgnz.co.nz/news/pr1123186626.html (accessed 1 March 2009).

The Council of Europe, Explanatory report on the European Charter of Local Self-Government, available at http://conventions.coe.int/Treaty/EN/Reports/HTML/122.html (accessed 7 June 2009).

The European Charter of Local Self-Government (ECLSG) The European Charter on Local Self-Government, available at https://rm.coe.int/european-charter-for-local-self-government-english-version-pdf-a6-59-p/16807198a3 (accessed 20 January 2009).

The Governing Council of the United Nations Human Settlement Program Draft Guidelines on Decentralization and the Strengthening of Local Authorities, available at http://www.citieslocalgovernments.org/uclg/upload/template/templatedocs/ENG_Annex1_Guidelines_on_Decentralization_revised_version.pdf (accessed 29 October 2009).

The IMF Good Governance: The IMF's Role, Washington DC: International Monetary Fund (1997), available at http://www.imf.org/external/pubs/ft/exrp/govern/govindex.html (accessed 2 July 2007).

The International Convention on Economic and Social Cultural Rights (ICESCR), available at http://www2.ohchr.org/english/law/cescr.html (accessed 23 May 2011).

The International Covenant on Civil and Political Rights (CCPR), available at http://www2.ohchr.org/english/law/ccpr.html (accessed 11 October 2010).

The Kigali Declaration on Leadership Capacity for Decentralised Government and Poverty Reduction in Sub-Saharan Africa, 8 June 2005, available at http://www.google.com/search?ie=UTF8&oe=UTF8&sourceid=navclient&gfns=1&q=Kigali+Declaration+on+Leadership+Capacity+for+Decentralised+Government+and+Poverty+Reduction+in+ Sub-Saharan (accessed 16 October 2009).

The OP 4.10 – Indigenous Peoples, available at http://web.worldbank.org/WBSIT E/EXTERNAL/PROJECTS/EXTPOLICIES/EXTOPMANUAL/0,,contentMDK:20553653~menuPK:4564185~pagePK:6 4709096~piPK:64709108~theSitePK:50 2184,00.html (accessed 10 August 2009).

The Rules of Procedure of the Parliament of Uganda, 2006, available at http://www.parli ament.go.ug/files/rules%20of%20procedure%20for%20the%208th%20parliament%20of%20uganda.pdf (accessed 10 March 2009).

The 2nd International Conference on Decentralisation available at http://www.ombudsman.gov.ph/UNDP4/the-second-international-conference-on-decentralization/index.html (accessed 9 April 2009).

The UN Governing Council of United Nations Human Settlement Programme/AGRED UN-HABITAT, available at http://www.unhabitat.org/downloadds/docs/170145838journ al04E.pdf (accessed 14 August 2009).

The United Nations: Uganda Population Sex Ratio (men per 100 women) (2008), available at http://data.un.org/CountryProfile.aspx?crName=Uganda (accessed 2 February 2009).

The Victoria Falls Declaration on Local Government, available at http://thecommonwealth.org/sites/default/files/history-items/documents/Victoria%20Falls%20Declaration%201994.pdf (accessed 20 March 2008).

The World-Wide Declaration of Local Self-Government (The Toronto Declaration), available at http://www.bunken.nga.gr.jp/siryousitu/eturansitu/charter/iuladecl_txt.html (accessed 25 October 2009).

The Yaoundé Communiqué on Leadership Capacity Building For Decentralized Governance and Poverty Reduction in Africa, 30 May 2008 http://unpan1.

un.org/intradoc/groups/public/documents/un/unpan031034.pdf (accessed 8 October 2009).
United Nations Centre for Human Settlement (Habitat) and World association of Cities and Local Communities Coordination (WACLAC), Towards a World Chapter of Local Self-Government, May 1998, available at http://www.unchs.org/unchs/english/feature/charter.html (accessed 10 March 2009).
United Nations Development Program: Governance Policy Paper, United Nations Development Program, New York, available at http://mirror.undp.org/magnet/policy/ (accessed 23 May 2011).
Workshop in Kampala, 3–4 October 2007, by hosted by the Uganda Local Government Association (ULGA) and the Ugandan Ministry of Local Government and supported by the Commonwealth Secretariat and the Westminster Foundation for Democracy, available at http://www.clgf.org.uk/index.cfm/pageid/12/type/Archive/view/128/Uganda+pilots+local+democracy+review+system (accessed 1 March 2009).

Legislation

Companies Act Cap 110.
Constitution (Amendment) Act 11 of 2005.
Constitution of Uganda, 1962.
Constitution of Uganda, 1967.
Constitution of Uganda, 1995.
District Administration (Districts Councils) Ordinance, 1955
Inspectorate of Government Act Cap 167.
Kampala Capital City Act 1 of 2009.
Leadership Code Act 168.
Local Administrations (districts) Act 13/66 (repealed by Act 18/67).
Local Governments (Amendment) Act 27 of 2006.
Local Governments (Amendments) Act 1 of 2008.
Local Governments (Amendment) Act 2 of 2008.
Local Governments Act Cap 343.
Local Governments Act Cap 243.
Local Government Administrations Act Cap 25.
Local Government (Declaration of Towns) (No.1) Order.
Local Governments (Financial and Accounting) Regulations.
Local Governments (Public Accounts Committee) Regulations S.I. 243–16.
Local Government (Rating) Act, Act 8 of 2005.
Local Government Revenue (Amendment) Regulations S.I. No.39 of 2001.
Local Government (Revenue Regulations) S.I. 243–16.
Local Government (Rating) (Amendment) Act 12/2005.
Legal Notice No. 1 of 1986.
Penal Code Act Cap 120.
Political Parties and Organisations Act of 2005 (PPOA).
Presidential Elections Act Cap 252.
Royal Instructions, 1920 (laws Vol. VI p 104), clauses XV & XXV.
Royal Instructions of 1920 (Amendment) Legal Notice No 314 of 1953, cl.XVA & XVB.

Trustees (Incorporation) Act Cap 165.
Uganda Order-in-Council No.1 of 1902.
Urban Authorities Act Cap 27.
Whistleblowers Protection Act, 2010.

Bills

Regional Government Bill No 20 of 2009.

Case law

Abdul Balingira Nakendo v Patrick Mwonda Court of Appeal Election Appeal No. 23 of 2006.
Amos Twinomujuni v The Attorney General & Another (CIVIL Suit No. 0413 of 2005) [2009] UGHC 145 (23 January 2009).
Attormey-General v Godfrey Katondwaki [1963] *E.A p 328.*
Attoney-General v Major General David Tinyefuza Constitutional Appeal No. 1 1997.
*Busoga-Asumani v Musa (*1969*) EA 274.*
Charles Onyango Obbo Andrew Mujuni Mwenda v AG Constitutional petition No. 15 of 1997 *(unreported).*
Daudi Ndibarema and Others v The Enganiz of Ankole and Others [1960] 54–5.
Electoral Commission and Another v Nambooze Betty Bakireke Court of Appeal Election Petition Appeal Nos. 1 & 2 07.
Dr James Rwanyarare and Another v AG Constitution Petition No. 5 of 1999 *(unreported).*
Esrom William Alenyo v The Electoral Commission and Another Court of Appeal Election PetitionAppeal No. 9 of 2007.
George Owor v Attorney General & Another (Constitutional Petition No. 038 of 2010).
Gladys Aserua Orochi v Kabalae District Government CHC Civil Suit No. 0093 of 2003.
Gole Nicholas Davis v Loi Kageni Kiryapawo Supreme Court Election Petition Appeal No. 19 of 2007.
Hajji Mohammed Baswari Kezaala v The Inspector General of Government and Others Miscellaneous application No.28 of 2009.
John Ken-Lukyamuzi v AG and the Electoral Commission, Constitutional Petition No. 19/2006.
Jowet Lyagoba v Bakasonga [1963] *E.A. p.57.*
Kakooza John Baptist v Electoral Commission and Another Supreme Court Election Petit Appeal No. 11 of 2007.
Kirunda Kivejinja Ali v Katuntu Abdu Court of Appeal Election Petition Appeal No. 24 of 2006.
Luya Idda Kasika v Kagimu Maurice Peter Election Petition Appeal No. 6 of 2006.
Major General David Tinyefuza v AG Constitution petition No. 1 of 1997 *(unreported).*
Mistry Amar Singh v Serwano Wofunira Kulubya [1963] 408.
Ndaula Ronald v Hajji Nadduli Abdu Court of Appeal Elect Petit Appeal No. 20 of 2006.
Nyali Limited v Attorney-General [1956] *(2) 1 Q.B at 15.*
*Onywello Ceaser v Pader District Local Government (*2007*) HCT-02-CV-CS-009.*
Paul Ssemogerere and another v Attorney General 2002 *Constitutional Petition No. 3 of* 2002.

Roland Kakooza Mutale v Attorney General Application No. 665/2003 arising out of HCCA No. 40/2003.
Rtd.Col.Dr.Kizza Besigye v Electoral Commission & Yoweri Kaguta Museveni (Election Petition No. 1 Of 2006) [2007] UGSC 24 (31 January 2007*).*
Rubaramira Ruranga v Electoral Commission and Another Constitution Petition No. 21 of 2006.
Susan Kigula & 416 others v the AG Constitutional Petition unreported case No. 6 of 2003.
The Katikiro of Buganda v The Attorney-General [1960] *E.A p 790.*
Tommy Obongo Ojok v Apac District Local Government HCT-02-CV-CS-0015-2005.
Uganda v Commissioner of Prisons Ex Parte Matovu [1966] *EA p 514.*
Victor Juliet Mukasa and Another v Attorney General, Miscellaneous Cause No. 247/06.
Zachary Olum and another v AG Constitutional Petition unreported case No. 6 of 1999.

Foreign legislation

Constitution of India.
Constitution of the Republic of South Africa.
South Africa's Local Government: Municipal Demarcation Act 27 of 1998.
German Basic Law.
Local Government: Municipal Systems Act 32 of 2000.
Organised Local Government Act 52 of 1997.
Municipal Demarcation Act 27 of 1998.

Foreign case law

CDA Boerdery (Edms) Bpk en Andere v Nelson Mandela Metropolitan Municipality (526/05) [2007] *ZASCA 1, [2007] SCA 1 (RSA) (6 February* 2007*).*
Fedsure Life Assurance Ltd v Greater Johannesburg Transitional Metropolitan Council 1998 *(12) BCLR 1458.*
Merafong Demarcation Forum and others v President of the Republic of South Africa and Others case cct 41/07.
Mkontwana v Nelson Mandela Metropolitan Municipality [2004] *(CCT 57/03) ZACC 9; 2005 (1) SA 530 (CC); 2005 (2) BCLR 150 (CC).*
Occupiers of 51 Olivia Road and Others v the City of Johannesburg and Others 2008 *(*5*) BCLR 475 (CC).*
Olga Tellis v Bombay Municipal Corporation A.I.R. 1986 *S.C. 180, 190.*
Re Certification of the Constitution of the Republic of South African 1996 *(10) BCLR 1253 (CC).*
Residents of Joe Slovo Community, Western Cape v Thubelisha Homes and Others 2000 *(9) 847 (CC).*
Uthukela District Municipality v President of the Republic of South Africa 2002 *(11) BCLR.*

Reports

ACHPR & ILO *The Overview Report of the Research Project by the International labour* ARD *Democracy and Governance Assessment: Republic of Uganda* (2005) Kampala: USAID.

*Organisation and the African Commission of Human and Peoples' Rights on the Constitutional and Legislative Protection of the Rights of Indigenous Peoples in 24 African Counties (*2009*)* Geneva: Centre for Human Rights.

Government of Uganda *The Commission of Inquiry into the Local Government System* (1987) Kampala: Government of Uganda.

Government of Uganda (GOU) *2002 Uganda Population and Housing Census Analytical Report: Population Size and Distribution* (2006) Kampala: Uganda Bureau of Statistics.

Government of Uganda Inspectorate of Government *Report to Parliament July–December 2007* (2007) Kampala: The Inspectorate of Government.

Government of Uganda *National Policy for Internally Displaced Persons* (2004) Kampala: Office of the Prime Minister, Department of Disaster Preparedness and Refugees.

Government of Uganda *Odoki Constitution Commission Report* (1993) Entebbe: Government Printer.

Government of Uganda *Public Service Review and Reorganisation Committee* (1993) Kampala: Government of Uganda.

Government of Uganda *Report of the Commission of Inquiry (Constitutional Review) Findings and Recommendations* (2003).

Government of Uganda *Report of the Rationalisation of District Boundaries Committee* (1990) Kampala: Government of Uganda.

Government of Uganda *Revised Framework for Monitoring and Evaluation (M&E) of the Future of JARD* (2008) Kampala: Local Government International Consultancy Division.

Government of Uganda *Summary of Recommendation to Strengthen Democratic Decentralisation* (1991) Kampala.

Local Government Financial Commission *Fiscal Decentralisation in Uganda: Strategy Paper* (2002) Kampala: The Fiscal Decentralisation Working Group.

Local Government Financial Commission *Revenue Enhancement Study* (2000) Kampala: Price Water House Coopers.

Ministry of Local Government *Joint Annual Review of Decentralisation (JARD) Meeting the Millennium Development Goals and Targets: The Critical Role of Local Governments* (2009) Kampala: Government of Uganda.

Ministry of Local Government *Annual Assessment of Minimum Conditions and Performance Measures for Local Governments: Synthesis Report* (2010) Kampala: Government of Uganda.

Ministry of Local Government *Decentralisation Policy Strategic Framework* (2006) Kampala.

Ministry of Local Government *Report on Streamlining Royalty Fees in Local Governments* (2010) Kampala.

Office of the Auditor General *The Annual Report of the Auditor General for the Year Ended 30 June 2009 Volume 3* (2009) Kampala.

Republic of Uganda *Proceedings of the Constituent Assembly: Official Reports* (1994) Entebbe: Uganda Printing Co. 383. The 2005/2006 Budget Speech by the Minister of Finance.

Uganda Local Governments Association *Accelerating Decentralised Response to HIV/AIDS: HIV/AIDS Workplace Program/Policy* ULGA Secretariat (2006) Kampala: Uganda Local Governments Association.

Uganda Local Governments Association *The Corporate Strategic Plan for July, 1 2007–June 30, 2010* (2007) Kampala: Local Government Association.

Uganda Local Governments Association *The Draft Fiscal Decentralisation in Uganda: Strategy Paper* (2002) Kampala: The Fiscal Decentralisation Working Group.

Weeks W *Pushing the Envelope: Moving Beyond 'Protected Villages' in Northern Uganda* (2002) New York: Independent Consultant's Report submitted to the United Nations Office for the Coordination of Humanitarian Affairs.

Foreign reports

The Federation of Canadian Municipalities Strengthening Municipalities: On the Path to Economic Sustainability (2002) Ontario: Federation of Canadian Municipalities.

Index